A Love Affair with
Life & Smithsonian

A Love Affair with
Life & Smithsonian

Edward K. Thompson

University of Missouri Press / Columbia and London

Copyright © 1995 by Edward K. Thompson
University of Missouri Press, Columbia, Missouri 65201
Printed and bound in the United States of America
All rights reserved
5 4 3 2 1   99 98 97 96 95

Library of Congress Cataloging-in-Publication Data

Thompson, Edward K., 1907–
    A love affair with Life & Smithsonian / Edward K. Thompson.
        p.   cm.
    Includes index.
    ISBN 0-8262-1026-0 (cloth : alk. paper)
    1. History, Modern—20th century.   2. Biography—20th century.   3. Thompson,
Edward K., 1907–   .   4. Life (Chicago, Ill.)   5. Smithsonian.   I. Title.
    D421.T56   1995
    069′.0973—dc20   95-31054
                                                                                      CIP

∞ This paper meets the requirements of the
American National Standard for Permanence of Paper
for Printed Library Materials, Z39.48, 1984.

Designer: Kristie Lee
Typesetter: BOOKCOMP
Printer and binder: Thomson-Shore, Inc.
Typeface: Times Roman

To my sons, with love:

Colin for his early encouragement and perceptive criticism of the original manuscript, and Edward, whose skill and patience were essential in getting this book into publishable form; working with him it became ever more obvious that he is what I always tried to be, a no-nonsense professional.

Contents

Preface

To those all-out converts to computerized journalism who declaim that "print is dead," I say, "Not so fast." Let's assume for now that what is important is getting information across, without worrying too much whether transmission is by fax, satellite . . . or even dog team.

Subject matter? Ever since Shakespeare wrote *Henry V,* journalists have been leaning on "What's past is prologue," with justifiable expectation of support. I bring to this narrative more than a half-century of experience. Few people have had a comparable professional life.

I have been editor and publisher of a four-day-a-week university (of North Dakota) newspaper; editor of a country weekly, the *Foster County (North Dakota) Independent;* city editor of a small daily, the *Fargo (North Dakota) Forum;* picture editor and assistant news editor (among other posts) of a metropolitan daily, the *Milwaukee Journal.* I didn't invent *Life*—that was done by Henry R. Luce and the first managing editor, John Shaw Billings, who set out to record the "pictorial history of our times." But I had a lot to do with its development into a giant, including almost twenty years as managing editor and editor (longer than any other person). I did invent *Impact,* a classified World War II Air Force picture magazine. And, at age sixty, I also invented *Smithsonian* magazine, as founding editor and publisher.

All this covered a unique era in American journalism. A lot of editing was still done with a fat, soft-lead pencil. I may never have yelled "Stop the presses!" in the *Front Page* tradition, but I junked all or part of an almost completed issue often enough (see Chapter 21 for graphic proof). The story of *Smithsonian* has not been told in book form before. The story of *Life* in its heyday has been told, but never from the perspective of its chief editor.

Along the way I was continuously involved with fascinating people. The reader of this book will meet many of them through my eyes. Some are world renowned (from the Luces, Winston Churchill, and Harry Truman to Ernest Hemingway, Whittaker Chambers, and the early astronauts). But just as interesting, and mostly a lot more fun, are the lesser-known people you will meet, the talented and often wacky journalists, photographers, artists, and others who contributed so vitally to the publications with which I was involved.

Now, nearly seventy years after getting my first paycheck from a money-making publication, I can't think of anything that has happened to me, in or out of journalism, that hasn't helped form my professional character. This surely includes my first almost twenty years of living in St. Thomas, North Dakota (population 500 then—it's smaller now). It might seem an unlikely springboard from which to leap into big-time editing, but I became inured, early on, to hearing, "You're from North Dakota? You have to be kidding."

Acknowledgments

◠ Special thanks to Philip B. Kunhardt Jr., who I am proud to say was also a managing editor of *Life;* his help in arranging for the publication of many of the photographs herein has been invaluable. Thanks, too, to Time Inc. and to a number of individual photographers for allowing me to use some of their photos. I am also grateful to my wife, Lee, to my daughter-in-law, Susan J. Thompson, and to Kenneth W. Price for their valuable contributions.

A Love Affair with
Life & Smithsonian

1

St. Thomas, an Adequately Obscure Takeoff Site

～ My paternal family farm in Norway was five acres of mostly rocks. In the 1850s, my paternal grandfather, Ole P. Thovsen, age eighteen, came to the United States and anglicized his name to Thompson. His father, Thov Olsen, was dead. Ole became a clerk in a McGregor, Iowa, store and then, with partners, started a dry goods establishment in Decorah, Iowa, the unofficial Norwegian capital of the United States.

He and his partners did well enough to set up a branch in St. Thomas, Dakota Territory. That store eventually became O. P. Thompson & Sons. My father, Edward T. Thompson, at age nineteen and with high school and business "college" diplomas, went to work there as a clerk. He came up from Grand Forks on a Great Northern work train—tracks were still being laid—in 1882. Houses were just going up, so he slept on a counter. Half a dozen years later he was a partner and, with other businessmen, started a bank; he was president. He subsequently served two terms as county treasurer, bought out his bank partners, and in a boom period became mostly an agent for buyers of land and a farm landlord.

My maternal grandfather, Charles F. Kramer, emigrated from Germany, also in the 1850s, to avoid conscription. He worked as a farmhand in Pennsylvania for one "Honest John" Hayes, an Orangeman and his future father-in-law. Grandfather Kramer was more of a patriot than Grandfather Thompson, who hired a substitute for the Civil War and escaped the draft. Grandfather Kramer enlisted in the Union Army and became a sergeant, but then spent the last months of the war in Andersonville prison. My

1

grandmother, Sarah Kramer, and two sons spent theirs on a backwoods farm. After the war Grandfather Kramer failed as a farmer in northwest Wisconsin but made a living as a maker of cabinets and coffins. I inherited none of his manual dexterity.

Sarah became an herb doctor and midwife and delivered almost all the babies born in Mondovi, Wisconsin, between 1870 and 1905. She often dispensed something called Aunt Sally's Painkiller, composed of 49.5 percent laudanum, 49.5 percent paregoric, and 1 percent pepsum (dried chicken gizzards). She was also a militant White Ribboner (prohibitionist) and such an aggressive Methodist that my mother, Bertha (the youngest of eight children who never met her two older brothers until 1920, when she was almost forty), reacted by joining the Episcopalians.

After graduating from Mondovi High School, Bertha taught all eight grades in a one-room country school. Then, "so she could make something of herself," two of her sisters staked her to tuition at Miss Woods's Kindergarten School in Minneapolis. In 1905 Bertha settled for teaching first and second grades in St. Thomas.

Grandmother Thompson's first name was Thonette (French names were fashionable in Norway in the first half of the nineteenth century). Something of an elitist, she named her four sons after the crowned heads of Europe: Edward, my father, after the British Prince of Wales; Charles after the king of Sweden; Theodore Albert after the king of Belgium; and Frederick William after the king of Prussia. She was a devout Lutheran and was most distressed when all of her sons joined the Masons, a fraternity frowned upon by her church. When she discovered that my mother was a terrible cook—until I was five, my parents ate dinner at the local hotel—she periodically sent large wooden boxes of goodies: jars of Norwegian meatballs (which she put through a hand grinder nine times before cooking), *lefse* (potato pancakes), and *fademonbockle* (very rich cookies that often disintegrated en route; still, the crumbs were delicious).

St. Thomas, where my family lived when I was born in 1907, was an unlikely environment for someone who would eventually go to work for *Life*. The town is in remote northeastern North Dakota, twenty-five miles from the Manitoba border, seventeen miles west of the Red River of the North. The well water was alkaline, but the rainfall was usually adequate for growing small grains, potatoes, sugar beets, and pinto beans.

Cottonwood trees served as windbreaks around most farms, but they couldn't really contain the periodic dust storms that filled ditches and postponed spring-cleaning every few years. Nor did the trees do much to mitigate the subzero blizzards that came roaring out of Alberta and Saskatchewan. In winter we could hear the howls of Canadian timber wolves outside town.

Vilhjalmur Stefansson, the Arctic explorer, in his book *The Northward Course of Empire,* somehow proved that in Pembina County, North Dakota, my native county, the average mean temperature was lower than on the Arctic Circle. (To be sure, he was promoting reindeer herding as a desirable way of life.)

School closed during blizzards but not in cold spells per se. At age eight I walked to school when it was 52 degrees below zero, Fahrenheit. I was wrapped ignominiously in a shawl Grandmother Thompson had used to keep bread dough warm while it rose. The school was only half a block away for me, but one farm boy walked a couple of miles from out of town. The cold is painful down to 30 below, when it is accompanied by northwest winds. But at 40 below or lower the air is deadly still. An exposed ear or finger freezes quickly and remains susceptible to freezing again as long as you live—every time the temperature gets much below 32 degrees.

The harsh weather, which included hail some summers, didn't prevent generally good harvests from the black soil—"more fertile than the Valley of the Nile," James J. Hill, the railroad builder, called it. For a couple of years in the mid-1890s, St. Thomas was the largest primary grain market in the world. There were few railway stations as yet, and long lines of horse-drawn wagons would wait for hours—sometimes a couple of days—to sell at the elevators.

To single women of that era, North Dakota had one attraction. Males outnumbered females. In St. Thomas the train with the year's teachers would come up from the south on the Saturday noon before classes started on Monday. A bachelor contingent would gather as the train unloaded. I doubt if my father would have been so undignified as to join the group, but his office in the bank looked out on the street that led from the depot. From that window in later years, he could spot his pet enemies—piano tuners and door-to-door book salesmen—and would phone home to have the doors locked.

He met the new arrivals soon enough. He, the teachers, and his eventual rival for my mother's hand, the cashier of the other bank, all ate at Mrs. Mike Van Camp's boardinghouse near the bank.

My mother would have felt kinship with the fictional Carol Kennicott of *Main Street,* if Sinclair Lewis had invented her by that time. Mother was in

A friend and I sit on the main street of St. Thomas, North Dakota (1909). Many frontier towns had this look.

the vanguard of a group of earnest women who formed the Study Club. She was a founder and the administrative force behind a public library, set up in a run-down Main Street building donated by my father, who had foreclosed a mortgage on it. In the 1920s, she became president of the North Dakota Federation of Women's Clubs. She credited my later facility with using pictures as a journalistic tool to my learning, at age four, to identify sepia prints of old masters' paintings, on loan to the club, hanging on our sitting room walls.

The Thompson family was by no means the only source of culture and other leisure-time diversion in St. Thomas. The schools had better teachers than the town deserved, and there were earnest and educated clergymen in the Methodist, Catholic, and Norwegian Lutheran churches. The congregations were tolerant of each other, and, of course, there were no blacks or Jews, hardly any in the whole state.

The Opera House featured home-talent plays, programs of the Lyceum circuit (the wintertime equivalent of the Chautauqua tent programs), community dances, card parties, and county-agent butchering lessons. It also served for high school basketball games. There were red-hot stoves in two corners and two pillars supporting the roof—around which the usually outclassed St. Thomas team planned its plays, hoping to fake opponents into painful collisions. (The baseball team never amounted to much either. It was no match, for instance, for an even smaller village, Icelandic, which fielded five Thorwaldsons and four Thorliefsons.)

There was a covered natural skating rink. In the warming room a Victrola sat with its horn cut into the wall toward the skaters. The single record had "Skaters' Waltz" on one side and "I Never Knew I Could Love Anybody" on the other.

The curling rink was a lot classier. It had a part-time paid caretaker who prepared the ice meticulously. Well water wasn't good enough. The surface was made from soft rainwater and pebbled with beads of warm water from a shaker so that the heavy granite curling stones could be guided with as much accuracy as the curler and his broom wielders could produce. St. Thomas was host to visitors in *bonspiels* (matches), but the big-league *bonspiels* were in Winnipeg and Minneapolis. My father carried his granite curling stones in a gouged-out block of wood with a handle—it was so heavy I never could figure out how he lifted it.

Schooling in St. Thomas had not been influenced by John Dewey's progressive theories. I was taught to diagram sentences, classify parts of speech, and conjugate verbs. My spelling was phonetic, bolstered by just plain memorizing words that weren't spelled as they sounded. I was a natural speed reader with some powers of retention. The long descriptions of Scottish scenery in Sir Walter Scott's novels bored me, so I skipped those passages. I read everything in the bookcases at home, plus almost everything in the library. I even got my hands on books that my mother considered unsuitable for general reading in St. Thomas.

The family trip was a staple with the Thompsons. My parents might have been excused for leaving me and, later, my younger brother, Bob, behind, but that possibility was never considered. Off we would go with my father's ritual remark "You're packing as if we were going to Europe."

In March 1912 we actually went there. An endowment insurance policy, on which my father's father had contributed the first premium thirty years earlier, was paid up. My father, who was pretty miserly on small expenditures, shot the works on occasion. My brother wasn't along in spirit, only physically. He wasn't born until September, shortly after our return.

Our itinerary was that of a Grand Tour. We sailed on a Red Star liner, passing literally within a day's distance of the sinking *Titanic*. I took walks around the deck with my father—my mother was seasick. Every morning a sailor would dip a thermometer off the bow to see if a drop in temperature indicated a nearby iceberg. Of course, a child of four and a half couldn't possibly remember a detail like that, but similar bits of family lore came up so often in conversation that it was easy to acquire the illusion that I did. I mostly remember the instances when I was scared, notably when I got onto an inter-urban train in Berlin and ended up alone in Potsdam, some twenty miles away.

Unfortunately there is no photographic record to serve as an aide-mémoire for this great experience. My father's camera was stolen in Gibraltar, our first continental stop. This made him so angry that he refused to buy a new one on that trip. We had to rely on occasional shots by street photographers.

In 1916 we made another trip outside the United States. My father was carried away by the 1898 conquest of Cuba. He considered annexation a sure thing and General Leonard Wood's continued administration of the island likely. My father had bought a quarter section of Cuban land, which produced no income, so we went down ostensibly to sell it. (He *did* unload it, taking a mortgage which he eventually wrote off as a bad debt.)

My brother and I were both recuperating from whooping cough. Between trains in Atlanta, we went to a matinee of *The Birth of a Nation.* The crowd booed when Lincoln appeared on the screen. My father, righteously outraged, grabbed me with one hand, my brother with the other, and stomped out. It was years before I discovered how the movie ended.

The Great War, later known as World War I, extended St. Thomas's outside interests beyond the prices in the Minneapolis grain pit. At first my father and mother were mildly pro-German—they felt they had been treated more politely in Germany than in England and France. With the invasion of neutral Belgium, the atrocity stories, and, finally, the torpedoing of the *Lusitania,* this changed. My father became chairman of the Pembina County Liberty Loan Committee, and my mother was president of the local Red Cross chapter.

Once we were at war, even St. Thomas wasn't too small for the attention of our new allies. An invalided British officer came through for morale building, stayed with us, and left an empty 75 mm shell casing, which my mother used to hold lilacs for years afterward.

I came out of the war with two pins attesting to the completion of two 100-hour stints for my mother's Red Cross—I had used my wagon to tote materials for bandages and wool for sweaters and for something called gauntlets; the latter were knitted tubes that covered a rifleman's wrists and upper hands but not the fingers, which of course had to be free so he could use his trigger finger. Also as part of the war effort I had patriotically used my allowance to buy war savings stamps, which, when enough were accumulated, could be used to buy Liberty bonds. And I had laboriously combed the town for tinfoil to fill an unspecified shortage of metals. The most productive area was outside the pool hall, a citadel of sin I had never entered. The loungers there were prodigious chewers of snuff (pronounced "snoose"), which came in heavy foil wrappings.

After the drama of the distant war, life in St. Thomas went back to its prewar placidity. With $2 wheat, the farmers had prospered, although they were angry at Herbert Hoover, Woodrow Wilson's food administrator, for not letting it go higher. Prices fell, and by 1921 a recession had developed.

Fires always provided the most visible drama in St. Thomas. The volunteer department was headed by a former Milwaukee professional, Jack Elias, whose first move at a fire was always to chop a hole in the roof of the burning building—for reasons that still escape me. To fight fires, the outlet of the nearest well was unplugged and attached to the fire engine. The stream of alkaline water smothered flames efficiently but ruined the furniture.

Most of the grain elevators burned down, one by one. Not-quite-ripe grain in the bins would heat up and ignite by spontaneous combustion.

The most dramatic fire was the burning of the schoolhouse, which was a half block from us. There was no doubt it was arson, motivated by civic responsibility. The aging building, made of yellow brick like our bank, had been declared unacceptable by state authorities, and the high school was about to lose its first class rating. And therefore graduates would no longer be able to get into state colleges and the university without taking entrance exams.

It wasn't as if St. Thomas was without warning. My father, who was president of the school board, tried to annex surrounding school districts to provide a tax base that would finance a new building. The effort failed because some farmers preferred their one-room grade schools and token tuition at the high school to paying higher taxes. The deadline for starting a new building passed, and every high school pupil who could do so was encouraged to graduate in three years so that the diplomas would come from a school that was still officially first class. I was one of these, and, because I had skipped the second and fourth grades earlier, I was a high school graduate at fourteen.

My father, my mother, my newly
arrived brother, Bob, and I in front
of our house in St. Thomas (1913).

The public-spirited arsonists wanted to make sure that the building was a
total loss so a new school would have to be built. In the dark, they chopped
the hoses that were attached to the artesian wells, so we had to climb up on
our roof and wet the shingles with pails of rainwater to prevent sparks from
setting our house on fire.

A new school had to be built, and my father took a gamble that there
would be enough taxes collected to pay for a gym to replace the Opera
House for basketball and dramatics. He got a few more districts to merge
with St. Thomas, but not quite enough. The new building was of red-brown
brick from Hebron, North Dakota, but the back, to which the auditorium
was to be a kind of lean-to, was in plain brick.

A little young to start college, I killed a year in "postgraduate" courses
at the high school, which was temporarily housed in the basement of the
Methodist church. I had been given a Corona portable typewriter, which then
had three rows of type, and I learned the touch system via a correspondence
course. I also took a mail-order course in solid geometry.

Even though I had been graduated, I was on the football team because there were only eleven boys in high school. Opponents would have been crazy to protest me as a ringer. When a player was hurt, he was taken behind an old threshing machine and his uniform was transferred to the biggest eighth-grade boy around. That year ended my participation in contact sports—except dancing.

At basketball games, I could devote my full time to being the cheerleader. There were five players on the first team, five on the second, and then there was me. For football games, I led the cheers between halves.

On a 1920 Shriners' convention trip with my father to Portland, Oregon, I came down with bronchial pneumonia and was put to bed at my uncle's farm in Banks, Oregon, where a country doctor prescribed drops of ipecac in warm milk direct from my uncle's cow. My feet grew three sizes while I was in my sickbed. When I recovered I returned home by way of Yellowstone Park.

And, in a modest way, I turned professional. I had taken a photograph of a bear eating garbage from the loading platform of the Yellowstone Lake Hotel, and I sent it to *Boys' Life,* the Boy Scout magazine. I was paid $1.

The next year we visited the Black Hills of South Dakota. My mother, a culture vulture, learned that the sculptor Gutzon Borglum would be there, and we booked into the same hotel. After dinner one night Borglum held forth in front of a man-high fireplace, sketching his idea for sculpting Washington, Jefferson, Lincoln, and Teddy Roosevelt on a mountainside. Much later he spent fourteen years carving those famous presidential heads on nearby Mount Rushmore. We were in on the prebirth.

Thereafter, the Thompson trips tended toward visits to lakes in northern Minnesota. My father chose cold, spring-fed lakes, supposedly because they are better for black bass. I never seemed to catch any fish, and the water was too cold to encourage swimming. I never got promoted from Second to First Class Scout because I couldn't swim 100 yards.

Beyond a thought, now and then, that it "might be nice," I did not in high school plan for professional journalism. I was not much inspired by the periodicals that reached us. There was a weekly, the *St. Thomas Times,* which had been owned by my godfather, Grant Sherman Hager (guess when he was born), but he left it in the hands of his printer when he moved fourteen miles south to Grafton and a county-seat paper. The *Times* was basically a few columns of local items, hand set and augmented by quantities of syndicated boilerplate (almost timeless material). It folded in the early 1920s.

The morning *Grand Forks Herald* came up on the noon train, and it had the Associated Press and *Chicago Tribune* comics. A Minneapolis paper, closing the previous afternoon, was on the same train.

The news magazine of the time was the *Literary Digest,* which culled material from the nation's newspapers, ending up with an "on the one hand and on the other hand" blandness. The *Saturday Evening Post* provided literature of sorts—the serialized fiction by such as Clarence Buddington Kelland, Octavus Roy Cohen, and Mary Roberts Rinehart was devoured by early Tuesday afternoon, the day of delivery.

Nor did a career in banking appeal to me. I had worked, part time, in my father's bank enough to want to try for something more than a future of balancing the day's accounts, staying up late at night to clear up a discrepancy of a nickel or two (it was unthinkable to just put in or take out a nickel to even things up).

So, with no clear future in mind, I headed, as the family had always assumed I would, to the University of North Dakota in Grand Forks, sixty miles south of St. Thomas. Whatever else, the price there was right: $16 a semester, not including room and board but with free tickets to athletic events and the *Dakota Student* newspaper thrown in.

" . . . my vife? You put dat in da paper?"

A state university offers a marginally larger world for a future journalist than a small town. It is a microcosm of a whole state, which makes it most useful for politicians because it contains someone who might be influential from almost every town in the state. Moreover, in those days the university could not be selective about its student body since it had to take graduates from every first-class North Dakota high school.

Hopeless incompetents usually flunked out at some point during the four years. The 1923 freshman class of 400 shrank more than 25 percent by the start of the sophomore year, and only half of the original class survived to receive degrees in 1927. Nonetheless, an education of sorts was there to be absorbed.

Even though those years were called the Roaring Twenties, it was a quiet time for me. I was sixteen. I was embarrassed, although I probably shouldn't have been, by my parents' decision that my mother should come with me to Grand Forks and take an apartment for a year, dragging my younger brother along, while my father "batched it" in St. Thomas. After all, the largest group in the university came from Grand Forks and lived at home.

I was trying to adjust to life in that metropolis of 15,000. That second largest city in the state impressed me more than did Milwaukee four years later or even New York only six years later, when I became, for a few months, a substitute correspondent there for the *Milwaukee Journal*.

Most students had little money. Farm prices were down. The average student spent less than $600 a year for room, board, tuition, and entertainment.

I was rushed by three social fraternities—ability to pay the house bills was a key factor in selecting pledges. Dormitory space was in short supply, and the fraternity and sorority residences were needed to house students. Room and board was about $50 a month, and the food was slightly better than that at the University Commons, so I joined a fraternity and moved into the chapter house the following year.

Jobs for students who were working their way through were mostly menial, such as waiting on tables. To support football and basketball players, the athletic department had a few cushy jobs at its disposal. One was that of station agent for the Great Northern's university stop. The pay was $40 a month, and the agent didn't even have to sell tickets—they were sold on the train. Even more important, there were no trains at night, so the station was used to house a poker game. The year I arrived, the agent was the star tackle, Aloysious Brodie. He had a round table with a hole in the center, and into that hole he swept 10 percent of every pot.

There were no perks for amateur journalists, but the four-day-a-week *Student* always needed reporters. A staff job was considered an extracurricular activity, worthy of a yearbook entry. My first story was a report on a weekly university convocation speaker. I wouldn't be eligible for journalism courses until my second year, but I had heard about the six Ws—what, when, where, who, why, and how—and squeezed them into the opening paragraph of my account. The rest, including what I thought the speaker said, was well enough organized to escape the rudimentary copyreading of the editor. I remember this as the moment when I said to myself, "This reporting isn't so tough," and was satisfied that I had communicated what there was to say in a tidy manner.

I looked around at the other freshmen on the *Student* staff, figured they offered a minimum of competition for the eventual editorship, and felt confirmed in my tentative decision to take courses in journalism the next year. It was only much later that I realized that if I had taken more courses in English, science, and history and fewer trade-school lessons in the journalism department (some of which I had to unlearn later), I would have been better prepared for my chosen trade.

The *Student* provided a taste of real-life newspaper production, of assembling enough copy to fill the pages (at least four), writing headlines, making layouts, fitting stories, and even selling ads.

In my time the *Student* was printed in a shop across the Red River in East Grand Forks, Minnesota. The issue editor gathered up the copy turned in during the day, took a trolley to Grand Forks, two miles from the campus, walked across the bridge, and had to finish everything in time to catch the midnight streetcar back to the university. The sometimes malty breath of an irascible, profane printer named Dutch confirmed that East Grand Forks, the sin section of that area, had several blind pigs (the term *speakeasy* came later) operating openly. I started editing issues in my sophomore year, became managing editor in my third, and editor-in-chief, in charge of both editorial and business operations, during my last year.

The minutiae of this sub-apprenticeship to a trade could be tedious, and there wasn't much political and intellectual activity on campus. The country was keeping cool with Coolidge, although in the Middle West there was some discontent represented by the La Follette Progressives in Wisconsin, the Farmer-Labor movement in Minnesota, and the Nonpartisan League in North Dakota.

The Nonpartisan League farmers in the western part of North Dakota filled most of the state offices, including that of governor, a potato farmer named Lynn Frazier. He was far from being a flaming radical, and he was such a superloyal university alumnus that he named his twin daughters Unie and Versie. They were in school when I was, and I was relieved to learn some years later that they had changed their names.

A short, muscular black girl athlete, who excelled in sprints and the weights, conducted a humor column for me in the *Student*. Years later she wrote me at *Life,* "Isn't it monotonous, all of us Thompsons are getting to be managing editors?" Her name was Eva Bell Thompson and she was then on *Ebony*.

In a few years Alfred E. Smith would be defeated for the presidency, in part because of anti-Catholic sentiment. So it should not be surprising that North Dakota, even though it was a northern state, had a vigorous and influential Ku Klux Klan. The Klan had been a large factor in the gubernatorial defeat of an able Catholic Democrat, J. F. T. O'Connor, who later became Controller of the Currency for FDR.

State politics was none of the *Student*'s business, and mixing in that wasn't what I had in mind when I remonstrated editorially with a local Presbyterian preacher, who incidentally was a state Imperial Wizard for the Klan. As in most churches, it was hard to attract a crowd for Sunday night services. He took out an eight-column ad across the bottom of the *Grand Forks Herald*'s front page, promising that the Reverend F. Halsey Ambrose would embark on a series of Sunday night sermons entitled "Sin at the

University." I hadn't noticed much sin on the campus, so I sent a reporter to audit the first installment.

The sermon consisted of vague generalities with no specifics at all, so I wrote an editorial suggesting that, if the series were to continue, Mr. Ambrose, to be credible, needed some demonstrable facts. There was no noticeable reaction to the editorial, either at the university or downtown.

In the next issue of the *Student,* however, a student who asked to be anonymous compared Ambrose unfavorably to Elmer Gantry (the Sinclair Lewis novel had just been published). I was called into the university president's office. Thomas F. Kane said he respected the paper's policy to provide anonymity on occasion, but that Ambrose was threatening to lobby the next legislative session to kill the university appropriation if I didn't reveal the name of the letter writer. I promised to think it over.

My instincts told me to start out being a fearless editor by registering defiance, however feeble, of the Klan, but I wondered whether satisfying my ego was worth the threat to the school. I was wrestling with the problem when the author of the letter himself, one Benny Johnson, solved it. He heard about the situation and volunteered that he would be proud to identify himself. He and I were excoriated only briefly in the next Ambrose sermon.

The *Student* was named the best paper in the North Central Conference and made enough money to pay tiny salaries. In the journalism department's curriculum there were courses in reporting and copyreading, advertising, newspaper history, and ethics. The only memory I have of the latter was a discussion of the sentence "There sat the Buddha, looking at his navel." It would sound worse, we were told, to substitute a blank for what Buddha was looking at. Fair enough.

The professor of journalism, Roy Laverne French, was a genial, lazy man with an outhouse sense of humor. He was popular with the editors around the state, so his department was useful—as are many similar departments and schools of journalism—as an employment agency for available jobs, mostly on country weeklies.

Before my senior year the department acquired a second teacher, a hot-tempered Irish-American named Ambrose Dominick (Pat) Gannon, a genuine professional, who was to have more influence than anyone else on my early career. He had gone from a tiny town, Sedan, Minnesota, to the University of Wisconsin, where French had been one of his instructors. Gannon then taught English in a North Dakota high school, worked on a country weekly in Algoma, Wisconsin, and got a job on the *Milwaukee*

Journal, to which he would return. Despite the fact that he threw me out of his classes a couple of times for impertinence (guilty as charged), he volunteered to check on the possibility of a job for me in Milwaukee when he returned to the *Journal.* Nothing definite. The Associated Press bureau chief in Minneapolis also promised to get in touch with me but didn't.

I was elected to Phi Beta Kappa, and as graduation approached, I knew I had to have a serious talk with my father about becoming a professional journalist. Although I loved and respected him, this would be our first such exchange. I certainly knew what he felt about the world in general and about specific items of my behavior. Even when angry he had a humorous way of expressing himself, but if I lost control and giggled, he could become furious. I knew that he bragged about me behind my back, and I found out after he died that he had even kept my old report cards, with their bad marks in penmanship. He himself wrote in a fine Spencerian hand and was in his element when he signed the paper currency that national banks could issue in those days.

Most people in St. Thomas expected me to take over the bank eventually, but my father never said so out loud. It would have been painful for me if he had, uncharacteristically, made an emotional appeal for me to join the bank. In fact, I felt fairly safe in chancing it.

"This newspaper business, how much would it pay you?"

"Not much at first, but I've heard of newspapermen getting $50 a week eventually."

"It looks to me as if you should try it. The banking business is no good any more. When I started, you loaned, let's say, $100 and immediately deducted $10 for commission. Then, when the loan was paid off you got 10 percent on the $100, so, a profit of $20. Woodrow Wilson and his Federal Reserve System messed all that up."

I realized that he was trying to make it easy for me to do what I wanted, and was truly thankful. He didn't know at the time that I was planning to marry a fellow student, Marguerite Maxam of Culbertson, Montana. I was convinced that there would be a hassle at home to try to talk me out of it on the grounds that I was too young to know what I was doing. So Marguerite and I decided to make it a fait accompli. Our marriage lasted thirty years—much longer than the bank.

It was a matter of faith with my father that St. Thomas was basically sound. Out of pride he refused an offer from a Minneapolis-based chain to take over his operation. He died in 1931, and soon after, with no one really running it, the bank was closed automatically by the Federal Reserve: the ratio of liquid assets to frozen (in farm mortgages, naturally) had fallen below its requirements. In spite of an inept nonbanker who got a political appointment as receiver, depositors were eventually paid more than 90 percent (as compared to about half that for the rival bank that had closed earlier).

I am indebted to Roy French's employment service for my first job, on the not very exciting *Foster County Independent* in Carrington, North Dakota. Carrington was at least a county seat, but since the job didn't seem all that permanent, Marguerite didn't come with me there. Instead she spent the summer at her family's home in eastern Montana, planning then to return in the fall to the University of North Dakota for her final year. The Carrington job did give me a start, and allowed me to acquire some of the basics of the trade. The *Independent* was barely into the Mergenthaler Linotype age, with one machine that set body type and small headlines but did not have a font for medium to larger size headlines, which had to be hand set from a case. This was back to Gutenberg, or at least to Ben Franklin, who started as a journeyman printer.

The *Independent*'s owner, George P. Collins, a kindly man with a froglike voice and a figure to match, greeted me: "I've been trying to take a vacation for twenty years, and I leave in a week or two." He was a printer who had worked on the *Traer (Iowa) Star Clipper,* which won prizes for its typography. Collins was a perfectionist in that area and was the proud owner of a set of all-brass column rules, leads, and slugs, some of which got melted each week when the printer's devil dumped the Linotype-composed metal into the hellbox, where it was melted down for the next round of type.

In my brief break-in period, Collins imparted two nuggets of wisdom: "To make a success in the newspaper business, work hard all your life, then inherit $90,000 and buy up all the papers in the county." As it happened, Collins had done just that, and the *Independent,* as Foster County's only newspaper, automatically had a monopoly on official legal notices at nine cents a line for the first insertion and seven cents—no resetting needed—for the two following weeks. This business took care of the overhead, and the revenue from other ads and subscriptions was gravy.

His other bit of advice: "If you must write editorials, don't pick a subject nearer than Minneapolis. I'm the only one in town who gets the *New York Times,* so I usually just clip something."

My professor Roy French had given Collins a somewhat erroneous assurance that I could hand set type because I had passed his pet course in the journalism department's type laboratory. The Linotype operator could do it, but he was too valuable elsewhere. In addition to his mechanical skills, he set in type the offerings from the correspondents throughout the county and edited their copy into English at the same time.

For the six weeks that Collins was to be on vacation, the staff would total four and a half: the combination reporter, editor, publisher, salesman of advertising and job printing, and hand compositor (me); the Linotype operator; a pressman who operated an ancient, clumsy flatbed; a part-time printer's devil for cleanup; and Cecelia, who was something else. She was the receptionist and bookkeeper. She took want ads and was the society editor. This last job consisted of calling every name in the local phone book every week to find out who had entertained, who had taken trips out of town, etc. It is a given in weekly publishing that everyone in the area should be mentioned in the paper at least once a year.

One weekend in July, Cecelia gave birth to a son. She left him with her mother to come back to work on Monday. The baby himself showed up in our office two or three weeks later, with an oversized wastebasket as a crib. Cecelia expected the father, a drifter who had left town, to come back "sometime."

My employment started in time for me to contribute to the Thursday, June 16, 1927, issue. I wrote a few stories, set a few headlines under George's wary eye, and saw a one-column portrait of myself, courtesy of George, on page 1. The other "art" on that page was a two-column engraving of Charles A. Lindbergh Jr., who had just made a triumphant return to New York from Paris and whose future plans were said to include a visit to his native state of Minnesota.

Straining for what is known in the trade as a local angle, I interviewed a young carpenter, Heldring Johnson, the nephew of a cemetery sexton, who had arrived that week from Sweden. The connection I hoped to establish was how Lindbergh's fellow Swedes reacted to the historical flight. The aviator's father was an antiestablishment congressman and was of Swedish descent. Heldring thought Lindbergh was, to be sure, a hero, but an American—not a Swedish—hero. That was my last try at the *Independent* for anything international.

A description of the June 23 issue, which I produced pretty much by myself, will illustrate a perilous aspect of editing a country weekly.

I checked the office of the county judge and was disappointed to find that only seven marriage licenses had been issued. The judge himself, a Norwegian immigrant, was considered a humorist. While running for his job he had said, "Getting elected to public office is like getting pickles out of a jar or kisses from a girl. It's hard at first but after that it comes easy." I asked him about marriage licenses, and he said, "There is too much red tape. It takes five blanks to get married, and you even have to get a license to fish suckers out of the Yim [James] River. I could get a couple married with one blank. I know of an insane couple that got married in Foster County. I never heard of anyone not passing the physical examination." I thought this slightly amusing and quoted him in a story.

The issue went to press Wednesday night and George Collins left by car on his vacation. Here I was on Thursday morning facing my first full week on my own. The morning was spent redistributing the type with which the headlines had been composed.

At lunch time I was walking on the sun-drenched, treeless Main Street toward the drugstore when the judge, small and redfaced, approached. A *High Noon* confrontation! The judge was sputtering mighty Norwegian oaths. His tongue-lashing attracted a crowd of small boys. Finally, I was able to interject, "But, judge, I only put down what you said." He shouted, "Suppose I tal you I fock my vife, you put dat in da paper?" This convulsed the giggling audience and left me speechless.

He stomped off, but the next day we got a notice that the *Independent*'s contract to print the county stationery had been canceled. Fortunately, he couldn't cut off the valuable legal notices.

Cecelia, in her role as society editor, wasn't turning up anything startling in the way of items for the "locals" column, but her notes filled part of the eight yawning pages. The gleanings included a birthday lunch for someone's mother, a lawn party for American Legionnaire children, a regular meeting of a women's lodge, and an auction. Cecelia needed only rudimentary editing, mostly devising various ways of saying that a family had visited a nearby town.

Other page 1 stories included the prospect of 200 district delegates from the pentecostal Church of the Brethren coming for a meeting. Members of nearby golf clubs would attend a Carrington tournament. Music lovers who wanted to hear band numbers played by their offspring were told that two months of practicing scales had to come first. More significantly, a tour of grain managers, including two from Carrington, reported the state's crops generally good, but there was not much optimism about prices.

Of genuine, long-term significance was the pending arrival at the Carrington city park of an educational tour headed by U.S. Senator Gerald P. Nye, who was in private life the editor of the weekly in adjoining Griggs County, with an army engineer and members of the state legislature. The group was to examine the possibilities for a mammoth Missouri basin project, which would start with an earthen dam at Fort Peck, in Montana, and continue with dams at Garrison, North Dakota, and on down the Missouri River until it joined with the Mississippi.

The James River, which flows past Carrington, is a tributary to the Missouri, and our whole area stood to benefit from this flood-prevention and irrigation project. At this point, however, the program was only a gleam in the eyes of the planners. Senator Nye, a leader of the Nonpartisan League of the Republican Party, had no influence with the Coolidge administration. (It took almost a decade and the New Deal to get the Fort Peck Dam into construction; a photograph of it was the cover of the first issue of *Life,* in November 1936.)

Filling up the rest of the June 23 issue involved rewriting some items that originated out of the county. For instance, a new state law required that the Ten Commandments be posted in all schools. Also from the state capital came the allotments for snow fences to keep drifts off the roads. Foster County would get less than four miles of them. The state's payment for local districts delivering pupils to schools more than two miles away from home would be $1.40 a day—under two miles was walking distance.

From the state agricultural college and the Federal Department of Agriculture, *Independent* readers learned that a mineral mixture helped prevent goiter in hogs. As if the farmers didn't already know it, I made items out of the information that potatoes and sugar beets require more labor than does grain, and that jackrabbits are capable of causing crop damage.

Syndicated columns filled more of the space. Aunt Louisa advised "A poor little innocent" not to be fooled by a "man of the world. His own brothers know he is a drinker and philanderer and always will be. A young girl cannot know the horror of having blind and afflicted children to rear."

Longer stories, called "bulldog," were available when needed. The National Geographic Society was a prolific source, and thus readers learned about a 1920 earthquake in the "wild west" of China, Kansu Province.

The total lineage to fill an issue was set in type, but a feeling of relief would have been premature. There was still the procedure of "sizing" all the columns. It was traditional to start with the shortest item at the top, then the next shortest on down the column, ending with the longest. The visual effect of paragraphs making their way symmetrically downward was pleasingly tidy.

I would get the galleys of type from the Linotype operator, select one event with which to lead the section on the correspondent's territories— Bordulac, Brantford, Cathay, Glenfield, Juanita, McHenry, Melville, and such. Subjects could include anything from a church picnic to a broken bat hitting a baseball spectator in the head. The headline story would be followed by a line in capitals: OTHER BORDULAC NEWS. This was followed by less portentous lines, arranged with the symmetry described above.

I am somewhat of a klutz mechanically, so it was a tense moment each time I lifted a headline I had set from the hand-held stick into the steel chase that held the page being assembled. Although I had wedged the letters tightly, there was always a danger that the whole thing would squirt out onto the floor—"pied."

Once the columns were locked into the chase, the pressman would take a wooden mallet and pound out a page proof for the final okay. This achieved, there were more breathless moments as each page was slid onto the flatbed of the old press. Although I was designated as the assistant pressman, I shudder to think what I would have done if anything had gone wrong. In my short reign, there were only minor delays in the press run of some 1,500 copies, but I stayed until the last one was folded, addressed, and ready for distribution from the post office Thursday morning. The June 23 issue was history.

I had the use of a 1920 Chevrolet coupe that George had bought for $50. In July International Harvester announced that it was about to market a "combine," which would revolutionize grain harvesting. This machine eliminated the process of tying the cut grain into bundles, placing the bundles into shocks by hand, and then taking these to the threshing machine, where they had to be pitchforked in. The following month, when harvest got under way, I used the car to cover an actual demonstration of this wonder.

Apart from the judge's, another set of hurt feelings awaited George on his return. Instead of using bulldog to make up for a shortfall of local editorial matter, I had concocted an ad calling attention to the availability of *Independent* classified ads for locating lost objects, as contrasted with using a fortuneteller. I had ignored a nearby "reader," an ad inserted in the column of local items (a common practice in country weeklies). It read: "Emil Wahren, well diviner, fortuneteller and finder of lost objects." Each morning as I passed Emil's house on my way to work he was sitting on his little porch, and he voiced his protest from there. The paper was competing unfairly with an advertiser, and he made his complaint personal by saying, "I see bad fortune for you."

Emil was tall and bent, almost cadaverous in appearance. He glared balefully each morning from eyes deep set in dead white skin. But then one day he burst into cackles of laughter. His hex was working. I had broken out with pimples, and Emil took full credit.

George had no trouble kidding Emil and the judge back into *Independent* customer status. I felt comfortable in having gotten my feet wet professionally but was embarrassed by a characteristic Collins kindness. Driving home in the office Chevrolet just before he returned, I had hit a cow lying in a prairie road. The cow had gotten up and moved on in apparent good health, but a fender had been bent. I had taken it to a town just outside the county for repair, but when I went to pick it up, the garage man said I owed nothing. Mr. Collins had come and paid for it. He must have done it on his first day back.

Among others, schoolteachers, preachers, and editors have no private lives in a rural area. But distaste for small-town life wasn't the only reason I was pleased with a phone call and job offer from an old friend who had been working on the *Fargo Forum,* the only paper in the state's largest town (30,000 at that time). I could sense that I was going to get on George's nerves; eventually we were bound to disagree on editorial approaches. Of course, I hadn't learned everything possible on the *Independent,* but I knew that openings on daily newspapers wouldn't come along often.

The pay in Fargo would be $25 a week, the same as in Carrington. George rather halfheartedly offered me $5 more a week to stay, which would have given me about twice what first-year reporters were making in Minneapolis. Still, I decided to leave. (It was not the last time I took a cut in pay for something I thought offered more opportunity.) The parting was friendly, and George and I corresponded intermittently for a number of years.

Moving from a weekly to a daily was no big deal. (Again Marguerite and I decided that it was best temporarily for her to stay in Montana.) Fargo was bigger, but the readers were the same kind of people as in St. Thomas, Grand Forks, or Carrington. I did, however, acquire a metropolitan-sounding and impressive title—night city editor. I was also all the reporters on the morning edition of the *Forum,* the A.M. paper being a kind of holding operation to keep competition out of town.

The controlling interest in the *Forum* was held by the biggest department store, Black's, but the visible figure in charge was H. D. ("Happy") Paulson, the editor. His brother-in-law was managing editor. Happy almost never came in nights. There was professional discipline of a sort from Glenn Parsons, the news editor, or slot man, in our night shift of four. We all had titles: telegraph editor, sports editor, plus Glenn and me. I was warned that if Happy called from a party and ordered a story about it to equivocate. If an editor refused outright, he might be fired over the phone. If he put something in the paper, he would probably be fired in the morning.

Glenn was a good journeyman newspaperman who introduced me to spiked beer—a measure of grain alcohol in a bottle of Minnehaha Pale near beer that was likely to cause morning-after headaches.

The night city editor's routine started in the afternoon. I walked to the office, stopping at three hotels to see if any visitor of note had checked in. Then I dropped by the police station and sheriff's office. Writing up what I found took me until supper, always taken at a home-cooking restaurant called the Bluebird Cafe. On the way back to the office I rechecked the police and sheriff.

Then there were telephone calls to the hospitals and undertaking parlors, to the sheriffs' departments in half a dozen neighboring counties. I had to make judgments on how long the stories should be, read my own copy, and write the headlines.

Most of my news gathering was by phone, although sometimes a tip picked up on my rounds or from others would be followed up by on-the-spot reporting. The *Forum* would reimburse me for taxi bills. On rare occasions there would be a story handled by the day staff that had come in too late for the afternoon edition. The collective judgment of the day staff was not infallible. For instance, the news that Lindbergh would visit Fargo on his triumphal tour drew an eight-column banner headline in the afternoon edition proclaiming: 1 MILLION TO GREET LINDY. I had to rewrite this story for the next morning, and an elementary calculation indicated that the earlier estimate would be double the population of the whole state. In my follow-up story, I omitted mentioning the size of the crowd. When Lindbergh did get to Fargo, there were perhaps 60,000 on the streets—twice the city's population—and they saw nothing but a closed car with the hero inside, whipping through town and back to the airport.

I soon gained the impression that, if a raise in pay was to be squeezed out of the *Forum,* a chance to leave had to be produced. Pat Gannon had been back in Milwaukee since June and in September wired me that there was an opening on the copy desk. Did I want the job, and how much would I ask? I took a deep breath and asked for $35 a week. My figure was accepted, and there wasn't much discussion about it. Marguerite was expecting a child in the spring, and my friends on the *Forum* told me to take it.

The managing editor, Happy's brother-in-law, allowed as how maybe $30 could be managed. The day city editor was more persuasive. He warned me that he had worked in Milwaukee, the pace was pretty fast, and I would never make it. That was a challenge I couldn't resist—even if I had wanted to. As I saw it, I was off to the "big time."

So I wouldn't miss a payday, Marguerite and I left Fargo on a Sunday and I reported to the *Milwaukee Journal* on Monday. In my eight weeks at the *Forum* I don't think I had learned as much as I had during a similar period in Carrington. I hadn't handled any difficult stories. My face-to-face contacts outside of the office had been mostly hotel clerks, policemen, and waitresses. My nightly telephone pals were undertakers, night nurses, and sheriffs' deputies.

Ahead was a big city and a demanding, albeit adequately recompensed, postgraduate education.

3

"Pope Elopes with Gilda Gray"

⟨∿⟩ The fast track of Milwaukee newspapering predicted by the *Forum*'s city editor did not appear menacing in October 1927, and less so as time passed. What was stimulating was that there were competing newspapers.

The independent afternoon *Journal* faced a Hearst rival, the *Wisconsin News,* and the official Socialist organ, the *Leader.* The longtime mayor, Dan Hoan, was a Socialist who had the tacit support of the business establishment. The Common Council (the city's legislative body) was Socialist, too. The morning paper, the *Sentinel,* was also owned by Hearst through Hearst's conservative editorial spokesman, Arthur Brisbane. Brisbane's father had been a Milwaukee Socialist—party headquarters was Brisbane Hall.

Powerful competition, especially for the *Sentinel,* came from the *Chicago Tribune,* ninety miles away, and papers in closer cities, such as Racine and Kenosha. In addition, there were German- and Polish-language dailies.

The *Journal* was a solid paper, about to emerge as number 1 in the city and state. It had a stubbornly independent editor and owner, Lucius (Lute) Nieman, a staunch Democrat in a then nominally Republican state. He was perhaps the last printer to parlay that craft into publishing success. His fortune was used to set up the Nieman Fellowships for journalists. He was (horrors!) pro-American when the country got into World War I. The competition was pussyfooting about being for the war, and the city's still pro-German elements had to read the *Journal* in order to find out what was being said about them. *Journal* reporters infiltrated ethnic societies and went as far as getting a brewery raided for hidden arms (there was nothing there);

the result was a Pulitzer Prize–winning series about pro-German sentiment in Milwaukee.

By 1927 Nieman was almost a recluse. An indifferent businessman, he had had the vision to recruit an advertising manager, Harry Grant, from New York. Grant was ruthlessly competitive and soon became publisher. He was personally choleric, but he propelled the *Journal* into financial success without, according to him, Nieman's being aware of it.

Key members of the editorial staff were more interesting perhaps than the newspaper itself. Marvin Creager, managing editor, was a former *Kansas City Star* Washington correspondent who demanded, with Grant's backing, full editorial independence—he never even allowed an advertising man on our floor.

Waldo Arnold was a news editor I greatly admired for his judgment and his mastery of his trade. He was nicknamed Scoop, perhaps in jest because he had never been a great reporter.

Basil ("Stuffy," because of his figure) Walters, the telegraph editor and my first boss, was an instinctive journalist. He was a master of self-promotion and was shortly to leave to become the editor of papers in, successively, Des Moines, Minneapolis, Detroit, and Chicago. He and I were the only ones to quit the *Journal* voluntarily between 1927 and 1937.

Vern Huston was a quiet marvel who ran the local copy desk. He was meticulous and humorous and had command of the language. He had neither the ability nor the inclination to push himself. When he retired he taught himself to operate a Linotype and worked on his son's country weekly.

Claude Manly, a star reporter who actually solved murder cases, was usually called Cap (he had commanded an artillery battery in World War I). His hobbies were singing Gilbert and Sullivan and punching cops while drunk. The policemen on the beat were given pictures of him and told to let him swing away because he knew too much about the Establishment. He had an explosive temper and wasn't a technically good writer. It was intimidating to have him glaring over your shoulder while you corrected his copy. He was reported to have been paid $125 a week.

Dick Davis was another star in the $100-to-$125 class. He wrote literate, colorful prose, reviewed plays, wrote a column, covered important public events, and was a man of always infectious, if sometimes misplaced, enthusiasm.

Manning Vaughn, a much-admired sports writer, rose above his Milwaukee-style clichés. To him, a home run by the Brewers (then in the Triple

A League) frequently landed on the Burleigh Street front porch of a Mrs. Hasenpfeffer. The *Chicago Tribune* once thought it had hired him away, but he sent his brother Irving in his place, and the brother was good, too. When Manning died, the opposition papers ran bigger stories than did the *Journal* to publicize our loss.

There were a number of good women writers, but their sensitivities were usually wasted on "sob sister" stories.

A spirited art department (layout and illustration) had internal feuds (the fiction illustrator and the political cartoonist hated each other and drew each other's faces on villains and dogs), but united against any lecher who approached the department's adopted daughter, a pretty young girl who pasted up the layouts.

The photographers were managed by a stern perfectionist, Frank Scherschel, who was about my age, twenty-one.

The paper had its share of time servers and dullards, but, until the full force of the Great Depression, hardly anyone was fired.

My first assignment was reading copy on the telegraph and cable desk under Stuffy Walters, who reigned from the inside (or slot) of the traditional semicircular table. Despite the *Journal*'s reluctance to fire people, the rim of the copy desk was rumored to be a dangerous place—three subsequent deans of journalism schools hadn't made the grade there. I succeeded a hapless practitioner named Hap, who reportedly never got a headline past Stuffy. He was safely ensconced as the church editor after I arrived and still had that job ten years later when I left.

In contrast to one deadline a week in Carrington and one a day in Fargo, the *Journal* had five editions a day plus a single-sheet "Peach" (the color of the paper) to handle the late afternoon sports events. Earliest—on sale by 10 A.M.—was the First, or Afternoon, edition, which was mostly for street sales. To prepare for this, the telegraph desk had to be at full strength starting at 7 A.M. A bigger edition was the Star Home, which, starting at noon, was distributed by a flotilla of trucks to the parts of the state within a 100-mile radius and was heavy on state and telegraph-cable news. By the 11 A.M. deadline, the working day in Europe was about over.

The bulk of the circulation was filled by the Home edition, which was delivered throughout the metropolitan area. Some of the local reporters would come in to write their stories, and others would phone in the facts to one of the three rewrite men. The city editor and his assistant would have time for no more than a cursory glance at the material before it went to the local copy desk. The Latest, or Financial, edition was for the stock market close and late-breaking news.

Much of the year there wasn't enough sports activity for the Peach sheet, so eventually it was abandoned. The very last, or Predate, edition, dated the next day, was mailed out to northern Wisconsin and the Michigan peninsula, which was geographically joined to Wisconsin.

Fairly soon I took on Sunday afternoon work in addition to my work week, producing a barely respectable Monday morning Predate, which was mostly filler material already set. I took whatever the lone Sunday police reporter phoned in, checked selected sheriffs' offices, took summaries inning by inning of the Brewers' baseball games or quarter by quarter of the Green Bay Packers' football games. The *Journal*'s Associated Press service was limited to weekday afternoons, so I would call the United Press in Chicago for a half dozen short stories to cover us nationally and internationally. The two printers, brothers, who composed and made up the front and sports pages, frequently stopped off at the neighborhood speakeasy for eye openers before work, and I violated union rules sometimes by guiding their unsteady hands as they put the type into the chases. All that was hard work, but I needed the $10 bonus I got for Sunday duty.

For the first two years I was at the *Journal* my basic skills had to include reading copy, correcting and cutting copy, and writing headlines that described the text and fitted the space indicated by the slot man. Street reporters were somewhat condescending toward desk men, but this didn't undercut the pride my fellow copyreaders and I felt in turning out well-edited, informative, and, we hoped, interesting news for the readers.

The most creative skill came into play in handling an unfolding story. Take something like the congressional investigation of Teapot Dome, comparable to the Watergate and Iran-Contra hearings. The copy editor started with the wire summaries from the day before for a midmorning edition. Witness followed witness, reported in a running account—a play-by-play. When something startling was divulged there was a bulletin that the copyreader could decide to make into a new lead or weave into the story at the last possible minute before the edition went to press.

The wire services also sent their own new leads from time to time. One service may have had a significant paragraph the other didn't, and there was nothing wrong with integrating material from two or more services. Stuffy gained recognition in the trade from this then innovative practice.

One example of the *Journal* copyreaders' esprit took the form of an informal contest for the perfect page 1, eight-column, banner headline. The

Ever the ham, I hold a fish in my mouth at a party celebrating the annual smelt run with fellow *Journal* employees at the Oneida Cafe in Milwaukee. Wally Lomoe is behind me with his arm raised; Frank Scherschel holds a prop while *another* photographer gets ready to shoot (1931).

ultimate, we agreed, should have surprise, national and/or world interest, religion, sex, recognizable names, and a local angle. It had to fit, too. The winner, alas not mine, was POPE ELOPES WITH GILDA GRAY. Gilda Gray was the undisputed national shimmy queen of the twenties. The local angle was that she had been discovered in a honkytonk on the South Side of Milwaukee; her real name was Mary Michalski. Her father was the frequent object of police attention on Saturday nights. "You can't arrest me," Mr. Michalski would say to the cops, "I'm Gilda Gray's father." They did anyway. His Holiness obviously was both religious and international.

At the *Journal,* single-column stories more than three paragraphs long had headlines no more than twelve and a half characters wide, and each line (three lines maximum) had to have at least two words—a rule that kept us scratching for short words. Moreover, the top line could not end with a preposition or a form of the verb *to be.*

Tuberculosis was a problem because there wasn't room for a second word in the line. *T.B.* was considered too slangy for a serious disease. An ingenious copyreader discovered *phthisis,* an obscure generic term for any pulmonary disease, and for years, in the days before antibiotics, a whole generation of Milwaukeeans departed this life via phthisis.

Most newspapers require a fresh headline for the main story in every edition; this can become a crusher. There was a copyreader who, in the winter of 1925, was assigned to the entrapment of Floyd Collins in a Kentucky cave. It was an eight-column headline for two weeks. The basic information was FLOYD COLLINS STILL IN CAVE—no more. Dozens of variations were hard to come by. Floyd died unmourned on the rim of the desk. The Collins copyreader had a breakdown and was nowhere to be found when I arrived in Milwaukee.

Two years as a copyreader left some gaps in my journalistic experience, but I seemed to be progressing. The telegraph and news editors usually accepted my judgment, and my headlines, if not prizewinners, were accurate, conformed to the *Journal* style, and fitted. I developed pride not only in my craft but in the *Journal* itself.

I did need one stern lesson in behavior as a *Journal* employee, however. A blizzard blew up one day, and since it was expected to last twenty-four hours, a skeleton staff of four was designated to stay downtown overnight to be sure the next day's earliest edition went to press. We took the last two rooms at the Republican Hotel, just around the corner. As a plaque on the exterior proclaimed, Theodore Roosevelt had been wounded there by a would-be assassin during his Bull Moose campaign of 1912, but the quality of accommodations had deteriorated so much that rooms were only a dollar each. Since I shared mine with another desk man, I put in for fifty cents on my expense account. A nearby tavern was serving free oxtail stew that night. I didn't know if alcoholic beverages were allowed, so I didn't claim the quarter I spent for a stein of beer.

Waldo Arnold, the normally equable news editor, approached, shaking my expense account. "You," he said, "work for the *Milwaukee Journal!* Our people do not stay in flophouses. No matter what you pay, never again claim less than $5 a night." Whatever class I have attained has never since been tarnished by a hotel room costing less than $5.

In 1929 along came a welcome change of scenery. I was scheduled to assist Pat Gannon in an expanded New York bureau, an idea that cooled when the stock market crashed. As a consolation prize I was sent to New York for a limited stay, while Gannon was brought home for some wholesome reacclimatization. Marguerite and our one-year-old, Edward, joined me.

The *Journal* was convinced that New York was a sinful influence. An earlier correspondent was the horrible example. One event that had to be covered was the annual college rowing regatta at Poughkeepsie. The University of Wisconsin crew usually finished last, but no matter. One year the correspondent went on an extended binge and no copy was sent to New York for relay on our leased wire. The Morse operator appropriated the race story from the *New York Sun,* the paper least likely to reach Milwaukee, and transmitted it. The correspondent later sobered up and, unaware that he had been protected, filed another version. After learning the awful truth, he vanished, possibly to provide ghostly companionship for the Floyd Collins copyreader.

In New York the work consisted mostly of selecting syndicated *Times* and *World* material and sending it to a night copyreader. There was an occasional event with a Milwaukee angle to cover in person. For instance, on one occasion Gilda Gray (remember her?) was due to arrive by ship with Gil Boag, a man-about-town to whom she might be engaged. I made an early morning trip on a pilot boat out to the ship for an interview, but Gil and Gilda were hiding out.

New York didn't prove to be scary. A raffish but stimulating bunch of correspondents from other newspapers around the country used the *Times* syndicate room. Sometimes none of the others would show up, and I would file to half a dozen or more papers simultaneously. My nightly companions included the *Chicago Tribune*'s derbied sports writer, Westbrook Pegler, and drama critic Burns Mantle (in dinner jacket).

After the crash, the cost of living didn't drop immediately. The *Journal* thought that a temporary allowance of $10 a week extra was sufficient for New York. I earned another $10 by filling in for the *St. Louis Globe-Democrat* man on his night off. Adequate pay or not, I figured I should take advantage of being in New York by going to the theater every Friday, my night off. It was a lively year on Broadway, and the shows were cheerful even though Fred Allen, playing a hotel clerk in a *First Little Show* skit, asked a banker whether he wanted a room for sleeping or jumping.

We had taken over Pat Gannon's single room and gas plate on West 73rd Street. When Pat came back from the antiseptic environment of Milwaukee, Edward got us a couple of extra months in New York by contracting measles, for which he was quarantined.

Back in Milwaukee, I talked my way out of copyreading and became a general reporter, starting with obituaries, the zoo, and golden weddings.

The *Journal* had a policy of publishing a photograph of every area couple who had survived fifty years together. Not knowing the policy, one husband offered me my only bribe ever: to get me to use his story, he slid a fifty-cent piece across my desk; I tactfully slid it back.

The depression arrived later in Milwaukee than in many cities, but arrive it did. The *Journal* usually hired a couple of University of Wisconsin graduates every year, so I began to achieve some seniority. But one day I looked around and found that I was again the youngest on the staff in point of service. Even though some banks were failing in 1931, there was no interruption in pay. However, when the paymaster gave us our envelopes they were often filled with nickels, dimes, and quarters from the newsboys.

Actually, anyone with a steady job was in relative clover—prices went down (pork loin was ten cents a pound). Originally I was the poorest tenant in a small apartment building full of salesmen on commission. Over a couple of months I became the richest at $55 a week.

Better reporting assignments came along. I learned that one got advance notice on court news if one included lawyers' names in stories. One could also discipline the lawyers by leaving out their names if they didn't play ball. They'd be reduced to getting themselves paged at ball games to get publicity. If the miscreant unwarily got on either side of a group picture, he was cropped off.

An assignment to the rewrite desk furnished some different kinds of duties. Taking facts by phone from "leg men" outside the office meant writing as many as three or four long stories in the last hour before the Home edition closed.

It would be satisfying for me to recall that, in pursuing a jack-of-all-journalistic-trades competency, I had recognized the largely untapped potential of photographs and other graphic means of communication. Instead, the chance to learn about this potent tool was thrust on me. The publisher, Harry Grant, believed that photography could pay off.

In the previous decade, picture tabloids had sprung up in New York. The *Chicago Tribune* had started the *Daily News,* which acquired the biggest circulation in the country. Hearst had the *Mirror,* and, for a while, there was the *Graphic,* which titillated its readers with composite pictures. It pasted the heads of "Daddy" and "Peaches" Browning on bodies in the positions described in the sensational divorce suit. Racy dialogue was provided in cartoon-like balloons. It was fakery that didn't fool anyone. This kind of thing was not done in Milwaukee.

Grant was scrupulous in avoiding overt meddling in editorial affairs, but the editors, like those on most other papers in those days, certainly weren't demanding pictures. Many thought pictures took space away from their words. Grant hoped that by providing a picture page for the display of photographs, editors could be converted to an appreciation of graphic values; in any case it would liven up the inside of the paper.

This was going to cost money, and so were other changes, such as upgrading the quality of the daily fiction serials. For those who would observe, Grant was teaching a valuable lesson in publication economics. In times of depression, with the opposition retrenching in every possible way, he operated on the principle that a dollar spent in improving the product brings in far more than that in competitive advantage. And, indeed, the *Journal* never lost money, even at the depth of the depression.

The first picture page editor was, briefly, the versatile Dick Davis. He mastered the simple geometry of the page—but his heart wasn't in it. He found the work drudgery, and he hardly ever ran a picture larger than a routine three columns wide. His choices followed the pattern of worthy women "planning" events and face-on shots of some club's new group of officers.

I had been out with photographers on assignment, of course. We had been booed by crowds when the flash powder accidentally blew off the gun after I had just blandly assured housewives that the powder was smokeless. I had helped photographers hurriedly pack their gear as the smoke curled to the ceiling just before descending to stain the curtains. In the police station the corridor down which suspects were led had scorched paint from powder flashes; almost all photographers had burn scars on their forearms.

I was at my rewrite desk one day in 1933 when there was a tap on my shoulder and the managing editor told me I was the new picture page editor. The geometry was easy, but what went into the different rectangles started to matter to me. And the fever spread: if a photographer's picture was made unusually large because it was good, he tried to take better ones—and so did his competitors on the staff. It became possible to plan eye-catching effects in advance. Photographers would try experiments on their days off. A Sunday rotogravure section, partly in color but basically an untidy grab bag, fell under my control.

The photographers themselves had the demanding Scherschel as boss. He would send a sloppy photographer back for a retake the minute he turned in a bad picture. Scherschel threatened, not idly, to beat up the chief engraver if the man refused to handle a hot news picture just because it was a few minutes after deadline.

The mid-thirties provided heady new opportunities for photographers. Miniature cameras (35mm) were coming in from Germany. The fast lenses and increasing film speeds made possible action pictures in natural light. The band of photographic pioneers in the Agricultural Adjustment Administration (Dorothea Lange, Walker Evans, Carl Mydans, and others, guided by Roy Stryker) were touching the sensibilities of Americans with their historic pictures of poverty, drought, and dust. Margaret Bourke-White was making industry look exciting in the pages of *Fortune*.

Cameras were becoming automatic so as to record sequences of action and making it possible to select just the right frame from a strip. In the past color had been confined to reproduction from unwieldy glass plates in view cameras, and it had been so slow that autumn leaves couldn't be photographed outside in bright sunlight if the slightest breeze was stirring. Now even air views could be made in color (at first the plane had to be stalled for a split second to get a still platform).

I tried to guide the *Journal* to respond in a non-clichéd way to these possibilities. For instance, hot weather was no longer indicated by polar bears panting at the zoo, and cold weather was no longer suggested by the polar bears romping in their icy pool. Photographers instead now went out onto the Great Lakes to show the drama of the spring breakup of the ice.

Current world news came by another new development, the wirephoto. Our Associated Press membership franchise allowed us exclusive use in Milwaukee of the technique—at a cost of $50,000 a year, as contrasted with the $5,000 we had been paying for a service mailed from Chicago. The extra cost fitted the Grant philosophy of spending money to make money. Events such as the death of Will Rogers and Wiley Post in an Alaskan air crash were a scoop on page 1. Surveys showed that the gamble on extra spending for photos was paying off. The picture page regularly outdrew the front page and the comics for readership.

In the roto section we learned that a color picture of the Dionne quintuplets would add 40,000 in circulation when advertised in advance. The use of color would also add circulation for something like a history of Wisconsin, using paintings from the State Historical Society, Currier & Ives–type lithographs from the Chicago Historical Society, and paintings of the French missionaries and voyageurs (perhaps somewhat fanciful) from Notre Dame.

This was a sample of what Henry Luce would later call magazine making. We were trying to give the people of Milwaukee and Wisconsin a new vision of themselves.

In the enthusiasm I developed for the pictorial, I found that the original *Journal* photographer, Bob Taylor, had kept all his glass negatives. We thought they would have nostalgia value, so we used them with the heading "Bob Taylor Remembers," complete with a drawing of Bob in his polka-dot Windsor tie. The trouble was that Bob Taylor remembered nothing. Fortunately, a rewrite man named George Archer not only remembered everything but could piece together enough material for a caption just from looking at the backgrounds in the photographs. Bob's file began to run out, but his pictures prompted readers to send in their own old photographs. We paid $5 each on acceptance.

In a journalistic setting in which photography had not played much of a role, work was bound to gravitate to anyone with a rudimentary grasp of its uses. As I became more confident in the possibilities of graphics, I began to get a glimmer of what an integrated combination of words and pictures could do. I worked with reporters to adjust for photographic coverage that would complement their words. In the national and international arena, it was possible not only to provide the current photographs of an event but to add explanatory historical and geographic pictures as background.

In straining to move forward, I sometimes stumbled. For instance, in anticipating a wedding spectacle that was not to occur as scheduled, I superimposed Edward and Wallis on a background of Westminster Cathedral (Catholic). I should have realized that the library had misfiled the view as Westminster Abbey.

We didn't have much guidance in our trial-and-error operations. As far as we could tell, we were discovering a mostly untapped form of journalism. To be sure, *Harper's Weekly* had covered the Civil War with line drawings that could be printcd on newspaper presses. The invention of the photo-engraving dot enabled newspapers around the turn of the century to reproduce actual photographs. The *New York Times,* using rotogravure, had introduced a Sunday pictorial review during World War I because it was felt that the photographs coming out of the war needed extended display, but the supplement had subsequently faded away. Many large newspapers had their own gravure sections, rather pallid, featurish, and dull.

In Milwaukee we used pictures to tell stories. I figured we were doing pretty well, but I still wangled an expense-account trip to New York for "education." At the *Daily News,* the picture newspaper, I was told, "Go away. You're better than we are."

I got no offers from the *News,* but the picture services, the Associated Press and Scripps Howard, began to take notice of me. Salaries involved were not as high as I was getting in Milwaukee. Photographic syndicates were losing money. So were newsreels. I made efforts to maintain my visibility in the trade, with a view toward whatever opportunities the future might turn up. For instance, the picture editor at the AP in New York got a Thompson letter periodically saying, in effect, "The AP has been lousy because . . ." My specific complaints were mostly justified.

Time magazine was, however, beginning to devote more space to photographs. Thomas D. McAvoy was getting scornful attention in Washington with his "toy," a 35mm Leica. Sheeplike, all members of the photographic corps then used four-by-five-inch Speed Graphics and frequently had a colleague "shoot a few for me," without even showing up for an event. They avoided strain on their technical knowledge by shooting indoors and out with flash bulbs, 1/200th of a second at f 5.6. They became believers when scooped by McAvoy's candid pictures. He even taught a congressman the rudiments of 35mm photography, thus furnishing *Time* with pictures taken on the theretofore sacrosanct floor of the House of Representatives.

Luce became a convert. He was quietly playing with the idea of a picture magazine, partly because of the success of photographs in *Fortune* and *Time.* Vague rumors of this reached Milwaukee in 1936. In due course the *Journal* was approached for photographs with which to experiment. I became a sort of unofficial agent for the photographers, collecting a modest percentage, and soon became the *Time* correspondent in Milwaukee as well.

A copy of a trial run for the new picture magazine (working title *Rehearsal*) was sent to me. On the whole I was not overly impressed, but when *Life* started publication in November it was a runaway success. Conceitedly, I figured to myself that I could have done better.

Life itself, though, provided me with some more national exposure. I had been wondering if Eleanor Roosevelt could be as bland as she appeared in news photos—there must be more to such an energetic person. As an experiment I assigned Robert Dumke to shoot absolutely all the 35mm frames he could of her during her appearance in Milwaukee. The cumulative effect of the hundreds of Dumke photographs was one of animation, but there was no time to arrange a layout for the daily, so I decided to hold the pictures of her visit for the Sunday roto. With an artist, I produced a collage, each picture cut out and combined by beveling down the edges with sandpaper so that the cracks wouldn't show, filling almost all of a sixteen-by-twenty-inch page. I had submitted the pictures to *Life* and had received no response, but when someone saw the *Journal* I got a wire asking me to send in the layout. I replied triumphantly, "But you have all of them sitting there." *Life* tried to duplicate our layout but didn't bother to do the careful sandpapering, so the result in the third issue of the new magazine was much cruder. I was credited by name in the text, and my colleagues were convinced that I was on my way to New York. No offer came.

The silence indicated to me that *Life,* in the flush of its runaway success on takeoff, had no place for me. Assuming then that I would probably stay in Milwaukee, I asked for and got a new job—assistant news editor—which meant that I was responsible for late editions and every other Sunday paper. I had begun to expect to become an overall boss somewhere, sometime.

I was almost ten years out of North Dakota but naive enough to be shocked when a very close friend and I were each taken aside and told we were competitors for promotion, with the suggestion that each should try to bitch things up for the other as the occasion arose. We did no such thing, instead comparing notes on continuing nudges of "let's you and him fight."

With the death of Lute Nieman in 1935, the future ownership of the *Journal* was in doubt. Grant convinced the executors that a sale to those who would maintain the *Journal* tradition was more in keeping with the spirit of Nieman's will than a vastly higher offer from Moe Annenberg, who seemed to crave respectability in his original hometown.

Grant had made being employed at the *Journal* a model of expectations for a comfortable financial future. He proposed that selected employees would eventually own the paper. Dividends of 25 percent enabled all of us to keep up payment of our installments on the shares. There would be more available in the future. To those who attained tenure, the *Journal* was Security Inc.

In the late summer of 1937, Wilson Hicks, the *Life* picture editor, offered me a job. It was for $100 a week, about the same as my Milwaukee take-home pay, including my moonlighting, by that time. Andrew R. Heiskell, future *Life* publisher and chairman of Time Inc., was a recent recruit from the *New York Herald Tribune,* where he'd been getting $40 a week. I assume that Hicks made the relatively high offer to me because I had turned down $90 from him earlier, when he was at the AP.

Now the *Journal* became more aware that I was a valuable property. Hands were laid on. Grant summoned me to his office and our session lasted several hours. He was alternately sarcastic (*Life* was a flash in the pan) and pleading (you're the kind we need for the future). When he gathered that I was serious about leaving, he offered me six months in which to try *Life,* with my job assured if I wanted to come back, no hard feelings.

I believe in clean breaks, and declined. *Life* was beginning to look professional, and I thought both it and I had a future.

4

"The Dalai Lama—the Unknowable Ectoplasmic Force"

꩜ "In the big time," Harry Grant scornfully termed the New York to which I moved when *Life* was only ten months old. As the *Time-Life* correspondent in Milwaukee, I had been in touch with the photo-collecting operation and regional reporting, but I didn't have a coherent overall picture. I asked myself, "Who's in charge here?" There was an answer somewhere amid the frequently aimless dashing around, but it took a little while to pin it down.

For starters, there could have been Wilson Hicks, who had signed the telegram offering me the job. Ostensibly, I was his assistant picture editor. I had managed my two previous moves, Carrington to Fargo and Fargo to Milwaukee, without missing a payday. This time, we—now a family of four, with the birth of son Colin in 1935—arrived at the Forest Hills Inn on Sunday night, and I reported to *Life,* then on the fifty-first floor of the Chrysler Building, on Monday morning, again in time for a full pay period.

Wilson was just back from a vacation and ruefully showed me a note left on his desk by Daniel Longwell, who had sat in for him. It was, if I had recognized it, an example of the infighting the management tolerated— even fostered—in the next-to-the-top echelons. Dan Longwell was one of the founding editors—an idea man responsible for many of the provocative stories that had surprised and delighted early readers. The note read: "Dear Wilson, I have just spent all of your budget for the rest of the year."

Had Dan been willing or able to take on the responsibilities, he could have been in charge. He engaged, however, in a feud with the business manager, Ralph McAlister Ingersoll, who persuaded Henry Luce to hire Hicks from the Associated Press as picture editor because of the somewhat loose Longwellian purchasing practices. (Example: Dan would simply turn over the top print of a set and say, "Buy it." Ingersoll proved that Dan had bought a couple of picture sets twice.) Wilson thus conceived his role to be that of a "no" man, which was too bad because he had creative instincts and was an excellent judge of photographs. He interpreted his mandate as an obligation to pinch pennies, although he would pay what he had to for photographs and the services of nonstaff photographers.

My previous experience had given me a rapport with photographers as a group, and I received almost immediate indications that my fellow working stiffs were going to make pleasant companions. The day I started, the women who made up the picture bureau were all wearing masks (props for a story that wasn't going to be published). I didn't know until later what they looked like. That behavior was typical of the fey quality that *Life* editorial would continue to exhibit during my years there.

On my second day at work a group of American-born photographers showed up to protest what they considered favoritism toward foreign photographers, mostly refugees from Nazi Germany. They blamed Longwell. One of them, Bernard Hoffman, brought in a cartoon of Dan, who had a nervous habit of punctuating his speech with "yups." He also raised dachshunds, so he was depicted walking down a corridor saying, "Yup, yup, yup," followed by a file of dachshunds, each with a Leica dangling from its neck and saying, in comic strip balloons, "Yup, yup, yup." A point of sorts having been registered, the delegation had to admit that some of the Germans were good photographers, and the protest dissolved.

By process of elimination, John Shaw Billings, the managing editor, had to be the one who picked and chose from the masses of material generated by Longwell, to a lesser extent by Hicks, and to a still lesser extent by the editors and writers of various editorial departments. The majority of the latter, in the early days, were transfers from *Time* and had very little interest in pictures. Billings was also a transfer from *Time,* but an issue of *Life* which emerged from his office showed that he not only appreciated good photography but knew how to use it.

As editor-in-chief, Henry R. Luce topped the masthead, of course—his office was on the *Life* editorial floor. It was close to a narrow, pie-shaped space that I occupied, along with two colleagues who were not destined to be around very long.

Occasionally, the staff would become exuberant, but it was impossible for us not to hear the stentorian voice of Luce's secretary, Corinne Thrasher, who would shout to the whole floor, "Quiet! Quiet! Mr. Luce is thinking."

By chance, I was invited to a lunch with Luce shortly after I arrived. On an impulse he decided he wanted to talk to "some photographers." He knew the stars from the original staff but had had no contact with the newer ones. As it happened, that day only two photographers were in residence, so I was tapped to help fill out the table in the Chrysler Building's Cloud Club. The photographers were the Germans that the American-born delegation resented, Alfred Eisenstaedt and Fritz Goro. Fritz had been an editor of a Munich illustrated magazine and, like Alfred, had fled the Nazis. In Paris, to support himself, he took up photography. He had an analytical mind and was to become the best science photographer in America.

Small talk did not come naturally to Luce, so, after several awkward exchanges, he used a characteristic ploy—a provocative question: "Compared to German publications, what don't you like about working for *Life*?" Goro replied immediately, "Those little girls who say 'eeck' behind me just when I'm going to take a picture." Eisenstaedt agreed.

The "eeck" girls were what we then called researchers. They accompanied photographers on assignments, helped set up situations when necessary, and gathered information for the text accompanying the pictures (possibly exclaiming "eeck" in bursts of enthusiasm, although *I* never heard anyone actually say it). They didn't actually compose the text, a task for the writers, but they checked the finished text and captions for accuracy. They weren't always girls, either. Sometimes they were young men at a stage between office boy and writer. (Today they are known, appropriately, as reporters.)

The lunch ended with no meeting of the minds between the proprietor and the photographers, and I don't remember that Luce ever again convened an all-photographer lunch.

I became an admirer, without qualifications, of John Billings's consummate editing abilities. In the areas he staked out for himself he was perfect. However, my personal affection for him, if stated, would have embarrassed him. He certainly had more than his share of crotchets, but his tastes must have been compatible with those of *Life*'s readership. To anyone who dared ask him how he sensed this, he answered with a scornful snort, "An editor without his own prejudices is no good."

My appraisal of this complex man, based on what I observed and what he told me from time to time, has been fleshed out by his private diaries.

At a staff party with John Shaw Billings, first *Life* managing editor (1942, photo by J. L. Burns).

He started them as a teenager and gave them, late in life, to the Caroliniana Library, University of South Carolina, to which I am indebted for some of the quotations I use. After he retired from Time Inc. to a family plantation, I was about the only person to whom he wrote. I was able to repay the library with letters written after he ceased keeping a diary.

Billings had not been scheduled to join *Life* at all. His co–managing editor of *Time,* John S. Martin, a flamboyant man and a hard drinker, had been assigned to the position originally, but his behavior with the *Life* planners was so erratic that Luce lost patience and named Billings as the first managing editor of the new magazine.

The Martin-Billings relationship on *Time* had been unpleasant, at least to Billings. Outwardly, he accepted the dual editorship, and his almost anonymous status seemed to fit in with his intense desire for privacy. When he thwarted an attempt of the *Time* promotion people to publicize him, he crowed to his diary, "I am the Dalai Lama—the unknowable ectoplasmic force." He was almost unknowable both on *Time* and as the unchallengeable shaper of *Life*.

Billings had gone to the prestigious St. Paul's preparatory school, where he was nicknamed "Josh," after the nineteenth-century humorist. He went on to Harvard but left, without graduating, to work in the campaign of a friend's father who was running for the U.S. Senate. The candidate sweated profusely, and Billings had the job of standing in the wings with a fresh shirt ready each time the candidate ducked out drenched.

Billings was an ambulance driver in France before the United States entered World War I. He did not get back there with the American forces during the war: he enlisted in the Signal Corps to be a pilot, but cracked up three planes in training. After that he never again in his whole life got into an airplane, military or civilian.

He went to work for a Hartford newspaper ("I was fired because I wrote prose that was too purple") and then moved on to the *Brooklyn Eagle,* eventually becoming its Washington correspondent. His fellow correspondents in Washington respected him. One of them, Henry Cabot Lodge, then reporting for the *New York Herald Tribune,* was also a part-time correspondent for *Time* and recruited Billings as his successor. From there Billings rose to *Time* national affairs writer and editor.

Billings had a sound cultural and educational background and excellent news judgment. His instinctive editing talents included a boldness to cut through the superfluous. At *Time* he once threw away a lengthy wind-up of the Lindbergh kidnapping story that his writer had submitted. Here is Billings's substitute version in full: "Last week in the New Jersey State Prison in Trenton Bruno Richard Hauptmann, 36, was executed in three minutes for the murder of Charles Augustus Lindbergh Jr. on the windy night of March 1, 1931."

Billings didn't seek the job on *Life.* Far from it. A sour entry in his diary reads, "We're to start experimenting with a new illustrated magazine for lowbrows"—not that he didn't have some lowbrow tastes of his own. He knew his strong points, however. Viewing some early layouts that Luce and Longwell had supervised, he observed to his diary: "I am a better picture picker than anyone on the new magazine." He was.

Luce's concept, as Billings interpreted it, was that *Life* was to be "a pictorial history of our times." Soon Billings would gloat that "Luce has turned *Life* over to me to run. I run it." In November 1937, he calculated that "after a year of hard work" he had put out forty-five issues, Luce seven. "I make my own layouts," he said, and he got rid of the art director, whose background had been in department-store window design. Billings tells how, when Longwell and the art director "would start tinkering I would back off sulkily. When they got bawled [*sic*] up I'd step in and do it in my simple way. You can't be too obvious with pictures." He advised (to his diary) "playing a picture small for fact, large for emotion."

He sometimes used the restrictions of a rectangular printed page to advantage. We seemed to have a plethora of half-page vertical ads, next to which it was impossible to get much impact out of horizontal pictures. For Billings-watchers, one of his solutions was a delight. He used the entire depth of a vertical half page to display a one-legged man on a mountain.

In another display of humor, he once used a right-hand page followed by a left-hand page to display head-on and tail-on photographs of a hippo named Lotus. The right-hand full page was headlined "Lotus Fore," the left-hand one "Lotus Aft." (The latter faced—or, rather, backed into—a Campbell's soup ad, and for the first time of several we lost that account.)

John edited the text, wrote the headlines, and organized each issue so that he could leave the office calmly in midafternoon of closing day (Saturday at that time). (When I became managing editor, my deadline was extended to midnight or later.) The staff did not have much insight into how decisions were made. Members would stand by silently while Billings was editing copy and listen when he said "This is fine" and then completely rewrote the block of text by hand between the triple-spaced lines on the copy paper. What he wrote almost always seemed to fit the allotted space to a letter. I was to have this exposure only later, because Billings, as part of his successful practice of remaining almost unknowable, took at least a year to get used to a new face. New arrivals were advised to keep a low profile.

Although the boss was reclusive, the members of his predominantly young staff generated plenty of gaiety among ourselves. We were deprived of All-American Saturday Night private socializing at home because we had to clean up odds and ends after Billings left for his weekend. As time passed, the *Life* party within the office became livelier than the "Life Goes to a Party" feature which ran in the back of each issue.

This all started on our first anniversary in 1937, two months after I arrived. Black Star, the photo agency, sent over an ice cream cake, a memory that horrifies some of the hard drinkers of later closing parties. Billings had a piece in his office, and the rest of us dripped ours off paper plates in the bullpen.

Christmas Eve that year started a long series of uninhibited office parties, an eye-opener for a new hand from Milwaukee. In the vain hope that gifts would influence the movie editor, then Joseph J. Thorndike Jr. (who was later to become managing editor), the movie companies sent whisky, champagne, and brandy. Thorndike didn't drink much, so he turned the loot over to the staff.

I had judged the female researchers as being rather mousy, devoted to torturing the writer-editors by making them prove that every syllable they wrote was literally accurate. But by after lunch they had metamorphosed into a predatory attack force, swooping into the men's offices and planting kisses indiscriminatingly.

Naturally, Billings had remained shut in his office working during the frivolity, as he did in the subsequent years when the company institution-alized the parties and picked up the tab for the refreshments. Personnel's odd (to me) theory was that it was good for morale to render the troops uninhibited enough to tell off the bosses.

My instinct to be wary about intruding on Billings ended one day in the spring of 1938. I was walking down a corridor of the then new Time & Life Building in Rockefeller Center, to which we had just moved, when I saw a spidery man with a shock of black hair, a batch of photographs under his arm, looking very angry.

He was Gjon Mili, an M.I.T. graduate in electrical engineering, who for ten years had been a lighting engineer for Westinghouse. What he had were some test shots taken with stroboscopic lights which Professor Harold Edgerton of M.I.T. had rigged up for him. We were all familiar with Edgerton's splash of a drop of milk and toe-dented football on a simulated kickoff, but those pictures seemed merely oddities. Mili witnessed some of these experiments and persuaded Edgerton to build equipment with a much stronger electrical charge so that, for instance, a whole human body could be photographed at extremely high speeds.

Mili had come in without an appointment and spent some time in the outer offices of both Hicks and Longwell without getting to see either one and was about to stomp away furiously when I happened along. I riffled through his prints and was struck by them. I didn't want him to go elsewhere. I said, "Let me have these for a minute or two."

I took them into Billings's office. I'm not sure Billings knew who I was, having met me only briefly at a party Roy Larsen, the circulation genius for *Time,* gave for the staff when he became publisher of *Life.* They were just single prints—a dancer sailing through the air with every muscle showing and a child blowing soap bubbles. Billings said, "I need a 'Speaking of Pictures.' Leave them."

Gjon Mili, using his revolutionary stroboscopic lights, catches me throwing my younger son, Colin, into the air (1938, courtesy Time Inc.).

So Mili the journalistic photographer was launched, and our long, if sometimes stormy, friendship ensued.

I expected no flak from Hicks, whom I had sized up accurately enough by that time to know that even if he was annoyed at being upstaged, he would accept a fait accompli. Indeed, a number of assignments were arranged to fit what we thought was Mili's particular talent. Mili didn't want to be on the staff but accepted a contract which provided him with financial security.

Mili had done his test shooting in a former church in Upper Montclair, New Jersey, but needed a bigger studio. He found a former Chinese restaurant on 23rd Street near Broadway which better suited his bohemian taste. It had a dance floor—he was an avid folk dancer. He arranged with a Ukrainian society to paint the interior of the dingy studio silver in return for use of his floor once a week. He had a composition-board bedroom constructed within the studio and lived there.

The following Saturday afternoon I was almost alone in the office, making assignments for weekend events, when two figures (one bulky, one slight) approached across an empty bullpen: one was Billings, one Longwell. The former asked me, "What do you know about railroads?"

"Only that the big event of the morning in St. Thomas, North Dakota, is the arrival of the northbound local from Grand Forks, and the big event of the afternoon is the arrival of the same local on its way back south from the Manitoba border."

"You're just the man," said the large Mr. Billings. Just the man for what? John was fascinated by railroads and had long wanted to play with a genuine system—no toy trains for him. That morning he had learned that one of the then three managing editors of *Time,* Frank Norris, had persuaded his father, president of the Southern Railway, to turn over to *Life* one whole division of the line for a week or so.

The shooting had to start the next Monday morning, a day and a half away. Billings wanted the Charlotte division "dissected," with only one specific request: dogwood was in bloom, so there should be a picture combining blossoms and a railroad scene. His knowledge of dogwood geography was not very precise. The wild dogwood bloomed so far away from the tracks that his suggestion was impossible to execute. Longwell then handed me a teenage-oriented book called *Train, Tracks and Travel,* by a professor of transportation at Columbia. I studied it overnight and acquired a vocabulary of enough technical terms that I could ask understandable questions.

For a job this important to the boss, I was to have two photographers, both prima donnas: Alfred Eisenstaedt for the 35mm work and Horace Bristol for big-camera subjects. Each had always worked alone. The three of us went to Washington the next afternoon and reported to Southern headquarters on Monday morning. The executive vice president loaned us his private car, which was hitched onto various passenger trains as we went, and came along with us. We meandered around in North Carolina, eventually to a mile or so outside the station in Atlanta, the southern end of the Charlotte division.

It became evident shortly after we left Washington that I had to keep the photographers separated as much as possible. My rough plan was to have one on the main line while the other worked the branches, and I had to divide my time equally between them or they tended to take offense. If I spent much time talking to Horace, for instance, Alfred would complain petulantly, "Ed, you do not like me anymore."

We recorded the appearance and actions of engineers, firemen, conductors, brakemen, dispatchers, area superintendents, etc. Southern hadn't been hiring during the depression, so the "baby" of the employees was thirty-three and owed his job to being a member of an established railway family. The private car would hook up to an electrical connection at each stop to keep the air conditioning in operation. Groups of employees would drift by to pay their respects to the executive vice president, who had come up through the ranks and knew many of them. These visitors were always fed, and thus the cook never knew whether he was going to have one or twenty for a given meal.

We had, by this time, plenty of pictures of people and of the details that railroad buffs drool over. Perhaps the best of these was by Bristol. Against the instincts of railwaymen on the scene, who were devoted to clean smokestacks, I got the engineer to belch out a cloud of black smoke just as the freshly scrubbed PS-4 Pacific-style locomotive, No. 1397, emerged from servicing at the Spencer, North Carolina, roundhouse. Forty-two years later, a boy who was eleven when the picture was published became the editor of *Trains* magazine, obtained a print from *Life,* and reproduced it as a classic.

We had worked our way through Georgia when I realized that no train had been juxtaposed against dogwood. The stationmaster at Tuccoa had a neat little garden, so I had a locomotive pulled up on a side track next to a spirea bush in bloom.

Alfred didn't think the spirea bush shot worth printing, but I found it in his contact prints and showed it to Billings, along with the rest of the take. Although the percentage of stories published from among those photographed was pretty low, there was no way that this story would not succeed. Billings laid it out for ten pages, using the almost rejected spirea picture as an opener and Horace's No. 1397 as a full-page ender.

John looked at the sheaf of dispatchers' records I had brought in and asked, "Do you understand those?" I told him I thought I did, so he said, "Assume it is a noon in April 1938. Have a map of the Charlotte division drawn and locate every train—passenger and freight." I did that, and he said, "This is too easy. Now figure out from those sheets when every train either will pass or meet the other trains and add that information to the other double printing on the map." This arcane touch didn't interest me much, but the result got by the nitpicking rail buffs in the readership without any challenge to its accuracy. And, of course, it established a rapport with Billings to the extent that I could call him to his face "the number 2 railway expert on *Life.*"

There were other Billings eccentricities. One, an attraction to movie star Shirley Temple, was rather poignant—he seemed to identify her with his only daughter, who had died as a child. A movie press agent became aware of a possible tie-in to the wildly successful *Life* and once, when Shirley

While we were doing a story on the Southern Railway, a very frightened Alfred Eisenstaedt cut and ran right at my camera after taking a picture of a train thundering by (1938). I accidentally caught him in reasonable focus.

was in New York, sent word that Miss Temple would be glad to receive Mr. Billings in her hotel suite. That was too much. The word went back that Mr. Billings would receive Miss Temple in *his* office. An impasse. The meeting never came off.

Billings had an aversion to American Indians as editorial subjects, partly because of what he called "romantic twaddle" about the Noble Red Man. This made him fair game for another less authoritative eccentric of *Life*'s early days, Alexander King. Alex had an appetite for bizarre humor and during a Billings vacation, conceived as a gag and laid out, in photostat form, a special issue solely on Indians. To open and close the issue were a "Speaking of Pictures" on Indian trail signs and an Indian party. In between were the ingredients of a normal *Life* issue, all related to Indians. As "Picture of the Week," Alex had unearthed a white man whom Billings also loathed, Heywood Broun, dressed as an Indian. The pasted-up layouts were presented as already partly closed, so it took Billings maybe ten minutes on the day he returned to realize that it was a joke. If he was amused there certainly was no ostentatious thigh-slapping.

Fun and games were all very well, but I began to wonder about my salary. I didn't expect a raise at the end of my first three months, and Hicks could well have resented my behavior, but he kept shifting more and more responsibility to me. I thought I was handling photographers and photographs well, and, as the fall of 1938 approached, I let friends know that my take-home pay in Milwaukee had been higher than it was in New York. I was not threatening to go back, mind you, but . . .

During *Life*'s first couple of years there were two significant Christmas Eve tableaus. One involved a group outside Hicks's office. Its members, including writers, were about to be fired. Longwell couldn't face that kind of unpleasantness. The other group, happy and expectant, waited for Billings. Although he didn't hire or fire, he reserved for himself the pleasure of announcing raises. I was in the 1938 Billings Christmas Eve group. He said, "I hear that it is costing you money to work here. We don't want that." My salary was increased 75 percent.

A few days later Hicks weighed in with, "I suppose you wonder why I didn't give you that raise."

"You're goddamn right I do."

"Well, Ed, you were doing so well I didn't want to hamper you by making you strain to be worth higher pay."

I didn't expect it to be a strain, and it wasn't. I took it to mean that I was on my way. The fact that I had helped Billings be a vicarious railway man hadn't hurt.

It must be obvious that John Billings had become my role model, eccentricities and all. I approved of his taste in pictures and was awed by his word editing. I envied his lofty position above the petty aspects of the Longwell-Hicks rivalry. I was amused by but did not wholly approve of the mischievous way in which he set one person against the other from time to time. The doubtful rationale, I suppose, was that the competition (or irritant versus counterirritant) brought out the best in each of them.

If my admiration for John Billings had been increasing, I had begun to wonder about Henry Luce. I was vaguely thankful that in acquiring an editorial page and bylined text articles, *Life* was free to report the news deadpan without worrying about any "message." In the editorials, the proprietor's views, it seemed to me, were clearly labeled as to what they were and left the magazine almost free of the charges of "slanting" facts. No one cared that I was a registered Democrat in Nassau County, Long Island, where the Republican organization used placement on juries as a payment to party workers.

It was unexpected but deeply satisfying to find Luce reacting to a situation the way I would have liked to be large-minded enough to do in his position. In February 1939, a hard-line Communist cell within Time Inc. surfaced— if publication of an underground newspaper can be considered surfacing— with *High Time,* projected as a monthly newsletter. The contents of the first issue included barbed gossip items with quotations about who said what about whom. My name was in the issue as being questioned by Hicks, "Is it true that everyone hates me?" This was not damaging because Hicks would ask this of just about anyone every once in a while, and I was not quoted as answering the question.

In an eloquent memorandum, Luce supported "the right of editors, writers and researchers to spout out to one another their views, well-considered, half-considered and ill-considered. . . . We have had people of all shades of political thought on our staff, and I maintain the right of every one of them to speak to every other member of the staff . . . to gossip, kick, criticize and laugh about what other members have said, done or written. . . . It would be intolerable if our editors had to feel that they could not open their mouths without having some half-uttered thought plucked out and used to stab them in the back."

One could not ignore Luce's strong political opinions, but if I hadn't believed in roughly the kind of world Luce wanted, I couldn't have worked at Time Inc. very long.

5

"I'm the Best Goddamned Photographer in the World"

◠◡ *Life* was mostly a picture magazine, so I had thought in Milwaukee that all of its editors would be designated as picture editors. Actually, the staff was small enough so that anyone with any claim to competence could latch onto tasks that needed to be tackled. Because my chief duties then were to assign photographers, it was logical enough that most of my professional—and personal—contacts were with that colorful fraternity.

Billings himself did not deign to join in the creative process of magazine making at the idea stage. Other top editors would have ideas for specific stories, but the assignments I made were mostly from requests by departmental editors: news, science, movies, parties, etc. Not all of these editors had good picture sense, so the picture editors theoretically had the option of adapting the details of an assignment to something that did promise to track as a story or of turning down requests altogether. Not enough suggestions were rejected, I believed, and the magazine overproduced vastly.

A composite character, the *Life* photographer, was taking shape in the public consciousness. From an international conference to a rural spelling bee, from a delicate surgical procedure to society high jinks would come the word that "the *Life* photographer is here." Whoever was there wasn't necessarily from *Life*. He or she might be an impostor who used the name to get cooperation and who hoped to sell photographs to *Life* or to one of its imitators. Or the photographer might be a legitimate freelance with a guarantee from the magazine. And there was, to be sure, a group of full-time practitioners who made up the *Life* photographic staff.

As individuals, none of these contributors could possibly have conformed to a composite image. If, in the late 1930s, I had been tempted to generalize, I would have said that because they were extroverts, the photographers were livelier social companions than some of my writer friends. Their practical jokes were occasionally tasteless, but I have to admit a perverse fondness for the schemers and deal makers among them.

My one-on-one experiences with photographers, during the period when they were adjusting to *Life* and *Life* to them, revealed individual qualities which added up to a revolutionary approach to journalism. I'm inevitably going to omit the names of some who have every right to be listed, and who, furthermore, are friends. Please forgive.

The original settlers, the first five on the staff, were there when I arrived, and antedated Wilson Hicks. They were Margaret Bourke-White, Alfred Eisenstaedt, Thomas McAvoy, Peter Stackpole, and Carl Mydans.

Although foreign accents in the photographic group would eventually abound, Eisenstaedt was the only member of the first five who had been born abroad. He arrived from Germany already a star and remained one. He had been an artillery corporal in World War I and had made a living briefly as a button salesman. He had somehow become an apprentice to the great Erich Salomon, the father of candid photography. Salomon usually covered white-tie events, so Eisenstaedt, a short gnome of a man, had a dress coat tailored with many pockets in the tails to hold the sensitized photographic plates for Salomon's Ermoflex. Eisenstaedt's infallible instincts made him a master at capturing the essence of human behavior, in composition and in the use of available light. He could hardly be described as an intellectual journalist, but when he did what came naturally he was unbeatable. In his late eighties he was still a star.

The contrast between Eisenstaedt and Bourke-White could hardly have been greater. She was strikingly handsome. She relied on an iron will and physical strength to succeed on any given project. A man dancing with her realized that she was all bone and muscle. Luce knew her from his days when founding *Fortune,* for which she took technically superior industrial photographs. The wisecrack in those days, not entirely unfounded, was that no one under the rank of corporate vice president ever got to carry her camera equipment.

Bourke-White expanded eagerly into the more varied subjects *Life* covered. She took the cover and lead article in the first issue, the Fort Peck, Montana, dam. It wasn't easy to like Bourke-White. It was always clear that she was using people, even though she may not have admitted this to herself. It was impossible, however, not to admire her as a serious journalist and a thorough professional.

The other three had also achieved early distinction in a journalistic world that had had no *Life* in which to display their work. As noted earlier, Tom McAvoy had introduced the Leica into the lazy Speed Graphic world of Washington photographers.

Peter Stackpole was the son of a widely known sculptor and had taken a notable set of photographs of the construction of the Golden Gate Bridge. His candid of Herbert Hoover dozing at a public function also made *Time*. The editors, though, tended to typecast him and assign him the glamor-girl stories that *Life* always seemed to need. For years, the Stackpole cover of showgirl Hope Chandler, captioned "Prettiest Girl in Paradise" after the nightclub of that name, held the record for the highest newsstand sales. Peter later became a pioneer in underwater photography.

Carl Mydans, whose journalistic career started as a Boston newspaper reporter, produced a solid body of documentary photography. On assignment, Mydans caught the tension of sandhogs tunneling under a river; he took on a photo essay on the whole state of Texas ("Texas Is Big," the headline said in appropriately oversized type); importantly, he became the first staff member to cover combat—the Soviet invasion of Finland in late 1939. It would be vastly underrating Mydans to typecast him as a war photographer, but his distinguished record in that grim but journalistically compelling pursuit puts him at least on a par with Robert Capa, W. Eugene Smith, and, later, David Douglas Duncan.

Mydans was in the Philippines before Pearl Harbor, was interned with his wife, Shelley, by the Japanese, and was released in time to record MacArthur as he strode ashore to fulfill his promise to return. He covered the entire Korean War. His sixth sense, augmenting the intelligence with which he handled all kinds of subjects, kept him intact through a long career.

Along with Mydans and others, Bob Capa was a personal friend—if he hadn't been, he probably would not have accepted my assigning him in 1954 to a story in Indochina, an assignment that cost him his life. Our first meeting was in 1938, just after his memorable coverage of the Spanish Civil War. I understood only a little of what he said. Capa had a thick accent (he used to joke that he won his English in a Shanghai crap game), mostly from living in Hungary, where he was born Andre Friedmann. He was trying to scratch out a living in Paris when, according to legend, an inventive girlfriend found that she could sell his pictures better if they were by that great American photographer, Robert Capa.

I tried—not entirely successfully—to find assignments for Capa that would be in character for him. He astounded an accompanying reporter, Don Burke, by making a scene in a railroad dining car because there was no vintage French wine. Capa had a "Nansen passport," named after Fridtjof Nansen of the League of Nations, a document issued by the still extant League to "stateless" people. The Hungarian quota for immigration to the United States was backed up for a couple of dozen years, so a begrimed, taped-together document—"if it was clean it would look fake," said Capa— was his shaky basis for being around. Eventually he solved that problem by marrying a nice American woman named Tony, which automatically gave him legal status as a resident. Capa considered the marriage temporary; Tony, sadly, did not, and was always wistfully asking me for news of Bob whenever I chanced to encounter her.

In May 1938, *Life* photographers John Phillips and Dmitri Kessel combined with Margaret Bourke-White to examine pre-Munich Czechoslovakia. The thrust of the fourteen-page essay was partly a consideration of how the Czechs would defend themselves if the Nazis parlayed a German ethnic presence in the Sudetenland into an all-out attack, and partly an explanation of the makeup of this rather artificially assembled country, carved from the Austro-Hungarian empire after World War I.

Like Capa, Phillips became valuable for his journalistic sense, which made technical consistency secondary. He grew up in North Africa and always had a slightly guttural tinge to his English, one of many languages he speaks. His mother was American. His father, who had a Ford agency in North Africa at one time, was as English as Eliza Doolittle's father. A former commercial photographer, he helped John get started as a London freelance by producing saleable prints from his early efforts.

Phillips developed an affinity for Middle Europeans and once played the unlikely role of speechwriter for Carol II, the playboy king of Romania. For *Life*'s essay on Czechoslovakia, Phillips talked his way into a supposedly secret military installation. He and Bourke-White portrayed the various types of Czech soldier—Sudeten German, Serb, Croat, and Montenegrin. Kessel wasn't even assigned to the story but turned up with some industrial pictures he had taken in Czechoslovakia on a *Fortune* trip. Phillips later photographed the almost unseen war of Tito's Yugoslav partisans against the Germans.

Kessel, a photographer's photographer, enriched the pages of *Life* for many years with his masterful lighting of art subjects, historic landscapes—including the Yangtze River—and the great churches of the world. A native of the Ukraine, he had served successively in the cavalry of three armies toward the end of World War I—the Czarist, the Ukrainian national, and the Communist.

John Billings started laying out the Czechoslovakian essay in his usual way but had one unexpected assistant. I had assembled the collection of pictures, so I stood by, with the foreign editor, his researcher, and the art director. We were silent unless asked for an identification. Billings was thinking out loud. "Now, what is Czechoslovakia famous for? Glass, the Skoda munitions works . . ." An electrician who was on a stepladder in back of Billings continued, " . . . and beer and shoes. Czechoslovakia, that's my country." Without saying a word, Billings dutifully dug out the suggested examples.

As the world found out, the Czechs did not have a chance to fight the ensuing Nazi invasion.

It should surprise no journalist to be reminded that man's inhumanity to man, even on a massive scale, arouses far less public outcry than man's cruelty to an animal. The shock caused by the first mass bombings of civilians in Guernica, Spain, did not engender an effective enough protest to make the Germans and Italians take a deep breath. But *Life* photographer Wallace Kirkland, a conservationist and animal lover, recorded the story of a fox hunt that drew a record number of protest letters—four thousand in the first ten days.

Even when compared to other colorful photographers, Kirk was an original. This hunt, sponsored by the sheriff of Holmes County, Ohio, featured a line of beaters who swept through a sixteen-square-mile area toward a circle of club-bearing "sportsmen." Kirk reported, "I failed to catch one look of pity on any face." Two foxes were clubbed to death by adults. The sheriff selected a boy to finish off the third in the enclosure. Billings, also an animal lover, wrote an inflammatory headline: "Big Brave Men Beat a Tired Beast to Death." Among the letters of protest were some that complained of *Life*'s bleeding-heart attitude, including one that demanded a "Hunt Kirkland Day."

Kirkland turned to photography after fifteen years as a social worker. He was never good technically. He wrote well, and frequently his accounts of why he didn't get a story seemed better than the story itself would have been. One time I assigned him to a bear hunt but specified that in addition

Tom McAvoy (center), Davie Scherman (right), and I reenact *The Days of 1776* at a party Gjon Mili gave to show fellow photographers how his strobes worked (about 1939, photo by Hansel Mieth).

to the pictures of hiking and beer drinking around a campfire, I wanted one more. "Get behind the hunter when he sights a bear and get his shoulder, the gun barrel, and the bear in the same shot." A few days later, Kirk called on a rural party line. "Ed, there's no bears here. I'm leaving." Then, before I could comment, I heard a muffled shout, "My God, it's a bear!" and Kirk hung up. He did not get the picture.

Kirk's humor was earthy, sometimes sexist, and not universally appreciated. None of my secretaries, for instance, would open his Christmas card when it came in April. Year after year he would ring changes on themes involving nude models. In the last one he was able to make before he died, he somehow got the model into his wheelchair and photographed himself pushing her.

The Kirkland legacy of projects was, nevertheless, serious and varied. His nature studies were meticulously researched and photographed. While on an assignment to photograph Gandhi for an essay, he combined a seemingly irreverent Kirkland touch with a sensitive appreciation of what the Indian leader stood for.

At a farewell party before he left for India, Kirk was asked how he would like to approach Gandhi, and he said, "Barefoot, over a half acre of women's breasts." A guest, Julio de Diego, painted an identification card for him with the breasts pointing upward, a fertility goddess with six more pointing out, a barefoot, one-eyed Kirkland, and Gandhi's goat.

Thanks to Kirk's sociological background with Jane Addams, whom the Mahatma admired, the assignment went well. At the end Kirk produced the Diego card and indicated where the holy man was to autograph. Amused, Gandhi said, "It's my goat. I'll sign where I want to," and wrote "M. K. Gandhi" across the animal's rear end.

Gandhi's protest against British rule was of course nonviolent and eventually successful. The Nazi protest in Europe—against what Germans considered the inequities of the Versailles Treaty—was turning out to be violent indeed and aimed at the Western concept of civilized existence. *Life* published photographs of Jews being forced to scrub anti-Nazi slogans from a wall. These pictures were arrogantly released by the government, but our headlines correctly characterized the storm troopers as "uniformed plug-uglies." We didn't have to look far for victims of anti-Semitism. Eisenstaedt, of course, was on the staff, and others found their way to *Life* assignments through photo agencies.

The refugee photographers were professionals, some having worked for German picture magazines such as the Ullstein group. A most dramatic example of adaptation to *Life*'s kind of Americana was Walt Sanders and his essay on the Hulls of Tennessee, the mountain kinfolk of then Secretary of State Cordell Hull.

Sanders had to take this important photographic essay on short notice. Originally it had been assigned to Eliot Elisofon, a New Yorker who had the temperament of a star before he actually became one. Elisofon insisted on taking a short skiing vacation to get himself in the mood for the story. On his way back to New York he suffered a skull fracture in an automobile accident, so Sanders did the story.

Walt's Bavarian Alps background seemed to give him an instinctive understanding of mountain people. His studies of Cordell's Uncle Bud and Aunt Louisa, Uncle Louis and Cousin Elmer, Cousin Edd's Cash Store with four other cousins hanging 'round, and Cousin Elmer's seventeen-year-old son, the barber, were masterpieces. He located the still that Billy Hull, godfather of the clan and a northern bushwhacker, had in eastern Tennessee, and contrasted all this with a Matthew Brady–type, Lincolnian portrait of Hull in his office.

Another refugee photographer, Fritz Goro, effected the hairiest escape from the Nazis I ever heard of. He was an editor on Ullstein's *Munich Illustrierte* but felt a purge coming and slipped into France, leaving his wife and infant son behind. He started supporting himself by photography in Paris, then made a clandestine return trip to Bavaria. He took his wife and son down a ladder from their bedroom, dressed them in peasant clothes, and caught what Americans would call a milk train. It started in Austria, entered Germany for some local stops, and wound back into Austria.

Thanks partly to his background as an editor and to his natural insistence on precision, Goro became a premier science photographer, probably the best anywhere. He wasn't always easy to deal with. He wouldn't be hurried—"I want to be known as the slowest photographer in the world." A Goro photograph or sequence went a long way toward illuminating a formula-laden text.

A remarkably talented pair of photographers, Hansel Mieth and Otto Hagel, came from the same small town in southern Germany, Felsbach. They had the rosy-cheeked appearance the Nazis claimed to cherish. Otto arrived in the United States first, illegally. He was working on a merchant ship and, as he told it, he became infuriated—he did have an explosive temper—with a Hitler speech he heard on the ship's radio someplace off Carolina or Georgia, jumped overboard, and swam to shore. He hitched to New York and got work as a window washer on a tall building. One day a prong on a defective safety belt gave way, and he found himself hanging by a single strap looking into a room. Someone pulled him in. Hagel was offered a settlement—he thought because the building owner had passed a safety inspection illegally and didn't want official inquiries into the accident. He may not have known that Hagel was an illegal alien.

Hansel followed, legally, with the sponsorship of a relative already in the United States. The two were reunited in California, both broke, but with cameras. After an unsuccessful attempt to support themselves by panning for gold, each began to make a little money selling pictures.

Mieth hit a jackpot of sorts with an essay on a sheep ranch at lambing time, just before I arrived at *Life*. Both came to New York, Mieth to join *Life*'s staff, Hagel to freelance, mostly for *Fortune* but occasionally for *Life*. Both were excellent technicians, Hagel superb. His industrial pictures were as powerful as he was; his portraits so sharp every pore showed (less gifted rivals called it "blackhead photography").

Mieth managed to instill her personal warmth into her photographs of people and animals. She was justifiably indignant at being typecast to the extent that we assigned her to do stuffed specimens at the American Museum of Natural History.

Mieth and Hagel were living together and responded to suggestions by Hicks that they marry with an offer to do so when Margaret Bourke-White and Erskine Caldwell legalized their relationship. Both couples eventually did so; actually Hagel needed an American relative, in this case a wife, so that he could leave the country and return legally.

Hagel, who didn't believe much in any kind of official authority and could have been called an intellectual anarchist, produced an eloquent interpretation of the American literary scene as perceived by Van Wyck Brooks in "The Flowering of New England." It was a photographic essay in the best *Life* tradition.

One Mieth project caused me to disagree with Billings's picture judgment. She had shot what we expected to be an essay at a Puerto Rican medical lab which used rhesus monkeys. It was well researched and full of eloquent pictures. Billings riffled through and came upon a lone male standing chest deep in water, looking forlorn but glowering. Apparently he had fled from amorous females. Billings, who usually disdained anthropomorphism, immediately labeled it "The Misogynist" and laid it out for "Picture of the Week," setting the rest of the photos aside. I protested feebly about all those other excellent pictures going to waste, and he brushed me off with, "Oh, those can run anytime." They never did, but Billings was right. The monkey was a classic and showed up on the walls of male hangouts like filling stations, machine shops, and bars all over America.

If there had been a composite *Life* photographer, which we have agreed didn't exist, there was one expression he or she would almost surely have used: "I'm the best goddamned photographer in the world." Take the case of the unnamed photographer with the broken wrist. The injured man hoped that his break would heal while on a ship carrying him to an overseas post. While waiting to embark, he became romantically involved with the estranged wife of a doctor. The wrist was not healing, and the doctor he selected to rebreak and reset it was his new friend's husband. The patient, worried, rehearsed what he wanted to say under the anesthetic.

Hansel Mieth shot this photograph of a male monkey standing in water just after he ran away from some amorous females. John Billings labeled it "The Misogynist" and used it as "Picture of the Week" (*Life,* ©Time Inc.).

After the operation as he became conscious he looked up and asked, "How did it go, Doc?"

"Okay, but you've been saying the strangest things."

"My God, what?"

"Well, you repeated over and over, 'I'm the best goddamned photographer in the world. I'm the best . . .' "

6

Sounds of Battle, at First Dimly Heard

⁓ For a special issue on the New York World's Fair scheduled for June 5, 1939, my editorial bosses decided to simply go along with the fair's theme, The World of Tomorrow. The issue, for which I assigned most of the pictorial material, was entitled "America's Future."

For the issue *Life* assumed the role of America itself, patting itself on the back for its splendid prospects and relative abundance of freedom. Virtually ignored were two more significant facts of life. One was the imminent war—the country was having to arm on a scale never before known in a time of peace. The other was that the Great Depression was ending, due in large part to war industries. In the single page of text covering the news of the previous week, one paragraph had headlines from the far shores of both oceans and the smug comment "Even America's bad headlines looked good compared to the headlines which continued from the rest of the world."

It would be more than a year and a half, February 1941, before Henry R. Luce himself squared off and made a five-page statement entitled "The American Century." Even though he cited the obvious—we were "in" the war despite our technical neutrality—he pointedly left to strategists the question of whether there should be an American Expeditionary Force sent to Europe.

Luce, I was to learn, made a distinction between working editors and thinking editors. The thinkers were exercising restraint in considering war, while the workers were paying some attention to the nuts, bolts, and personnel of the military—more, I would say, to an exposition of military science than to one of national policy.

I was a kind of amateur "expert" in a world where "God protects fools, drunkards, and the United States of America." Because the University of North Dakota was a land-grant college, ROTC was compulsory, and I graduated as an officer in the U.S. Army Reserve. Since then, by taking correspondence courses and a few tours of active duty, I had attained the rank of captain. "Active duty" had included serving as a guide to foreign military attachés when the Wisconsin National Guard "invaded" Michigan in a cross-lake, car-ferry operation.

The army had adopted the triangular form for a division—three squads to a platoon, three platoons to a company, three companies to a battalion, three battalions to a regiment, three regiments to a division. The old "square" division, with two brigades and four regiments, was on its way out. The Second Infantry in Fort Sam Houston, Texas, was the first to make the change. Billings sent me off with two photographers—Tom McAvoy and Horace Bristol—with no instructions, although he did say vaguely that he would like, sometime, to see a whole division in one picture.

Life at Fort Sam, near San Antonio, resembled the peacetime army described later by James Jones in his novel *From Here to Eternity*. Senior officers, led by Colonel Laurence (Gee) Gerow, division chief of staff, seriously discussed the tactical and strategic implications of the new formation, while the younger regular officers were mastering the alternatives to "squad right" in close-order drill. We methodically recorded the details of how the new division actually worked.

The main problem with getting a picture of the whole division was that a portion of the Second Infantry was in Wyoming at Fort Francis Warren. With a mighty assist from Gee Gerow, we finally produced a convincing facsimile.

We divided the drill area into three parts, each to represent one regiment, and photographed each part separately, moving troops from one to another as needed to fill it out. Almost every available soldier appeared twice in the resulting paste-up, a few three times. Signs were painted to indicate what kind of unit was "occupying" each block. This took a day out of training, so the division staff prudently selected a day when the commanding general, Walter Krueger, was temporarily off post. The requisite number of troops in units for the full-strength divisions—the squads, platoons, companies, and battalions for each regiment, plus supporting units, such as artillery, signal corps, and medics—showed in the finished view as it appeared in *Life,* properly identified as a composite. We turned about 6,000 soldiers into 13,000.

The result wasn't great photography, but Billings got his whole division, after a fashion. The soldiers could amuse themselves by looking for repetition of their own faces in the composite.

My personal military experience took a turn in August 1939, when I was ordered to two weeks of active duty with the Seventh Cavalry Brigade, Mechanized, on maneuvers near Plattsburgh, New York. The Seventh Cavalry was Custer's unit and was the nucleus for what would become the Armored Force. At the time it contained all the operational—if one used the word *operational* loosely—tanks in the U.S. Army, perhaps twenty.

I was of no real use even among the former horse cavalrymen, who weren't too handy with machines. The tanks were light and fast, and I did get some orientation from a fifty-mile-an-hour ride across the rough terrain in the area. In a demonstration of how the vehicle could leap a ditch, our tank didn't quite make it, and my chest was thrown against the butt of the turret machine gun. It hurt me to breathe, but the brigade medical officer said, "We have decided to have no injuries in these maneuvers. There's nothing wrong with you." After I returned home, X-rays revealed that my ribs had been cracked a bit but not broken.

After Plattsburgh, Marguerite, the boys, and I went directly on vacation to Montreal, to Winnipeg, to St. Thomas, North Dakota, and back to pollen-free Isle Royale in Lake Superior. (Hay fever has been my lifelong bane.) There, on September 1, I got word from Coast Guard wireless operators that Germany had entered Poland. When I got through to New York I was advised to finish my vacation.

On a mid-September Monday we returned home, and I was told, "Go home and pack." Tom McAvoy and I had been booked on a ship leaving the next day for Panama to cover a Pan-American conference. I protested that conferences usually were pretty dull. The answer was, "The Germans will have observers there. Keep an eye on them and, as long as you're there, why don't you do the U.S. canal defenses, too?"

Doing both stories at once involved long days but turned out to be possible because the military was on a peacetime schedule that started at 6 A.M., with everyone knocking off at noon—the hour when the diplomats were just getting started.

The conference seemed to be ongoing news, so we dutifully sent off an air express package of film, captions, and running reportage every night.

It was a good thing for me that the president of Panama (center) didn't turn around just then (1939, photo by Thomas J. McAvoy, courtesy Time Inc.).

The actual proceedings were as routine as I had expected. The Germans were extremely circumspect. Tom Stokes, a Scripps-Howard columnist, and I, acting on a rumor that a meeting was being held in the apartment of a resident German, got nowhere, possibly because we asked to be shown the *lebensraum.* It did not, we found out later, mean the sitting room of a private dwelling. It was the word Hitler was using in his moves toward expanding the Third Reich.

It was hard to take the conference seriously. An International Day was held at the Panama City race track. No delegates showed up, so McAvoy and I became VIPs. We had been betting a few dollars on each race—and losing. "This won't do," the chief steward said. He named a horse for the last race and suggested we bet enough to make up our losses. Then the race was held up until a messenger could reach the starting gate. Surprise—our horse won.

The conference itself was important to the United States, if only as a stage on which to exhibit the exterior amenities of FDR's Good Neighbor policy toward Latin America. Undersecretary of State Sumner Welles was there, and when we found that he was going to visit every delegation in one day, McAvoy and I obtained a copy of his itinerary and managed to be at each embassy when he arrived.

One delegation had a pet burro in its courtyard, but McAvoy failed in an effort to have the animal driven into the foreground as Welles was greeted. Nevertheless, the cumulative impression of the sequence represented Welles as the hardworking diplomat he truly was. It was almost the only coverage of the conference which got into print, but Welles, at least, was aware of us. As he opened his late afternoon briefing for the U.S. correspondents, he pointed and said, "This is the only place all day I have been ahead of you two."

Every delegation had to have a reception during the week, so there would be as many as three parties an evening at staggered hours. When the president of Panama wanted to entertain the press corps, he had to settle for a noon cocktail party. El Presidente had rather racy tastes in art. His public rooms were decorated with murals depicting primitive Panama as perhaps he would have liked it to be—a jungle inhabited by bare-breasted Amazons.

Why the *Christian Science Monitor* correspondent, who was equipped with a Rolleiflex as well as a notebook, thought a picture of the party would be appropriate I don't know, but he asked us all out on a balcony where the light was better. He cautioned that his paper wouldn't like anyone in the picture to be holding a glass. I just held my drink behind the president, and, when the *Monitor* picture had been taken, I lifted my glass over the presidential head. McAvoy stepped out of the front row and snapped. It was a gag for my personal memento file, but the picture prompted the lone home office reaction. "Why," a cable asked, "is Thompson only one with glass in picture?"

The canal story was definitely something else. As the coverage developed, we realized that we had an important exclusive which showed the Canal Zone as it had never been seen before. The zone, then U.S. territory, cut the Republic of Panama in half. A governor general, by tradition a brigadier general in the Corps of Engineers, administered what would have been, in a normal territory, the civilian affairs, but he was outranked by an army major general who had the final word on security.

We argued to ourselves that the taxpayer was entitled to know about how we could keep commercial shipping moving from ocean to ocean and how the canal allowed us to be reasonably flexible in shifting parts of the fleet to the ocean deemed most vital to our naval operations. (Since the locks were designed early in the century, they didn't have the capacity for handling the big battleships and carriers, which had to go around the tip of South America.)

Our ally, it turned out, was the vanity of the major general. He was due to retire shortly and viewed a story in *Life* as recognition of his services. We realized that we could ask for almost any help we wanted and get it. Psychologically we got off to a proper start by photographing the general on his horse. For good measure, but not for use, McAvoy shot one picture that included the general's son-in-law (and aide) windmilling his arms so that the horses's ears would be properly erect.

A preliminary trip in a small boat revealed the difficulty in showing *Life*'s readers just how the locks raised and lowered a ship through the canal. On a ship we were at water level, and there were no elevations alongside the banks that were high enough to show the progress. We hitched a ride on a spic-and-span Dutch ship, but from it one could see only the sides of the locks we were in, even from the mast. How could we get high enough to photograph a ship at successive levels? There were no blimps closer than the Goodyear headquarters in Ohio, and helicopters were not in use yet.

The mast of a minesweeper might be high enough to show a sequence. An experiment with McAvoy in a bo's'n chair proved that it was practical, so he spent a day up there photographing a large ship getting closer and closer as it passed through a lock. We tied up a crew of forty-odd in the process, which the local press later deplored—wasting all that tax money because of a "smooth-talking city slicker" (meaning me). My reply was that local photographers weren't offered such an opportunity because no one had ever asked. We had. We had the same cooperation in taking pictures of obsolescent biplanes flying air defense over a lock. This was a little touchier, but the major general had the authority to clear it, and he did.

Then there was the matter of the sixteen-inch naval guns the army coast artillery had set up in a jungle. The Japanese knew the United States had them, so it would be okay to photograph them if we were careful to avoid showing any identifiable features of the landscape. When unlimbered, one of these cannons was indeed a fearsome sight, even more so with its muzzle's diameter exaggerated by a wide-angle lens. There was no way of telling that it was aimed toward the Pacific to interdict possible Japanese naval action. I casually offered to buy beer for the gun crew and found, from my PX bill, that it numbered more than ninety.

The afternoon and late-night diplomatic activity (mostly in air conditioning, to be sure), plus our forays in the humid jungle heat in which the military worked, had been an enervating experience. We had decided to carry the film back to New York instead of trusting air express. I was glad to take a Pan Am flight home, a two-day trip with an overnight stop in Guatemala.

McAvoy, however, had contracted amoebic dysentery, then very difficult to treat. Tom was a Washington institution, though, and the president's office saw to it that he was admitted to Walter Reed Army Hospital, which had the world's most knowledgeable experts on tropical diseases. Thanks to them, Tom recovered.

Our twelve-page canal essay was rushed into print as soon as I returned to New York. The "news" of the conference we had so diligently shipped ahead of us ended up in a later issue as a short article on how diplomacy (by Sumner Welles) was practiced. By that time, nobody much cared about the Declaration of Panama, which emerged from the conference. War raged in Europe.

7

From Stetsons to a "Rain-in-the-Face Cap"

A natural tightwad, I didn't buy any new civilian suits during 1940 and 1941 because I expected to be wearing a uniform sooner rather than later, convinced that the United States would have to get into the war.

But in the meantime, I was a journalist, and 1940 was a presidential election year—FDR was about to challenge the two-term-only tradition. The voters may not have realized which way they wanted to be led, but the man who was leading them was a formidable candidate. The Republicans needed a charismatic rival.

Time Inc. practically invented Wendell Willkie. Russell (Mitch) Davenport of *Fortune* brought him to national attention. Willkie's roots were in Indiana; he was the boss of a large utility. He held surprisingly liberal views for a Republican ("the barefoot boy from Wall Street," Harold L. Ickes called him).

Taking charge of *Life*'s staff photographers at the Republican convention in Philadelphia was the kind of assignment I had left Milwaukee for. Unless there is a genuine contest and some suspense, a political convention is Dullsville, as millions of television viewers in later years can testify. All the elements of a horse race were in this one. Senator Robert A. Taft was the party's Establishment candidate. Thomas E. Dewey had a lock on the law and order issue—he had successfully prosecuted the malefactors of the New York political machine (Tammany Democrats!)—and was looking ahead to the governorship of New York. The hooves of the principal dark horse, Willkie, were audible. The man who was to become history's most durable

Republican candidate, Harold Stassen, was in the Minnesota delegation, ready and most willing.

Willkie, of course, won out. One small thing that damaged Taft was what Bob Capa did with what is now called a "photo opportunity." Taft wanted to prove he was a regular guy by going fishing. Capa's pictures showed unmistakably that Taft's catch was already dead and stuffed when he pulled it in. In later years Republican candidates would have more reason to be wary of the mischievous impulses of *Life* photographers, reporters, and editors. For instance, one photo taken from the side showed Tom Dewey sitting on a dictionary to bring his chin a little higher above his desk.

Willkie's candidacy involved a number of Time Inc. executives personally. I was sitting in for Wilson Hicks when an executive vice president came in to demand a *Life* portrait to use for a Willkie campaign poster. I said, "Sorry, we can't release an editorial picture for commercial use." He exploded. "I know all about rules. You'll be sorry." He stomped out, and I didn't hear any more about it. Later I found out that Billings had placated him by producing a nonstaff photographer who did work both for *Life* and for commercial customers. The v.p. later apologized to me.

Judgment of what is news is more subjective than differentiating between editorial and advertising material. Dan Longwell had a problem with Luce on the subject of Willkie. That year Longwell had an apt idea—a special issue on the U.S. Navy for the October 28 issue. This would coincide with Navy Day, on the birthday of Theodore Roosevelt, considered the father of the modern U.S. fleet.

The project was undertaken with all flags flying, and an admiral and his staff showed up at a Time Inc. company dining room to meet our planning staff. Longwell had rehearsed the rationale for a special issue so often that he delivered it at tobacco-auctioneer speed.

The navy should cooperate with *Life,* he argued, so that it could become more a part of the national image. "Look at the British. There are all those kids in sailor suits with 'H.M.S. Courageous' on their cap bands." After he had gone on in this fashion for a while, he wheeled around and said, "Isn't that so, Admiral?" The Old Salt found himself unexpectedly on his feet. He came out with, "I don't quite know what this little man is saying, but if he says we have the best goddamn navy in the world, he's right."

The best damn navy became, during the preparation of the issue, a branch of *Life.* None of the various editorial departments could get an item into the issue unless some naval connection was implied. The fashion department even talked a consortium of designers into coming up with women's clothes and accessories displaying naval motifs.

Everything was proceeding more or less according to Dan's plan, but the October 28 issue was the last before the election. Longwell realized that he had to break the news to Luce that there wouldn't be a political feature story—navy special issue, you know, timed for Navy Day and Theodore Roosevelt's birthday. "Why did he have to be born then?" Luce burst out indignantly. Much of the issue was already closed, so Luce had to settle for a few pages of campaign news.

The pranksters in the *Life* layout room prepared a risky practical joke on Longwell, who had wrung himself out in planning and editing the special issue. There was a double-page color photograph of a battery of naval guns being discharged. The large-type headline yelled: B O O M! In the first copy that Longwell opened, the headline had been changed to B O O! I've both perpetrated and been the butt of jokes, which were one of the things that made *Life* enjoyable. I felt this one, though, was dangerous because the Longwell family had a history of heart ailments. Predictably, Dan was shocked, but no heart attack ensued.

I couldn't vote for Willkie, attractive and reasonable though he seemed to be. My opinion was probably the result of a simplistic interpretation of what I had been taught in high school civics. A president is the representative of a political party, and since the Republicans had failed by only one vote to kill a renewal of the draft and Willkie was running as a Republican, I couldn't vote for him.

Although the "thinking editors" weren't yet prepared to talk out loud about fighting overseas, the "working editors," those fearless chair-borne combatants, were proceeding as if what the magazine was reporting was a prologue to formal involvement. A few staff photographers and correspondents were actually beginning to hear shots fired in anger.

Carl Mydans was shifted from icy Finland, where he had photographed the war with the Soviet Union with alternating cameras (producing one from inside his clothing every other shot to keep the shutters from slowing down), to "sunny" Italy. There, with Tom McAvoy, Mydans produced an essay of the country where Mussolini "at least made the trains run on time." A caption writer, from the safety of the Time & Life Building, made their stay untenable by calling a strutting Mussolini "the aging bully boy of fascism."

Mydans and his wife, Shelley, were in a small Time Inc. group which, as France was collapsing, made it out to a Pan Am plane in Lisbon. The group included Andrew R. Heiskell, soon to become publisher of *Life* and later chairman of the whole company, and Ralph D. Paine, future managing editor and publisher of *Fortune.*

We were not organized well enough for staff coverage of the French defeat and the British evacuation from Dunkirk, but William Vandivert, a genial staff photographer from the Midwest, threw his considerable bulk into poignant coverage of the aerial blitz on the United Kingdom. Freelance cameramen who supplemented Vandivert's take included the elegant Cecil Beaton, then and later famous for portraits of the royal family. Beaton's little bombing victim in a hospital, her head bandaged, holding a doll, made a *Life* cover. A Vandivert picture of a Welsh child, also heavily bandaged, her life saved by the protection of her dead mother's body, had vastly more emotional appeal than Beaton's well-lit, perfectly composed portrait.

Images like these were only a taste of what was to come. In the meantime, a variety of jobs seemed to be attaching themselves to me. Some were trivial. Others led to my taking on more and more responsibilities.

The man who originally handled photographs from newspapers and amateurs, and who was my contact with *Life* when I was still in Milwaukee, drank himself out of his job—even though he had taken the precaution of keeping an extra hat around to hang in his office when he was out at a bar. I took on his work. He had six secretaries, all of whom were named as co-respondents when his wife sued him for divorce (he gloated: "She didn't get the right one"). I already had one super-secretary, Peggy Smith Sargent, who took on the work of all six. Later she was *Life*'s film editor and made the indispensable decisions, mostly from 35mm contact prints, on which frames were to be enlarged for the editors.

The *Life* concept of a departmental editor who would both generate stories and write them didn't always work. Lincoln Barnett was growing into one of our most distinguished writers (he later wrote the series "The World We Live In"), but he could not produce enough news stories to satisfy Billings. I got the creative part of Barnett's job and added the de facto title of news editor. I was designated, perhaps whimsically, as the joint assistant to the rivals Wilson Hicks and Dan Longwell. I informed each of them that my accepting the job proved that I had no character at all. I was wearing quite a few hats, all literally 2½-gallon Stetsons, which Roland Butler, press agent for Ringling Brothers, used to pick up for me when the circus hit Wichita Falls.

I drifted almost casually into what was my single most visible prewar achievement, organizing and editing a special issue on U.S. defense. *Life* by now recognized the military and industrial build-up for what it was— preparation for World War II. Longwell, a promising young editor named John Field, and I set out to scout the country for stories. When we came back I was made the editor of the issue, or at least put in charge of collating the material and making layouts. As usual, Billings was to edit the text.

Longwell wanted to augment photos of war with paintings by known artists, and this issue was the place to start. He had lined up representational painters including Peter Hurd, Aaron Bohrod, Tom Lea, Fletcher Martin, Paul Sample, and Barse Miller. Their early efforts were confined to subjects such as marines firing machine guns, a battleship, pool shooting in a service club, a mess line, and a shell factory, but their paintings would eventually show grimmer action. Longwell also located some patriotic women's fashions (red, white, and blue) and found that Dorothy Lamour was a pin-up favorite. The bathing-suit picture of her was taken by Bob Landry, who later photographed what became the actual no. 1 pin-up of the whole war—Rita Hayworth kneeling on a bed in her nightgown.

Field and I concentrated on what we considered more serious subjects. A number of photographers moved in on the burgeoning military industry to produce a series of stunning full-page pictures, topped by a double truck (two facing pages) of the assembly line of the new fighter plane, the P-38 Lightning. That also was taken by the versatile Landry. His creative impulses extended to expense accounts, and he complained loudly for years about my lack of imagination. I disallowed a claim for daily taxicabs while he was at sea on an aircraft carrier. He countered with, "It was a long deck."

Since my duties ranged from the ideas to the assignments to the layouts, I had a chance to make hands-on, mid-course corrections. For instance, I assigned Eliot Elisofon to do what I thought would be one of the major components of the issue, a photographic essay on the Armored Force, which had grown from the Seventh Cavalry Brigade, Mechanized, to four full armored divisions. Elisofon's first installment came in, and the pictures were rather nondescript and static. We still had some time before deadline, so I spread out on a light table the color film of another military story, by Dmitri Kessel.

"I think this is a good way to shoot a military story," I told Elisofon. He looked for a little while, said nothing, left the office, and took a plane back to Tennessee, where the Second Armored Division had a part in ongoing maneuvers. When he returned, he had most of a highly pictorial, action-packed eighteen-page article. And for good measure, he took the photograph that would become the cover for the special issue. It was of Major General George Patton, commander of the Second, in his specially painted (red, white, and blue, plus yellow—the cavalry color) light tank. Patton's famous pearl-handled pistol was prominent in a shoulder holster, his two stars unsheathed (which would not have been proper in combat) in front of him. (Elisofon later covered Patton's operations in North Africa, where the general nicknamed him Hellzapoppin.)

Life's radio editor negotiated with NBC for advance release of a poem by Stephen Vincent Benét, "Listen to the People." It was a patriotic rouser: "We made this thing, this dream, this land unsatisfied with little ways. . . . we made it, and we make it and it's ours. We shall maintain it. It shall be sustained!"

For the week of the July 7 issue, the Germans turned on their cosigners of the nonaggression treaty, the USSR, and invaded. The only photographs available were radioed propaganda shots from the Germans. We published seven of them on a page, small because in those days the transmission lines in radio photos were rather coarse.

Following that were three pages of maps, ending with one in which the menacing arrows of the German advance pointed at Moscow. The maps were prepared under the supervision of another *Life* military expert, the redoubtable Garry Underhill, who was so convinced of German victory by his G-2 (army intelligence) sources that he devised a diabolical bet with Dmitri Kessel. Underhill agreed to pay a dollar for every day the Germans were not in Moscow. Although he was a refugee from Communist rule of the Ukraine, Kessel had confidence in the stubbornness of his former countrymen and said he would pay a dollar for each day the Germans were in Moscow. Kessel let Underhill's losses build up for five years before mercifully calling off the bet.

A couple of future photographic greats surfaced in time for token representation in this defense issue. They were similar in only two ways—each would unhesitatingly take on any assignment without protest, and each had a mother who would call me up to find out where her son had been sent on assignment.

One was W. Eugene Smith, a cult figure among young photographers today (see Chapter 22), whom I assigned to a frothy story on the Fort Leavenworth, Kansas, officers' club. Dues for belonging to this $800,000 installation, built with WPA funds, were $5 a month. It included a hunt club with stables and kennels. The master of the hunt and the riders wore pink coats. The huntsmen were black corporals dressed in green who herded in the coyotes that the officers pretended were foxes. It was all suitably recorded in color.

The other was Ralph Morse, a bouncy extrovert who became pictorially eloquent in every kind of photography, from candid human pictures taken with available light to science and sports pictures taken with strobes. When I am asked whom I would choose if I could have a staff of only one, I answer, "Ralph Morse—for his versatility." His contribution to the issue was the opening of the Chrysler tank-assembly line at Willow Run, Michigan.

After the issue closed, Billings noted in his diary, "Thompson is being bossy—that's what you get when you give someone a chance to get ahead." If I was being bossy, though, it was no doubt a preview of how I would eventually operate.

Certainly Billings was entitled to be the bossiest of bossy bosses. I was awestruck with the way, later, in which he handled the pressure in closing a story about the *Zamzam*, a decrepit Egyptian ship which was seized by a German surface raider. Aboard the *Zamzam* were David E. Scherman, a *Life* photographer and erstwhile promotion man, and Charles J. V. Murphy, a star writer for *Fortune*. They, other passengers, and the crew were interned in a small Biscayne Bay city in occupied France.

Murphy, who had been second in command of the second Byrd expedition to Antarctica, was the spokesman for the civilians. When there was no milk available for the children of a group of missionaries, he shamed the Germans into finding milk for the infants by sneering at the German reputation for efficiency.

Scherman spotted the Gestapo chief, one Schmidt, in the town and delighted in calling out, "Hello, Herr Schmidt," whenever he saw him even from across the street. Scherman somehow convinced the Germans that he was a buddy of Schmidt's, even though his greetings were never acknowledged. He was, naturally, taking pictures surreptitiously.

The internees were released and reached New York. Scherman had gotten his film developed somehow and hidden the negatives in a toothpaste tube—a timeworn but in this case effective ruse. Murphy normally had total recall and was pressed into service to write the lead article. But as the deadline neared, he was immobilized with a case of writer's block. Billings had him locked in an office, gave him Scherman's diary for guidance, and shuttled in relays of stenographers. Murphy dictated, and Billings took the raw narrative and edited the short takes into a coherent account.

This was not the way the Great Murphy was treated on *Fortune,* where the lateness of his copy sometimes caused the printing of an issue to be delayed. His colleagues there called the discipline to which he was subjected at *Life* "the Billings treatment."

In my last peacetime contact with soldiers, I helped cover the mock battles in Louisiana between two American armies in September 1941. With Dmitri Kessel, I reported on the Blue side; John Field, teamed with Ralph Morse, covered the Reds.

The Blues hired taxicabs to carry correspondents to and from the action. (Marshal Joffre taxied his soldiers to save Paris in World War I, didn't he?) We weren't told ahead of time what our side was attempting. Actions at various points in the designated battle were decided by on-the-spot umpires, a large group of officers commanded by Mark Clark. He was said to be "a comer" in army gossip, as was the Blue team's chief of staff, Dwight D. Eisenhower. The umpires' tactical rulings—this bridge has been knocked out; this crossroads is out of action; this side has aerial superiority—confused correspondents, and most of the uniformed participants as well.

One night while following a tip that a cavalry unit from Texas was about to enter the action, Dmitri and I got stuck in the mud in front of a Red outpost. Fortunately the Blue flag we were supposed to carry had snapped off in an earlier accident, and the Red soldiers, bemused by Dmitri's Ukrainian accent, pushed us free without taking us prisoner. The other *Life* team, Field and Morse, were captured and held a couple of days, so Kessel got the most pictures into the eventual layout.

On the fifth day, the "war" was called off, with the Blues officially victorious. The maneuvers would have been laughable if they hadn't shown how unprepared our army was. The vehicles stuck in ditches and swamps all over the area and couldn't have done much to repel invasions such as those the Japanese mounted against the Philippines, Hong Kong, and Singapore.

The troops, particularly those conscripted, were not being given any convincing reason for being in uniform. "OHIO" (over the hill in October— that is, desertion) was scrawled on walls in military installations throughout the country. Many officers had a feeble printed riposte on their office walls:

"Morale is a dirty French word." There was nothing official from the Roosevelt administration to contradict campaign statements that American boys wouldn't fight on foreign soil.

Then Pearl Harbor made the morale problem moot. I ordered a new uniform from a military tailor, but there wasn't any immediate call for a thirty-four-year-old reserve captain. I busied myself trying to locate wartime personnel for the magazine. I believed that, ideally, it was better for *Life* to recruit people who were somewhat office broken and had had some journalistic experience. But I found that Northwestern University's Medill School of Journalism, for instance, like other such schools with a job placement responsibility, just wouldn't talk about recent graduates who were doing well. Northwestern had a long-standing arrangement with the Inland group of small daily papers, which supplied jobs for the newly graduated. The trip I took to the Midwest and South yielded only a couple of recruits. Suggestions from me for a Thompson replacement from the staff elicited no reaction from my superiors.

Of much more use to *Life* was my participation in organizing the still-picture pool for war coverage. Hicks, to his credit, must have realized that the Associated Press, United Press, and International News Service would automatically have the priority transportation status that was necessary for spot news coverage. To get that same status, *Life* had to share its pictures with the daily press. Luckily the daily papers did not copy our technique of using sequences of photographs to tell stories. *Life,* which bought all three syndicates' product anyway, needed only to get its photographers into action. Many of the syndicates' photographers didn't particularly relish danger, so the low men on the totem pole, making perhaps $50 a week, were the ones sent to work in the pool. The best *Life* photographers *volunteered* to go.

The preliminary meetings by which this system was set up seemed interminable, but it worked out, and *Life* became, with no further help from me, *the* publication covering the war. The credit truly belongs to Wilson Hicks.

All this was vamping-until-ready for my part, whatever it was to be, in the war itself. I had learned enough about bureaucracies, both commercial and military, to realize that the details of one's future need not be left entirely to chance. From being on the other side of the desk, I disliked public relations work. Most persuasive to me was the complaint of unwilling draftees that a lot of older people were deciding that the younger men should go to war.

I argued to myself that, if I wasn't to consider myself hypocritical, I should at least be someplace where I could be shot at.

Some management types offered to convince the army that I would be more useful to the war effort on *Life*. I said no thanks. I had accepted the reserve commission in 1928 without reservations. I wasn't adamant about becoming a hero, but I did believe I should—if I had the cunning to bring it off—serve in a capacity in which I could find the most direct way to make a contribution toward winning the war. I realized that my civilian record indicated a public relations billet, so I went to the highest-ranking officer I knew in that area.

Major General Alexander Surles, the former commander of the First Armored Regiment of Fort Knox, Kentucky, was serving unwillingly as War Department director of public relations. "General," I said, "I bet you wish you were back in the Armored Force."

"You're goddamned right I do."

"You're stuck here, but you can send a kind of substitute. Could you get out my 201 [personnel] file and expunge every reference to my employment by newspapers and *Life* and then have me ordered to active duty in your Armored Force?"

He could. He sympathized with my feelings, and in the spring of 1942, I received a telegram ordering Captain Edward K. Thompson, 0-256492, to active duty at Fort Knox, for Armored Force orientation.

The parties that followed threatened to make me unfit for that active duty. One started with a visit to a Swedish folk dance session with Gjon Mili and went on through the night with Burl Ives, the folk singer, and Peter Hurd, one of *Life*'s war artists, who had once made a living singing in Mexican night clubs. I drove back to Long Island with the rising sun hitting me right in the eyes.

The climax was an office party which would have been a surprise if the foreign news editor, with whom I'd had some differences, hadn't stopped me in the hall to tell me he couldn't come but had paid his $5. John Billings overcame his resistance to fraternization and did come. He confided to his diary that he also paid $5. (The company did not subsidize parties in those days.) Billings did not exactly boost my morale by telling me, "You know, I never could quite figure out. What were you doing? I've abolished your job." He may have intended that as a compliment. I had worn a number of hats, now to be exchanged for an army brimless, called by members of the Armored Force a "rain-in-the-face cap."

The layout room started what was to become a staple idea for decorating such affairs. There were plenty of pictures of my face around because photographers used to test the synchronization of their flash guns on me. My face appeared on posters in composites of all kinds of military poses, from Rita Hayworth patching my trousers as a GI to a chiefs-of-staff group in which my face was substituted for those of each of the generals.

It seemed to be anticlimactic to return to the Time & Life Building after the party, so my secretary met me at the Pennsylvania Hotel bar with the final memos I had to dictate. She was Lynn Monroe Tate, whose application had come to me from the personnel department with the notation "Too exotic for any magazine except *Life*." She was one of a number of Thompson secretaries who were smarter than Thompson. On my recommendation she received a university scholarship and went on to become a highly skilled *Life* reporter. She subsequently married and divorced a *Life* editor and then, ditto, a *Life* photographer. Last I heard, she was teaching mathematics at the University of Nevada.

So I was off to Fort Knox, where armored vehicles did not come equipped with exotic secretaries.

8

An Assignment Protested but Fortunately Completed

✆ A theory behind having the reserve, or a citizen's army, is that years of gainful employment as a civilian develop qualities of leadership and flexibility while one keeps up with military affairs through correspondence courses and tours of active duty. The trouble was that during the Great Depression there wasn't enough federal money available for training, even every two years. Thus, starting out in the Armored Force in June 1942 was in effect launching into an almost new profession.

It was rather a relief, after the hectic days of winding up in New York, to have everything in our month's orientation sternly scheduled. In a class of one hundred, ninety were 1942 ROTC graduates, including all the Louisiana State football seniors. Those ninety seemed to revel in the physical training periods, whereas when I heard reveille, I would peer out, hoping it was raining too hard to work outdoors.

There was no mental challenge. With visual aids such as oversize gears painted in various colors, the army taught us some basic things, including what makes an internal combustion engine work. Each of us had to drive and service every vehicle: motorcycles; trucks; peeps (which is what the Armored Force called what everyone else called jeeps); jeeps, which were ungainly command cars; and General Grant tanks. The rationalization for this training was, "We know you won't be driving and servicing vehicles, but we don't want you to expect troops who are out on the road all morning, washing and greasing, to be on time for lunch in spic-and-span uniforms."

Members of the class were then ordered individually to various armored units for two months of summer maneuvers in the California desert, where operations had to be suspended every noon because the motors vapor-locked.

In the desert, I was assigned in rapid succession to the Second, Third, and finally the Fifth Armored divisions. The Fifth was learning how to fight a desert war that would end before it even went overseas. I respected my battalion commander, not just because he was the poker champ of the Fifth and had put in a request (which was ignored) that I stay on in his outfit, but also because of the transition he had made from being a Texas high school teacher to being a crafty fighting officer. (He must have goofed somewhere, though, because when I met him later in France he was in command of a grave-registration unit.)

Personally, I developed a whole new set of concepts as to what constituted luxurious living:

Item—I slept like a baby during the fifty-nine nights I had no bed because I learned that if I dug a hole for my hip in the rocks my hip bone wouldn't be driven into my body.

Item—Between specific maneuvers, our supply trucks would catch up to us and bring an apple box out of which someone had carved a comfortable toilet seat and which we would carry out into the desert at night so we could avoid thigh-straining crouches.

Item—I got one of two baths I managed during the sixty days when we passed a point in a huge pipe where the Los Angeles water supply flowed in from the mountains. The engineers had constructed a shower off the pipe, where I was able to wash my fatigues with my body in them and then take an ice-cold bath myself.

Item—We stopped off in Palm Springs, where a USO troupe was performing, headed by Victor Borge. Gjon Mili and Helen Morgan, out of the Los Angeles bureau, were covering the show for *Life*. I played hooky from my unit, occupied the extra bed in Gjon's room in the Desert Inn (the only first-class hotel there in 1942), and took a hot shower.

Item—The maneuvers ended in Needles, California. A poker game for the railroad workers (it was a division point on the Santa Fe) had been in progress twenty-four hours a day for years. My battalion commander bet $10 on a good-looking hand; the next player called and raised him $1,000.

The ultimate luxury was that I could catch the Santa Fe Superchief for civilization and Fort Knox again.

A troop command awaited my return. It was a replacement/training company in the Eighth Armored Division composed of new draftees, mostly from the hills of Kentucky and Tennessee, who were getting their thirteen-week basic training. In taking over a company, the new boss has to sign for all the equipment the outgoing commander turns over. The watchword is "Don't trust your own brother. Count it."

The more or less permanent first sergeant took me aside and said, "You're going to see a power lathe and a movie projector on the inventory, bought with company funds. You won't find them. They're in my house. But you go along and sign. When it comes your time to check out, I promise everything will be in order. If you're short of spoons, blankets, or whatever, I'll go out and steal them from other outfits." The sergeant, who really ran the company anyway, proved trustworthy.

At Fort Knox, I was shifted to the G-1 (personnel) section. This didn't make much sense to me, but the personnel officers said that anyone who had worn shoes and had any office experience at all had little chance of avoiding duty as an administrator.

My family joined me at Knox. All those years in the reserve gave me enough seniority to get a house on the post—a former sharecropper's house that had been moved in from the artillery range and set on top of an oversized hot-air furnace. We had to keep windows open—the orderly in charge of coal and snow shoveling pointed to a sheet of dittoed paper: "It says here I fire up four times a day, so that's what I do."

Some sticks of furniture were rented from the officers' club: metal government chairs and cots, pieced out with orange-crate cupboards and tables. It beat driving to a hotel in Elizabethtown, twenty miles away. My older son, Edward, was at a prep school on a scholarship. My younger son, Colin, age seven, went to the third of four schools he would attend that year.

Toward the end of 1942, my military service started to take the kind of direction I had hoped it would. I was designated as part of the cadre for a new armored division, the Twentieth, as assistant G-2 (intelligence) and was under orders to take a six-week cram course at the Command and General Staff School, Fort Leavenworth, Kansas. Eventually I was to report to Camp Campbell, Tennessee. But my plan to hide my civilian profession unraveled. I would never see Fort Leavenworth or Camp Campbell.

Just before Christmas of 1942, a wire from the War Department to Armored HQ, Fort Knox, directed that I be prepared for transfer. On the assumption that this meant a mission in North Africa, I was given a series of unpleasant inoculations, issued a pup tent (with poles and pegs), blankets, a gas mask, and a .45 automatic pistol. The confirming written orders got lost, so, after a couple of weeks, another telegram announced that Thompson was AWOL and should report (yesterday) to the assistant secretary of war, not mentioning which one, in Washington.

After a two-day winter drive, Marguerite, Colin, and I arrived at the Pentagon parking lot. Leaving my family—and equipment—I hurried to sign in, not wanting to be AWOL an extra day. I was told, "The secretary is waiting for you," and taken to the E wing, barely noticing that the sign on the office door said "Assistant Secretary of War for Air." I had never even been up in a military plane.

Behind the desk was Robert A. Lovett, who remarked in a low-key voice, "You were rather hard to find." It turned out that he had asked Luce to provide someone to run a classified picture publication. By this time Luce was tired of losing people to the military and, not knowing about the combat service I had plotted, blew my cover. Now I was being told that, even during a world war, I would still be putting out a picture magazine.

I expressed my reaction to Lovett in a manner that probably stretched the limits of how a presumed officer and gentleman ought to address a superior. Lovett, however, was tolerant and sympathetic. He didn't have to, but offered to see that, once I had his project successfully underway, I would be sent overseas. I sensed accurately that I was talking to a man of superior intelligence and integrity, and calmed down.

Then a few days later I met Luce on a Washington street, and he asked, "How do you like that good job I lined up for you?" I blew up again, in an even less inhibited way than I had with Lovett. Luce seemed suitably shaken.

It was time to stop griping and go to work. Lovett was convinced that his combat people could do their jobs better if they could be kept up to date on Army Air Force actions against the enemy. But he was also convinced that these predominantly young men had been so crammed with textbook material during crash courses that they would be loath to read anything more. How to get their attention? The best way, Lovett felt—but he sounded a little vague—would be to regularly disseminate classified aerial photographs in an easily understood format to the men in the field.

That was my job. To assemble tools, I had only a hunting license. Among necessities were 1) an editorial staff, 2) sources of editorial material, especially pictures, and 3) printing facilities. I could involve the clout of the assistant secretary as needed.

The staff of the magazine-to-be would be part of A-2 (air intelligence). I was outranked in my section by a full colonel, who had shifted from the cavalry to the AAF, where he believed promotions came faster, and by a former Boston stockbroker. Both tried to be helpful and in part overcame their concern about standard operating procedures.

Pending the completion of the Pentagon, A-2 publications was stashed in one of the many Washington buildings made of composition board, which were temporary during World War I and remained occupied until well after World War II. Ours was on Gravelly Point, near National Airport. Before the safes for classified material could be moved in, an engineering survey was used to place them so they would balance each other and not plunge through the deteriorating floor. When you worked late, you had to face armies of rats, which swarmed in to feed on the scraps of brown-bag lunches left in the wastebaskets.

My previous experience had conditioned me to work against deadlines, so April 1 was arbitrarily set for Volume 1, No. 1. In order to have it ready, the material would have to go to an as yet nonexistent printer in early March. By chance, I had met two former (and future) *Life* writer-editors already in the AAF corridors and requisitioned them.

It was best just to plunge in and produce something—the war wasn't waiting for us to attain a perfect set-up. In the process of being produced, the publication would develop a character of its own, I told myself.

In contrast to my experience at *Life* and at the *Milwaukee Journal,* there was no existing pool of skilled engravers, compositors, and pressmen to tap. The Government Printing Office was so jammed with work that it couldn't possibly do the job. Furthermore, its bureaucratic rules would not allow the display of the unusual photographs I envisaged to capture the attention of the textbook-weary flyboys. So almost unilaterally I began to check out printing plants in the area.

We found a third-generation family firm in Baltimore with a deserved reputation for quality work. The owner, C. William Schneidereith, wanted to participate in the war effort, so we negotiated what amounted to a "cost-plus" standard contract with minimum quibbling over *whereas*es and *wherefore*s. When the GPO found out about it months later, it threatened to have my colonel disciplined for bending the regulations, but the project was, by that time, too popular with the top brass to touch via a court martial.

There was no central unit which could serve up a collection of photographs for editorial selection, but there was a laboratory in a Pentagon sub-basement which made prints from the thousands on thousands of ten-by-ten negatives routinely shot from high-level bombers on missions. The lab also could turn out photostats ordered to the size necessary for page layouts. On order, it would produce prints in seven to ten days. That wasn't fast enough, but, thanks to the other half of my initial staff, my secretary, the lag problem was solved.

Kitty's professional qualifications were six weeks of high school lessons in stenography. But what she lacked in routine skills she more than made up for in honey-dripping southern charm.

Even in the days before the women's movement made sexist tactics a no-no, I had better sense than to suggest she vamp the lab boss, a first lieutenant. She realized I was in a hurry, though, so she would stay around the lab, usually until she came back with the prints or photostats the same day. The other women in A-2 told me that Kitty became engaged to the lab man—and to four other first lieutenants, too. She wore a silver bar on her dress, each of her "fiancés" thinking it was his. When one of them made captain (two bars joined) all five engagements became unsupportable.

One could estimate which missions would produce good material by reading combat reports, by word of mouth in Pentagon offices, and indeed by reading sanitized press reports. So there was an ample supply of high-level bombing and reconnaissance pictures to choose from—too ample. The world from 30,000 feet was hard to read, even for fliers, so it was desirable to mix oblique photographs from low levels, when available, with the high-level verticals that frequently needed 3-D photo interpretation to explain them.

We selected the publication's name just before the first issue closed. It was somewhat surprising—to me—that the Boston stockbroker came up with the winner, *Impact*. It connoted action and was general enough to cover both operations and intelligence.

In the first issue, the sinking of a Japanese cruiser by B-17s was the most arresting article. It was acquired in a most unbusinesslike way: I saw a young brigadier general in a corridor with photographs in his hand. He was glad to loan them to me, having hand-carried them to Washington because he claimed that Admiral Nimitz, commander of all forces in the Pacific, wouldn't allow proof of the Army Air Force's successes to pass Pearl Harbor to Washington.

AAF Commanding General Henry H. ("Hap") Arnold found *Impact* to be an invaluable visual aid when testifying before a House appropriations subcommittee. A congressman told Arnold, "I have a brother-in-law in the navy in the Pacific, and he tells me the B-17s can't hit anything." Arnold triumphantly reached into his briefcase for Vol. 1, No. 1, and said, "This is classified confidential, Congressman, but I think you ought to see . . ."

On a catch-as-catch-can basis, the first issue turned out to be a fair representation of the AAF's overall activity. There were photographs of high- and low-level bombings, MacArthur's airlifted capture of Papua, a captured Japanese fighter plane being put through its paces, and downed German reconnaissance planes sticking up out of the snow in Iceland.

We assembled the first issue with an absolute minimum of waste motion. I gathered, laid out, checked, and wrote virtually everything. Armed with government-issue T-square and rubber cement, I composed each page. There were no time-consuming conferences because there wasn't anyone with whom to confer.

After that involuntary self-sufficiency, though, I was glad to welcome proven professional help. Lieutenants Maitland Edey and Tom Prideaux would be the mainstays of the *Impact* staff while I was there and afterward. Later, at *Life,* Edey would be my assistant managing editor. Prideaux, an erstwhile English teacher, Egyptologist, and *Life* drama critic, would become entertainment editor. *Impact* also acquired an art director, John Burton Brimer of *House & Garden.* He had a civilian contract with the AAF and agreed to transfer to *Impact.*

By the second issue, *Impact* began to take on a coherent form, spiced up by attention-getting headlines. I found puns, alliteration, slang, and general cornballery acceptable as long as the message was conveyed. Within the AAF readership good taste seldom reared its ugly head.

A lead article was ideally a narrative in photographs. In the second issue it was the battle of the Bismarck Sea, March 1–4, 1943, in the Southwest Pacific. Each day's action was indicated by a simulated calendar page, from the time the Japanese convoy was sighted until the last of the twenty-some ships was hit and sunk. The convoy had been transporting an entire infantry division. Included in the seven-page article was a Weather Information Bureau reconstruction of the conditions and a complete box score, which included the planes engaged, the weights of the bombs dropped, and our own casualties (very few). Shorter stories, most of them two-page spreads, on a variety of subjects completed the thirty-six-page issue.

Thoughtful subjects gave substance to *Impact.* What made it exciting were single great photographs. From the beginning, we published instructions on how to speed pictures that operational units thought were good through channels for the direct attention of *Impact.*

The search for material may have been a little over-aggressive at times. On a trip to the combat zone in North Africa, Lovett seemed amused by what happened during the attack on Pantelleria, an Italian island off Sicily, which the AAF undertook to conquer by bombing alone. Before Lovett left, I had asked him to ginger up units in the area because *Impact* was not getting many submissions.

He said he would do what he could. As he told the story: "I was standing on a little hill with some officers. The atmosphere was tense. Our allotted time, after which the navy would land ground troops if the bombing failed, was about up. A courier from the nearest message center approached with a radio message which I thought must be news of the surrender. It said, 'Where are the pictures? Thompson for Arnold.'"

Pantelleria, which had been bombed by eighty AAF missions between June 1 and June 10, 1943, ran up a white flag on its fortifications and showed a white cross on its battered airfield. Thus the AAF was saved from the ignoble fate of having to accept help from the navy.

From the beginning, the *Impact* style of graphic display had appealed to AAF headquarters. I was summoned to General Arnold's office, stood at attention in front of his desk, and saluted. Apparently the commanding general's office was not considered saluting territory, because he didn't return it. While I was, I hoped unobtrusively, slithering my hand down to my side, he said, "You're the president of the United States."

"Sir?" I quavered.

The general glanced at a copy of *Impact* on his desk and said, "That's good." Then he tossed three photographs at me and repeated, "You're the president of the United States. Fix these up so *you'll* like them." The pictures showed the first significant mission inside Germany itself. The target was a submarine shipyard in Vegesack.

The perception, accurate or not, was that President Roosevelt's attention could not be held for much more than thirty seconds, so John Brimer and I stayed up most of the night preparing the layouts. We obtained enlargements from the lab. We put a one-word headline on each picture: "Before, During, After" and a very few lines of information—date, place, number of bombers, altitude, number and type of bombs. A brief summary of the damage went under the "After" picture.

I didn't consider the photographs the most compelling I'd ever seen, but when presented by Arnold to FDR they must have held his attention for the magic thirty seconds because Arnold called on me to prepare similar presidential presentations at intervals thereafter. One I delivered surreptitiously at night at a White House gate for Elliott Roosevelt. The AAF had commissioned him to counteract his father's presumed preference for the navy.

To the president and to the public, General Arnold correctly emphasized strategic, precision bombing as the most direct way to affect the enemy's ability to make war. For starters, there were durable long-range vehicles, the B-17 and later the B-24, supposedly well armed for protection and equipped with the supersecret Norden bombsight.

Something crucial was missing at first, though. There was no Allied fighter plane with sufficient range to go all the way with the bombers on long missions into Germany. The bombers' own machine guns did destroy German fighters, but our losses over Schweinfurt and at the aircraft plants near Regensdorf proved to be of unacceptable magnitude. It wasn't *Impact*'s business to lecture, but I thought it essential to maintain credibility by recording the bad news. Then, when we had good news, we would be believed.

It wasn't until 1944 that the P-51 Mustang became operational. Then a staggered arrangement of escorts, duly diagrammed in *Impact,* could be set up. The rugged but short-range P-47s would cover the first leg; then P-38 Lightnings would arrive for the middle miles; finally, P-51s would accompany the bombers over the target.

Impact's method of producing photographs to show what happened to fighters in action was devised by Captain Erich Schlaijker, whose name had popped out of the personnel files as a magazine writer. Actually, he was by trade a paleontologist, but he *had* once written an article for *Natural History.* The usual pictures of fighters in action showed them as tiny dots. However, successful pilots were now coming back from combat zones and were available for detailed interviews. Complete sets of scale models of both our forces and the enemy's planes had been made for recognition training, so Schlaijker found that, after reconstructing dinosaur bones, it was child's play to devise gallows-like arms to which model planes could be attached with almost invisible threads in the proper relative positions and angles for each stage of the combat being described. Only the distances between the planes were altered.

Dancing up a storm with Marguerite (probably 1943, photo by Carl Mydans).

A retread from World War I, Donald Hough, was another useful addition. He was about to be retired for being over age in grade when I got him orders to join *Impact* in Washington. He started driving in from the West but got into a big-time poker game in Chicago and lost all his money, his Cadillac, and his house in Palm Springs. His orders got him a rail ticket, and he arrived at my desk in Washington, bummed a cigarette, and borrowed thirty-five cents for lunch at the officers' cafeteria. He had found himself stranded earlier in other towns and had written his way out by selling freelance articles to, among other publications, the *Saturday Evening Post.* He did a good professional job for *Impact* and didn't have enough money to get re-hooked on gambling in Washington. Hough spent his evenings in searches for bars with bowls of hard-cooked eggs—"A saloon without them isn't worth drinking in."

Less colorful characters came to the staff, and they shared in one way or another the curiosity which provided the variety necessary to make the meat and potatoes of deadly serious matters such as bombing, air defense, and logistics more digestible. We varied photographs and diagrams with comic-strip narratives. We reprinted the propaganda leaflets our planes dropped.

Impact was lavish with instructions on how to bail out, how to ditch, how to survive in enemy territory, how to minimize the danger of flak, the right and wrong ways to bomb at deck level—all with photographs of actual events. I must admit, however, that no grateful survivor ever showed up in the office clutching a salt-soaked copy of *Impact* and saying, "You saved my life."

Still, the photograph can be a startling, if sometimes brutal, way of teaching lifesaving lessons. We looked for a significant AAF goof for every issue. In publishing a picture of a B-17 scattered in hundreds of pieces on a landing strip, we pointed out that this kind of mistake carried the need for air safety precautions "grimly beyond the cartoon and funny jingle state."

It was also important for the operational troops to realize that the damage from enemy action was often survivable because of the sturdy construction of the planes. Pictures of equipment that had made it back appeared periodically.

Early in 1944, after a full year in Washington, I suggested that *Impact* could now continue without me. Lovett kept his word and arranged a transfer to the indisputably useful War Department's G-2 Special Branch, which provided interpretations of high-level intercepts of enemy messages to various commands. For once, the system had fitted a square peg into a square hole.

Through the ensuing years, I kept in touch with Mr. Lovett (I was too much in awe of him to address him directly as anything but Mister or Boss). He would chide me on my predilection for the mass journalistic audience. Better, he said, to have a few influential readers who made things happen. He was thinking of the Air Forces' top echelon, which found *Impact* useful, and my audience of one, FDR, when I concocted the presentations for General Arnold.

9

From Ultra to the Bulge
to Victory in Europe

◠◡ Going to the Special Branch meant I would satisfy a natural taste for snooping. I would contribute something to the military effort, and my presence at high-level planning sessions would give me a fly-on-the-wall view of the great men of my day as they fashioned history. But to achieve this I had to learn a new military skill: interpreting enemy messages.

The British knew that the Germans had an encoding machine, Enigma. The Allied cryptanalysts tried unsuccessfully to read the German messages using a commercial model the Germans had sold before the war. Then, just as their country was falling to the Germans, Polish secret service agents got hold of a military model. The Enigma machine was smuggled to Britain, where clone machines were constructed. It then became, basically, a matter of rotating the machine drums when the Germans routinely changed codes.

Assistant Secretary of War John McCloy was the top boss of the Special Branch. My more immediate boss was Colonel Alfred McCormack, the administrative director, also a Wall Street lawyer but an outspoken freewheeler.

I knew Al was okay after the following incident: An officer was being sent to handle Ultra material (the British cover name for all high-grade signals intelligence) at General Douglas MacArthur's headquarters. Al decided to have this man deliver some classified orders and produced a mailbag, weighted to sink if the plane ditched, and a .45-caliber pistol. "If this gun fires accidentally and kills General Willoughby," Al said with a straight face, "you will have rendered an inestimable service to intelligence." Willoughby,

MacArthur's G-2, was known to slant intelligence reports toward what *he* thought his boss wanted to hear.

I stayed in Washington only long enough for a full FBI security check, and in early spring 1944 was off to London. I signed in at the U.S. Embassy and emerged onto Grosvenor Square (Eisenhower Platz to Londoners). There, just as if it were West State Street in Milwaukee, I ran into Frank Scherschel. I had hired him for *Life* when he found out that the *Journal* wouldn't cover combat. I couldn't tell him what I was doing, but he didn't care. He had survived U-boat attacks on a convoy to Russia and a crippled B-17 from which he covered the costly AAF attack on Schweinfurt. He swept me off to a party Bob Capa was giving that evening.

Capa had sublet a luxury flat for himself and his then girlfriend, Pinky. There wasn't much furniture, so most of the guests stood or sat on the floor. Bob introduced me to a bearded guest with, "Ernst, this is Ed." I didn't pay much attention because many of Capa's friends were bearded and the name Ernst seemed to fit them. When we emerged, however, this Ernst was trying to kick his way into Scherschel's Morris Minor. Frank guided him gently to another Morris Minor, where his key was found to fit. Next morning's paper revealed that Ernst was Ernest Hemingway, who had fractured his skull by driving into a lamppost in the blackout after he left the party.

My dip into my past (and future) *Life* incarnation was brief. Next day the embassy cut orders to send me to British codebreaking headquarters at Bletchley Park, near Bedford, for a cram course in what Ultra and the German Air Force were all about. The existence of the Bletchley operation and its importance remained a deep secret for thirty years, until publication of William Stevenson's book *A Man Called Intrepid.*

Two Royal Air Force officers were my instructors for a few weeks at Bletchley. One was a former advertising man/literary critic, Wing Commander (Lieutenant Colonel) Rose, called Jim in place of his three initials, none of which was J. The other, Peter Calvocaressi, was an attorney who later became an assistant prosecutor at the Nuremberg trials. Peter had helped break the Enigma codes, but fortunately was not required to teach me that skill. After the messages had been rendered into English, I would explain them to those who needed to know.

I was tentatively ticketed for the German Air Force section at SHAEF, Supreme Headquarters Allied Expeditionary Force, headed by General Dwight D. Eisenhower. First, though, I had to go through an "inspection" by the section chief, my prospective boss, RAF Group Captain (U.S.

Army equivalent: full colonel) Harry Humphreys. The SHAEF staff was split between American and British officers—a British boss would have an American assistant who, in turn, would have a British assistant, and so on. Humph recoiled from the spartan atmosphere of Bletchley. Four British services were stationed there: the British navy, the British army, the Royal Air Force, and the Foreign Service, so no one of them would take responsibility for the food. The canteen, for lunches, was serviced by an outside contractor, who had a predilection for dishes such as tripe and brussels sprouts in their soggiest, most odoriferous forms.

My "inspection" meeting with Humph was at a London hotel. He was an accomplished linguist in French, German, and Spanish and worked hard at avoiding work. Dinner was a bibulous affair that lasted well beyond midnight. Present was Humph's crony, Air Commodore "Tubby" (referring to his figure, not his initials, none of which was T) Grant. My role that evening was to listen to scurrilous anecdotes that Humph and Tubby told each other about RAF comrades. I was not questioned about what I had learned at Bletchley or about what I already knew about the American Army Air Forces. It was rather a test of durability and capacity for scotch, gin, and brandy.

Jim Rose elegantly described the encounter as "the Thompson cow being presented to the Humphreys bull" and triumphantly informed me when I returned to Bletchley that "the bull had accepted."

While my orders assigning me to SHAEF were being cut, I spent a week with the British Air Ministry. I was introduced to the resident guru of Ultra interpretation, Wing Commander Asher Lee. He looked at my silver lieutenant colonel's leaves (my rank was equivalent to his) and said loudly, "Oh, Americans—overranked, overpaid, overfed, oversexed, and over here." He did not smile when he said it.

Apart from Asher Lee, none of the other air intelligence people I met were anti-American. All were very helpful. They also exhibited, in a concentrated form, the kind of intelligence mind-set which seemed to make them feel that they were part of the enemy. One striking example: I came into the air ministry V-1 section the morning the first German buzz bomb hit London, wrecking a commuter rail station. A V-1 had been expected for months, ever since a young photo-interpreter, Constance Babington Smith (who later worked for me at *Life*), had spotted an early model on a Peenemünde air strip. The reaction of the British V-1 section: "By God, we have finally done it."

Thereafter, the V-1s fell increasingly on London. They were powered by a primitive jet engine, and you were safe if you could hear it buzzing—it would overshoot you. But when it went silent, it was time to dive for cover. Hitting a specific target with the relatively small bomb was impossible. The tension in the streets was considerable. The British antiaircraft ammunition in those days did not self-destruct, so falling pieces of our own shells did more total damage than the V-1s. When American, electronically controlled antiaircraft guns came in, almost all the V-1s on the predictable path toward London were destroyed, something that power-diving Spitfires could accomplish only occasionally.

The day I reported to SHAEF, a V-1 arrived in the vicinity of Bushey Park, near Hampton Court Palace. As I walked toward the adjutant general's office to sign in, a giant bullhorn blasted out: "V-1, V-1, all personnel to slit trenches!" It was raining, but all ranks, including generals, piled into the muddy ditches.

I had only one uniform and I was wearing it, so I didn't jump. My footlocker, shipped by sea, hadn't caught up yet. My hastily thought-up alibi would be that I was a new boy, not officially part of SHAEF, who hadn't read any regulations. The bomb barely cleared the SHAEF offices and slammed into an adjoining barracks, killing several.

There was no Group Captain Humphreys in my new office, but an RAF squadron leader, Victor Cross, greeted me. He had been flying bombers in Egypt and explained his presence with, "Those planes aren't insulated—the roar of motors affected my ears. What does the RAF do with a deaf pilot? Put him into intelligence." Obviously we were going to get along well. Before the war he had managed a tobacco plant for Players cigarettes and was better qualified than most lawyers or even the journalists that I got to know in the Ultra group.

Victor and I were immersed in the moves the German Air Force was making as the Allied Air Forces pounded bridges, airfields, and probable defensive assembly points in preparation for D-Day. We were much too busy to take time out for getting into slit trenches during V-1 alerts, so we worked under tables and desks to evade the military police who patrolled the halls, seeking to enforce the stern standing orders that we protect ourselves. The code name for access to our invasion plans, which we had to have, was Bigot. One soon got accustomed to answering "I am Bigoted" when challenged.

Humphreys would appear just before the 9 A.M. SHAEF staff meeting started, grab whatever Victor and I had written, and, I suppose, embroider it for the assembled generals. We wouldn't see him again until the next morning.

The Germans were led to believe the D-Day landings would take place in the Pas de Calais area. Allied wireless traffic, meant to be intercepted by the enemy, was for a phantom army. Our air strikes sealed off the Pas de Calais, as well as the rest of the Normandy beaches, where the landings did take place. (Back in New York, *Life* editors were badly fooled too. When the flash came that the invasion was on, the magazine went to press with carefully prepared maps and an artist's conception of the attack the Germans had been led to expect.)

General Walter Bedell Smith presided over the SHAEF morning staff meeting as chief of staff for Eisenhower. Ike disliked formal meetings and showed up only periodically, without advance notice. Smith was called Beetle by his intimates. I never got more familiar than addressing him as "sir." He was the kind of executive I admired—brisk and stern. He was sometimes brutal toward other generals, and though outwardly gentle he was no less demanding with lowly lieutenant colonels. It was not likely that the facile but basically shallow Humphreys would fool him for long. Humph didn't, but in the meantime he had twenty-four-hour-a-day use of the section jeep, while Victor and I could draw only bicycles.

SHAEF Main was a rather unwieldy bureaucracy, so directly after D-Day the actual running of the war was split off to SHAEF Forward. We in SHAEF Forward were sent to the Forest of Bere in southern England near Portsmouth. Working and living quarters went under canvas. This was not Humphreys's idea of gracious living, so he stayed at SHAEF Main—with the jeep—broadly hinting that a frequent passenger was a high-born leydee, as the song went.

Meetings were at 9 A.M. (you'd better believe, sharp), seven days a week. The staff I addressed, in addition to the formidable Beetle, included Air Chief Marshal Arthur Tedder, deputy supreme commander to Eisenhower, the assembled Gs (1, 2, 3, and 4), at least one admiral, and brass hats from lower commands who happened to be passing through and who were cleared to receive Ultra.

As each of us completed his briefing, he would return to his seat behind the general staff members. We stayed on in case someone wanted more information. We could listen to the discussion leading up to decisions or perhaps hear about a decision made since the staff meeting of the previous day. Just watching and listening to how the SHAEF general staff conducted the war was a tremendous learning experience.

SHAEF Forward was the operating unit of the whole Allied Expeditionary Forces, although the "offices"—tents with rolled-up sides because of the summer temperatures—did not look very military. The Ultra material came to me on flimsy onionskin sheets. We had been thoroughly scared at Bletchley Park about the dire consequences of loose security. So when a general strolled into the intelligence tent one day with an Ultra flimsy in his hand, my heart almost stopped. He was the SHAEF inspector general and not cleared for Ultra. He asked, "Did you lose this?" and I snatched it out of his hand. Very shortly thereafter I was called back to the U.S. Embassy in London. Had another flimsy blown out of the tent?

I called a friend who was an assistant air attaché at the embassy. Why was I being called back? What was up? He called back, laughing: "You're getting a medal, for God's sake." It was the Legion of Merit for creating *Impact*.

By any conventional military calculations, SHAEF Forward, the major headquarters, should not have gone to Normandy as soon as we did. In post-landing fighting across the channel, Field Marshal Montgomery's British weren't advancing according to plan. The American part of the advance was also stalled. But Beetle Smith was considered to be the only Allied general who could handle the abrasive Montgomery. We were airlifted to another tent camp near Granville, on the coastal cliffs.

Group Captain Humphreys made a one-day visit to Normandy, and, after a notable lunch at a country inn where his elegant French charmed the landlady out of some vintage wine she had hidden from the Germans, he returned to London, permanently. I became head of the GAF section.

While preparations for a breakout from Normandy were proceeding, with Patton and his army on the right flank and Montgomery with his army group on the left, we had a real scare. General Eisenhower was learning to fly a light plane and had a forced landing on the beach below our cliffs. The tides in Normandy are second only to those in the Bay of Fundy in height. The general had to run for it to escape being inundated and barely made higher ground; in the process he wrenched a knee. In the next morning's planning session, Beetle announced with no attempt to conceal his satisfaction: "General Marshall has grounded the Supreme Commander for the duration."

In the breakout, General Patton's army started down the Normandy penin-sula, imaginatively substituting fighter planes for what would have been a traditional right flank on the ground. Montgomery started his carefully prepared advance on the left. The allocation of fuel was the prime concern of the G-4 (supply). Laying a fuel pipeline under the channel, code-named Pluto, had been an engineering triumph, the first drops being hailed by Beetle with, "Pluto pissed."

The gasoline indeed developed into a mighty stream, but delivery to the troops was limited by the number of tanker trucks and planes available. Choices had to be made. Patton did not favor tank-against-tank fighting. Even our armored partisans considered the German Tigers and Panthers to be better than a one-on-one match for the American Shermans. "Never get into a pissing match with a skunk," Patton said. His tactic, then, was to probe for a soft place, ram his Shermans—vastly more numerous than the German tanks—through the hole, fan out behind the lines, and cause havoc with the German infantry. He did this repeatedly in his rapid advance and was virtually out in the open, bypassing Paris, when, according to the previously agreed upon plan, Montgomery was to get the bulk of the transportable fuel. Patton saw his breakthrough as a chance to continue and wrap up the whole operation in Europe.

Montgomery aimed at the bridges near Arnhem, the Netherlands, and thence to the Ruhr industrial complex. The original allotment was honored, and Patton was screaming protests from eastern France. When Montgomery's thrust stalled short of Arnhem, he blamed bad weather, which had deprived him of air support for a period. Most SHAEF generals felt strongly that Monty should have pushed ahead anyway.

Armchair strategists may be somewhat surprised to find that the severest critics of Montgomery's failure were the British members of SHAEF. This was due in part to Monty's bad manners in dealing with the man who had the job he thought ought to have been his, Eisenhower. Monty never, as far as I know, showed up at SHAEF. "Ike knows where I am. He can come and see me," Monty was quoted as saying. "Where I am" was a caravan or trailer, usually hidden in the woods with a staff that, compared to the overblown infrastructure of SHAEF Main, operated with a minimum of waste motion.

With the Patton sweep past Paris, the city was liberated and SHAEF Forward was reunited with SHAEF Main at Versailles. Beetle had toyed audibly with the idea of making the Louis XIV palace SHAEF headquarters, just to rub it into the Germans, but there was no central heating. Instead, SHAEF took over a luxury hotel, the Petit Trianon. The women's services were quartered in the unheated palace stables. My secretary, Margaret Hopkins, and her WAF friends regularly used my office's plumbing facilities to take hot baths.

My choice of a Briton as an assistant was Victor Cross, whose base rank in the RAF was flight lieutenant. In the British forces, however, the job determines the rank, so Victor jumped two levels to wing commander to match my rank of lieutenant colonel.

The air operations briefer, Roger Francis, and I were assigned quarters in a rather seedy hotel near the railway tracks in Versailles. We took one look and Roger said, "Let's try Paris. I know the manager of the Crillon." It was my birthday, September 17, and we had finished the morning briefing. Why not?

The Crillon put us up in a suite with two bedrooms and a living room. We arranged a predawn pickup service to take us to our office in Versailles. At the hotel, the canned breakfast juices were cooled in silver buckets. The Crillon chefs were, miraculously, able to make powdered eggs into palatable omelets, with the help of canned tomatoes and garlic. This luxurious existence was not to be for long. A memo from the chief of staff's office said it had come to the attention of the Supreme Commander that a number of SHAEF officers were in Paris. The memo directed that if such residence was in line of duty, proof should be submitted. If not, the officers involved would be in assigned quarters by 1700 hours, that day. The Crillon was hastily evacuated by Francis and Thompson.

Roger immediately wangled a posting to the SHAEF mission in Paris. I found an apartment on the Seine in St. Cloud. Since the building, which had housed German occupation officers, was full of generals, I figured it would surely be well heated. But all the brass couldn't prevent the floods which kept pulverized coal, needed for the heating plant, from reaching St. Cloud by canal.

An even chillier experience served as a stern lesson in military speaking for me. General Eisenhower made one of his unexpected appearances at a briefing. He edged into the far end of the semicircular staff table right in front of the gigantic war room map. Beetle Smith was in the center. I had to deal with a lower corner, and rather than shove my rear end into the Supreme Commander's face, I addressed him and Beetle alternately, walking a few steps as I turned from one to the other.

Beetle told me to wait after the meeting and seemed almost hesitant about speaking, a rare phenomenon. "Your material and how you use it has been okay," he said, "and I wouldn't say anything if I hadn't had the same trouble as an instructor at Fort Benning. I walked, too."

I tried to explain why I had, but he cut me off. "They made me stand in a tub to keep me still. Now I won't do that to you, but for God's sake don't walk anymore." From then on, pointer in hand, I delivered what I had to say from an erect, fixed position with my feet, as prescribed by the manual, at an angle of forty-five degrees "or as near thereto as the formation of the man allows."

The fall months of 1944 were relatively quiet, a period of consolidation, with Patton's army probing tentatively at the Siegfried line in the Saar area. I got a firsthand insight into Patton's thinking at a meeting where I was the intelligence briefer. The attendants included the American and British fighter and bomber commanders, representatives of the British Air Ministry from London, and assorted ground generals, including Patton. Patton was trying to figure out how he could utilize the strategic bombers.

These big planes were used from time to time against fortified ground positions. For the sake of our own troops, there was the so-called bomb line, safely ahead of our front ground units. Carpet bombing did stun the defenders, but by the time the ground troops could advance to the bomb line, the acute effects of the bombing had dissipated.

What if, Patton asked General Jimmy Doolittle, commander of the Eighth Air Force and a kindred spirit, a thin line of American tanks was stationed right on the bomb line to move in immediately while the enemy was still in shock? Only a direct hit would kill a tank crew. At X yards, what were the statistical chances of a direct hit on a tank? Would the casualties be less than if troops back of the bomb had to face recovered German defenders? The two generals proceeded to sketch out the situation on the backs of envelopes, and each left with the intention of working out the details. The Battle of the Bulge forced Patton to scurry north to relieve embattled Bastogne, so the experiment never came off.

The failure to forecast the Bulge advance should have weighed on the conscience of every Allied intelligence officer in the European theater. It did on mine, although I was strictly responsible only for the German Air Force, which was not used in this operation. I was about to enter the War Room for the 9 A.M. meeting when an officer from the "Y" service, which did low-level intercepts, handed me a note reporting a lot of wireless traffic in the Ardennes, a theretofore quiet area. The report was unevaluated raw material, and I didn't use it in my day's report—only to find out later that the material indicated that the German Bulge offensive had been underway.

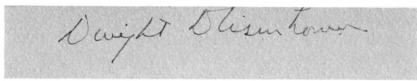

Talking with General Dwight Eisenhower at a Supreme Headquarters Allied Expeditionary Force reception (1944).

The Germans had, by night movements, switched an entire army from the Russian front, maintaining complete radio silence.

I suggested to my titular superior, an amiable RAF air commodore named Colin Grierson, that he might want to have me transferred because of my failure to mention the "Y" flash. He tut-tutted that the warning had come too late to stop anything. I heard, however, that some intelligence officers were saying that their warnings about the Bulge attack went unheeded. I dug up their so-called forecasts and found that they had listed an Ardennes advance only as one of six possible developments and then dismissed it. Still, I remain troubled about that blind spot in my intelligence.

I actually saw the Bulge later with a young pilot who was assigned to fly me around to the various SHAEF air commands with which I maintained contact. It was almost always easier to requisition a plane than a car. The pilot had four fighter victories, which left him one short of being an ace, but he had been relegated to chauffeur duty for "psychological reasons." He would shortcut over the Bulge every chance he had, unlimbering his .45 automatic and opening his side window, looking for that fifth plane. Fortunately, we never saw one.

I thought the pilot was just trying to kid me when he warned that some of the plywood courier planes like ours occasionally lost a wing. Once, when we were turned back by weather over the Vosges mountains, my pilot had to make a particularly hairy landing. When we came into the operations tent, there was Admiral Richard E. Byrd, the polar explorer, on some kind of inspection tour for the navy. "Nice landing, son," said the admiral. "How do you like that plane?"

"It's okay, I guess."

"The reason I asked," Byrd said, "is that the navy has grounded its version of it. The wings were falling off."

SHAEF was scraping the bottom of the barrel to get every possible assistance to troops in the Bulge and decided to use the antiaircraft artillery that was supposed to be defending Paris. I was assigned to soothe the French command for the defense of Paris, which was understandably jittery. I assured a meeting of six or eight colonels and generals that they really didn't need the ack-ack, that the German Air Force was out of the sky anyway.

A few nights later, when an air-raid siren sounded in St. Cloud, I wondered whether I would have to go back and apologize. It was a few days before Christmas, and I could see lighted trees in windows along the Seine. There were a few bomb pops, and the tree lights went out one by one. It turned out to be only a reconnaissance plane getting rid of its few bombs before returning to base. Fortunately, Patton's forced-march relief of Bastogne ended the Bulge threat.

SHAEF—and this was in the perceived character of General Eisenhower—treated the egos of commanders such as Montgomery, Patton, and De Gaulle with the respect their performances had earned and bore their histrionics with equanimity—up to a point. Beetle Smith revealed at a staff meeting one of his tactics for handling Montgomery. The Netherlands were under Montgomery's military command, and Queen Wilhelmina had asked to return home. Smith said, "Churchill wants it. The president wants it. But Monty doesn't want any rival attractions. I will draft a message from the Supreme Commander directing Monty to receive the queen with appropriate ceremonies. I will find Monty's trailer in the woods, drop the directive at his door, knock, and run like hell." However delivered, the message was effective. The queen returned to her throne.

Once the Bulge was neutralized, SHAEF Forward again broke off from SHAEF Main and set up in a Reims technical institution, which the press later called "the little red schoolhouse." The generals and full colonels were quartered in the Lion d'Or, the only good hotel in town. The lieutenant colonels and majors had considerably less elegant quarters. Some lower-ranking officers drew former brothels. Reims was used by the 82nd and 101st Airborne divisions during rest periods, and the paratroopers did not appreciate the new residents.

Preparations continued for Montgomery's big push toward the Ruhr. It was several weeks away when one of those breaks that good teams sometimes force occurred at Remagen, on the Rhine. American troops, clearing out the German forces west of the river, found the Ludendorff bridge standing. They swarmed across, and the Rhine was crossed before Montgomery could proceed with his cautious set-piece battle. This success enabled the Allies, with Montgomery on the left, Bradley on the right, to encircle the Ruhr.

Studious generals have pet battles from history that they use to prove points. Preferably, they should be so obscure that opposing views won't have a chance. For the capture of German forces on the Ruhr, Beetle Smith reached back to 216 B.C. and characterized it as "the greatest double envelopment since Cannae." A peek at a reference book revealed that Hannibal had wiped out the Romans in that one.

The Low Countries and then parts of Germany itself were cleared of German combat units. SHAEF Forward was scheduled to move to Frankfurt, and we inspected the offices in the I. G. Farben Building, but we were never to occupy them. Word came that an airfield near Weimar, the capital of the post–World War I German Republic, had been captured with a unit of German ME-163 jets intact. An inspection team of a few officers, including an expert in technical intelligence who could presumably understand them, was assembled. We flew in in a C-53 with a jeep which could be rolled out of the fuselage.

We made an approach to the grass runway of the base where the jets were held but were waved off by American airmen who pointed frantically at signs of "Minen! Minen!" Besides that legacy of departed Germans, we also found, when we reached the field by jeep, that other Americans were crating the planes for shipment out before the area, as scheduled, would be turned over to the Russians. We never did get to see an assembled ME-163, though we did look at some parts.

The military billeting officer in Weimar warned us to stay out of sight the next morning because the area was to be cleared for General Bradley, who was going to a formal meeting with his Russian counterpart in Torgau, on the Elbe River. We decided that no one was holding his breath in Reims for a report on the ME-163 that we'd never examined, and therefore we could hide as easily in Torgau as in Weimar, couldn't we? As we approached Torgau, we were surprised by a five-mile stretch lined with soldiers, in battle dress and armed, standing at intervals of five yards. Our overloaded jeep was mistaken for the point of the Bradley entourage. As we passed, each GI came to present arms, and we saluted in return.

Arm weary, we reached Torgau and posed for a picture in front of a billboard painted by an outdoor advertising artist showing the Stars and Stripes and the Red Flag, an American and a Russian infantryman. Russian troops had arrived, but the only Russians we saw were muscular women traffic directors, and we prudently escaped without seeing the Bradley group. We toyed with the idea of making a one-day dash to Berlin, seventy miles away, but prudence prevailed over exuberance.

The formal surrender came less than two weeks later. When German Field Marshal Alfred Gustav Jodl entered the school building on May 7, 1945, to meet SHAEF Chief of Staff Smith, the SHAEF Forward staff, tipped off by the rumor mill, crowded the entry area and the stairways. General of the Army Eisenhower refused to meet with Jodl personally—Jodl was considered, for protocol purposes, roughly equal in rank only to Smith. We watched quietly as Jodl walked out after signing the surrender.

I had some odds and ends to clear up with Ninth Air Force intelligence, so I went to Wiesbaden and found myself in a military bar that evening. A certain amount of off-key singing encouraged me to try "Marching through Georgia" in honor of my maternal grandfather's service with Sherman. An almost instant objection developed from an unreconstructed young lieutenant from South Carolina, who punched in my general direction. He stirred up only air. When he saw the silver leaves on my shoulders, we quietly observed Appomattox-at-Wiesbaden.

The next day, in Reims, the victory announcement, delayed at Russian request, became official.

I attended a dinner the champagne industry of Reims gave for General Eisenhower and staff. At each place was a magnum. The general spoke, apparently extemporaneously, and seemed to be saying just the right things. I turned to one of his political advisers and asked, "Did the general ever vote?" The answer came back instantly, "Yes. Abilene, Kansas, in 1912." Someone was thinking about domestic politics.

Members of the Ultra group expected to be rotated to the Pacific once European combat was over. It was early May and my older son was to graduate from the Lawrenceville School in June—the rest of the family had sat out my overseas time with relatives in Wisconsin. I tried to time my arrival in the States for the happy event. I nudged where I could and attained priority on a list of officers directed to report back to the embassy in London, then to be sent to G-2 in the Pentagon for probable redeployment to the Pacific.

I did make the graduation, but then settled into a period of boredom at the Pentagon, part of what amounted to a G-2 pool. A memo circulated that officers who had been confined to the Pentagon while the rest of us had gone to the ETO would get a taste of field duty, for which the memo implied they had been yearning. Some of the lawyers, as they feared, were pressed into handling claims for damage by our troops in the Philippines—wounded water buffalo and such. The rest of us sat.

Life, not at my request, made an effort to get me released. Roy Larsen, president of Time Inc., and Dan Longwell, who had become managing editor when Luce made John Billings editorial director for the whole company, came to Washington. The wartime staff replacements on the magazine were wearing a little thin. G-2 apparently figured that Time Inc. knew something good about me that the army didn't and refused to let me go.

Then came the bombing of Hiroshima and V-J Day. After that, my separation papers began to move. I received a lapel pin signifying my discharge (known, from its shape, as a ruptured duck) and started worrying about getting a second civilian suit—they were scarce.

Although I had several months of accumulated leave, I just took the pay for it and reported to the Time & Life Building in New York.

Was what I did in Europe—interpreting Ultra's intercepts to the people who could use the information as a basis for action—worth all the scheming I did to try to get into combat, as I kept saying I wanted? No. Technically, I was not in combat. The shots I heard fired in anger overseas were not aimed at me, and I confess to a liking for whatever luxuries I was able to find, including breakfast at the Crillon. But it is undoubtedly true, as our top generals repeatedly insisted, that our work advanced the date of our landing in France, possibly by a year or more. So I was one part of a complicated setup that greatly reduced the German danger to our troops. One cog on a wheel. Fair enough. I have no trouble believing that my bit counted.

At the least, the sophisticated world of Ultra forced me to be flexible enough to learn a new trade.

10

"We Have a Managing Editor"

∾ I returned to *Life* with a Supreme Headquarters point of view. I wanted to run something, and *Life* was at hand. But no one was going to just hand me anything.

The military and Time Inc. both had powerful bureaucracies to overcome. The difference, I once told Luce, was that in uniform you couldn't say, "I quit," whereas at Time Inc. you could. He pretended to be mildly amused the first time I said it, definitely unamused when I later exposed him to that crack again.

The *Life* I lined up in my sights was a diffuse target. I couldn't complain about the kind of creative work I found to do. I was heartened by a substantial raise in pay, which I suppose was comparable to what I would have received if I hadn't quixotically exposed myself to military living, Pentagon stultification, V-1 fire, and soggy English food for three and a half years. Everyone, in varying degrees, seemed glad to see me.

For a while after peace came, Luce's guidance was almost invisible. He took a long tour of the Pacific, and on his return, he sequestered himself with his thoughts about the future of the company and the world. Meanwhile, the *Life* editorial staff was, as before, gregarious and bubbling with cheerful confusion. Only a few of the wartime substitutes survived.

It has been said that *Life* edited itself during the war, but that is a considerable oversimplification. Editors frequently junked laboriously thought-out articles at the last minute when censors cleared a batch of photographs and dispatches from the combat zones. Those shipments didn't just happen. As related earlier, the groundwork for the coverage had been laid by Wilson Hicks, the picture editor.

In the office, the talented copy editor, Joseph Kastner, struggled with an inadequate staff. From reading the issues overseas, it seemed to me as if Joe had written the whole magazine.

The trouble for us in 1945 and 1946 was that readers weren't responding with consistent enthusiasm to the stories about a country at peace. Longwell was uneasy about making choices, even among his own large pool of ideas. He would, for instance, select a couple of stories for each single vacant space on a closing day and have them both laid out, written, closed, and sent to the printing plant in Chicago. His decisions could then be delayed until the next morning. This was bad for the morale of a staff that was not very sure of itself. A survey was made of where the story ideas came from and what proportion survived. Longwell bragged ruefully that his ideas were by far the most numerous, but that he, when he became managing editor, rejected practically all of them.

I felt that peace didn't have to be boring. The atomic age had dawned. The skyline of America was changing. For example, Houston power Jesse Jones said that we would look back at the late 1940s as the good old days, and—despite advice to wait until the prices on scarce materials came down—his city sprang to life. Badly needed new homes were begun all over the country. With more leisure, a boom in self-improvement was getting underway. European and Oriental art treasures were again on display and some extraordinary exhibitions were coming to America. Sports, both spectator and participant, were in full swing, and another sport, politics, was being pursued without the restraints that wartime patriotism had put on it.

Life—with a circulation of over five million—had, for some time, been the country's biggest weekly magazine. It had passed the *Saturday Evening Post* after Pearl Harbor, when the *Post* was still saying, in effect, you'd better watch that Roosevelt—he may get us into a war one of these days.

Longwell superstitiously was loath to change the masthead, the column that listed members of the staff, so I was anonymous for about a year. I would get letters addressed to me "c/o *Life,* please forward," saying, "It's too bad you lost that good job you used to have." One correspondent who had been fired and had a new job asked to have his name removed. He wrote, he wired, he phoned. Nothing doing. His name stayed on.

As soon as I had been back for a while, I decided that I might be out of touch with the country, so I should take a trip. Ohio had almost everything—industry, farms, universities—so I went there, alone, and spent a useful month of company time ranging from Cleveland south, east, and west to

Akron, Wooster, Ashtabula, Columbus, and Cincinnati. I had tried while overseas to keep my American outlook. Two of the books I had had shipped were George Stewart's *Names on the Land,* for its poetic folk poetry of American places, and H. L. Mencken's *The American Language.* I had gotten a bit worried when the British university dons in SHAEF Intelligence seemed to understand me and I them, although the fact that one from Cambridge could sing all Groucho Marx's lyrics was reassuring.

There was nothing in Ohio up to Stewart or Mencken, but I did learn that:

• Approaching Akron on an early morning, one would see a dark, dome-shaped cloud—from the carbon black used in making tires—hiding the city. This made it impossible to manufacture clear plastics there.

• It was inadvisable to have lunch, say, at Goodyear without also arranging to visit Goodrich, Firestone, et al. The word spread fast.

• Ohio State University was crossing Aberdeen Angus and Hereford beef cattle to produce, with "hybrid vigor," faster-growing and heavier steers.

• A newspaper strike can drive florists to the financial wall—with no obituaries published, funerals are not decorated with donated bouquets.

• An ad salesman who answered the *Life* phone in Cleveland and who later became publisher of a Time Inc. magazine had never met an editorial employee.

• A roadside milk bar near Massillon had the thickest malted milks and the fattest straws in the state.

It was reassuring to return to the type of trivia which kept *Life* in touch with its everyday readers, but I had the uneasy conviction that "winning the war" had by no means removed sources of conflict in the world—within the U.S. and within Time Inc. itself. From the outside, *Life,* in particular, seemed to me to be an assemblage of free spirits, ready to break into cocktail parties for the slimmest of excuses, such as the move of an office two doors down the hall.

Wartime restrictions—wages had been frozen—severely limited effective activity by the editorial union, the New York Newspaper Guild. The Guild did not seem about to win the traditional position it sought: a closed, or at least a union, shop to which all employees had to belong. Luce had let it be known that he would close down before he would force all hands to join the union, no matter what their personal preferences. Oddly enough, when the Guild first organized at Time Inc., Luce wanted to join. It was a body of professional journalists, wasn't it? He accepted reluctantly the argument that if anyone was management, he was, but his feelings were hurt, however briefly.

Now, in 1946, there was serious danger of a strike. Contract negotiations were stalled over "maintenance of membership." In lieu of a union shop, the company offered to deduct, on behalf of the union, dues from each member's paycheck. The local rejected this and voted to authorize a strike. Longwell announced that *Life* would publish and was accused of intimidation. A practice picket line, which included fur-coated researchers, marched, and people of goodwill began to worry that in the bitterness strikes sometimes leave, the old staff camaraderie would disintegrate.

It didn't happen. An ad hoc committee composed of former Guild members, headed by Kastner, and management figures other than professional labor-relations types produced acceptable compromises. Intrastaff cordiality was not fatally damaged. The flag—a cocktail glass with an olive—that the foreign news department hung out to signify that something notable was being celebrated again flew on occasion.

At the time of the threatened strike, I had come out of my masthead anonymity as one of two assistant managing editors. The other was Joseph J. Thorndike Jr., who had joined *Time* and then come to *Life* in its experimental days while he was still fairly fresh out of Harvard.

I immediately told Longwell that when he vacated his job (as he often said he was about to) I wanted to be considered for it. His "Yup, yup, yup" was not very reassuring. I did get an issue to edit during the strike scare, but coincidentally, R. R. Donnelley, which printed *Life,* was suffering power interruptions. Some forms could not be printed. I tried to make each of the articles self-contained within its form, but the issue lost one form with a story ending in its middle, and another story mysteriously started in the middle of what should have been the adjoining form. No matter who was at fault, the issue did not demonstrate that I would be a good managing editor.

The time for the selection of a new managing editor arrived. Joe Thorndike was and should have been the odds-on favorite. He had stuck on through the war; he had refused an offer to edit *Collier's.* His candidacy for the job didn't warp my appreciation of his character, his basic honesty. During the discussions, Billings noted in his diary, "Luce hardly knows Thompson."

In late 1946 Thorndike won the job, but I gained enough stature in the discussions to be bold enough to tell Billings, "You have the wrong man."

It wasn't as though I took this lying down. Bruce Bairnsfather, the great World War I cartoonist, had his protagonist, Bill, advise a fellow Tommy in a flooded shell crater, "If you knows a better 'ole, go to it." I thought that a "better 'ole" for me might be the purchase of a small daily newspaper, where I would be my own boss.

In the first of several searches, I found no paper—I had prudently not said that if I didn't get the managing editorship I would quit. I believe that when one bluffs one must be prepared to have the bluff called. I was not so prepared.

Thus Luce was quite accurate in writing to the staff, "Thompson would be full-out to do his part in making a great new team."

He might have had a momentary qualm when he drifted into the managing editor's office one Saturday afternoon as I was closing an issue. Thorndike, like Longwell before him, liked a normal Saturday and Sunday weekend, and, in a split into divisional editorships, I was in charge of foreign and domestic news, sports, and science. I wanted to cover events as they came up, with no special attention to ideology.

That afternoon I had laid out a story showing a column of Chiang Kai-shek troops which had been passed by a truck carrying a *Life* reporter-photographer team. The officer had gotten out of his jeep, screaming, and his soldiers, with feet and fists and cranks and tire irons, had attacked the truck driver. I had laid out Mark Kauffman's pictures and John Purcell's text on two facing pages.

I spread out the layouts for Luce. He stopped abruptly at the sight of Chinese faces. "What's all this? Don't you have something better? This is completely out of character. Chinese are gentle. They're so wise, artistic, and humorous."

I wasn't about to argue but just said, "I think we should run it."

Reluctantly, he said, "Well, there is that violent side sometimes, I guess." He walked out, and the story was published.

A substantial development during this period was the start of the first of *Life*'s major cultural series, "Western Man," written by Whittaker Chambers (of whom more later). His copy would come in—almost always late—from his farm in Maryland, pasted in strips on Western Union sheets, sheaves of them. Usually Kastner would have to rush the copy through, editing from the telegrams themselves. The prose was eloquent and erudite, and

Chambers always seemed genuinely contrite about the tardiness. The series was Luce's idea and was not at that time intended to start a trend toward formal series.

More down my alley was the first closing of an issue out of the Chicago office. This was to save the time of sending pictures and text of a story originating in Chicago to New York and back again. The tryouts for the 1948 U.S. Olympic team were held at Northwestern University in Evanston, Illinois, on a Friday and Saturday. I took a skeleton staff to Midway Airport, where our Chicago office had paid a pair of policemen to escort us in style.

We arrived with sirens blaring and lights flashing. The Chicago police department did not keep very precise track of its patrol cars, and since the cops sensed a festive atmosphere, they attached themselves to the operation through Sunday, eating deli food, drinking *Life* whisky, running pictures and copy from Dyche Stadium to the Michigan Avenue editorial office and photo lab to the Donnelley plant farther south.

Olympic officials had not yet learned about the profits to be made selling rights to the media, so they allowed us to photograph whatever we chose. For instance, we were able to photograph the 100-meter dash at night with strobe lights. There was a rehearsal Thursday night, with puffing *Life* staff members making a picture at each 25-meter mark. The four photographers Gjon Mili had tripping shutters performed flawlessly in the real race, and the strobe lights didn't seem to bother the runners.

Not to be outdone by Mili's electronic wonders, Wallace Kirkland rigged up four Rolleiflexes for sequence shots of the pole-vault trials. They worked, but Kirk, not a great technician, was fiddling with one Rollei when, on a track alongside, the great Harrison Dillard disqualified himself by knocking down a high hurdle. Somehow Kirk swung around and got the action picture.

Technique was all very well, but the innovative touch to the story was supplied by Leonard McCombe, a sensitive British photographer who later became famous for photo essays like "Career Girl." He noticed that after an event, the contestants would wander off under the stadium seats. The emotional and physical stress caused them to gasp, retch, and vomit. His recording of all this gave us a notable set of photographs.

More important in many ways, including journalistic, was my project for a series on the atom in kitchen-sink terms. Americans, I believed, needed to understand the complex scientific ideas that more and more were shaping their lives. David Lilienthal, head of the Atomic Energy Commission, made

In the early morning hours, Ray Mackland and I wait wearily for late *Life* copy (1950, photo by Martin Iger, courtesy Time Inc.).

it sound deceptively simple by observing that every boy of our generation who knew how to fix a Model T could understand the atom. "It's no more complicated than a double play in baseball." I realized how obscure that was when I took an English friend to a Yankee game. The execution of the "simple" idea for explaining atomic fission also was complicated. To take only one picture, the photographer, Fritz Goro, used four lenses and thirty-three exposures on one plate moved into fifteen different positions. The result, however, actually simplified the point and did justify the title: "A Layman's Primer."

The 1948 election taught me a lasting lesson in the hard school of experience ("fools can learn in no other"). Contrary to everything I'd ever learned, I carelessly allowed a caption referring to Dewey as "the next President" to get into print. This would have been outrageous even if Dewey had won. Smothering ourselves publicly in sackcloth didn't help much. If I had been Luce, I would have considered firing me. He confined himself to saying, "Confidentially, Ed, who wrote the caption, and who checked its accuracy?" I refused to tell him. I had been the last to see it. I had initialed it. I should have known better. I was responsible. Period. I don't think he ever found out anything beyond that.

Luce's attention in the months that followed, however, was turned more toward tinkering with *Life*'s mode of operation. Thus, at the beginning of 1949, I was made a full-time assistant managing editor without the added responsibility of running any specific editorial departments.

There were no critical rumblings from Luce's office when I filled in for Thorndike while he toured Western Europe. Thorndike-Thompson relations must have been fairly good because Thorndike patiently tolerated a doubtful practical joke. He habitually left dirty laundry in his desk drawer, so I sent a batch to his ship by pilot boat.

But Thorndike became increasingly irked with what he considered Luce's erosion of what the managing editorship should be. Luce didn't agree with Thorndike's concept. "Does he expect me," Luce once asked Billings, "to retire to the Riviera and be editor-in-chief from there?" Still, Luce approved efforts to talk Thorndike into remaining when he threatened to resign. Billings told me it happened four or five times—possibly an exaggeration.

The climax came on a hot Friday afternoon in early August, one day before an issue closing. The ostensible trigger was a memo from Luce specifying that major policy decisions would be made by the Editor-in-Chief's Committee: himself, Billings, Thorndike, Longwell (whose title was that of a meaningless chairman of the Board of Editors), editorial writer John Osborn, and myself. The memo arrived on our desks shortly before lunchtime. Thorndike wrote a short memo of resignation and walked out (again leaving his laundry) for good.

Luce summoned Billings, Time Inc. president Roy Larsen, and *Life* publisher Andrew Heiskell. He "was trying to feel guilty," Billings reported, "but we wouldn't let him."

Then I was called to Luce's office and asked if I wanted the job. I said that of course I would at least close out the issue as usual, but I asked for a little time, saying that if there was something that Thorndike, whom I admired, couldn't stand, maybe I couldn't either. Luce said he would wait.

My delay wasn't just a posture. I did try to find out more from Thorndike by phone, but got nothing significant. I figured I could somehow handle such annoyances as the editor-in-chief's policy committee, knowing that such groups don't really get much done. It did soon shrivel away.

Billings knew more about the background than I did at the time, although in reading his diary, I find him unnecessarily spiteful about Thorndike. Billings reported Luce as "looking tired and whipped down—gray and bleary. This has been a blow to him." When I had gone to see Billings and Heiskell, Billings had opened with, "When Joe was made managing editor, you said that we had the wrong man. You were right."

His diary records my conversation as "stilted and oblique," with my concern seeming to be what sort of a job I was taking. That was correct. "A tense, nervous, exciting three hours," Billings reported. "My eyes sting as if I'd been crying. I feel the change is for the better if Thompson will let us help him and not try to be a solo performer." That was a legitimate worry.

After a day of closing the current issue and a day of thinking, I called Billings to rehearse my call to Luce accepting the job. "Longwell," Billings told his diary, "had already called me twice. His worry is that Luce will give Thompson too much authority as M.E. and squeeze Longwell out. I wouldn't interfere. . . . Thompson wanted to be sure the M.E. job hasn't been downgraded. He warned he'd be difficult. He wouldn't change his spots. He said he was sorry for Luce—'I feel paternal toward him.'"

It wasn't being cynical or overmodest to figure that Luce didn't have much choice but me. He was owed a statement of intentions. After a couple of weeks I wrote a personal memo. I quote it here at length, along with Luce's reaction, because it turned out to be a fairly accurate outline of what *Life* would be as I ran it. It follows, with corny overtones intact:

> If I had been forced to write a platform on which to run for the job, I'm afraid it could have been described as "Me, too, but I can do it better." I am not like an out-of-office politician seeking to turn the rascals out, because I think (unoriginally) that my predecessors did a hell of a good job. Of course I'm prejudiced because I've personally been involved in producing the magazine since it was eleven months old and before that I was showering my betters with unsolicited advice from Milwaukee.
>
> I once thought that it would be impossible to improve the promise of the prospectus, "to watch the faces of the poor and the gestures of the proud; to see strange things . . ." Now, though, I will stop saying "me too" long enough to state my strong belief that we mustn't be that detached. We must make the reader feel that his 20 cents gives him something more than a seat in the bleachers, he should feel a sense of participation in what the editors see and think.
>
> *Life,* to me, is a friendly neighbor, almost one of the family. He is kind of gabby, asks a lot of questions, always wants to get into a discussion, so there are bound to be some anti-social folks who don't like him too much. But where he is welcome he sidles up to the picket fence and says:
>
> "Let me tell you about that big fire I saw on my way through the county seat tonight . . ."

"I've been studying up about this fellow Tito, and I have a Jugo-Slav brother-in-law who tells me . . ."

"Say, have you heard of a wonderful man named Schweitzer over in Africa? Well, he's doing fine things for those natives, but he's an expert on Goethe, too, and here's what he thinks . . ."

And he ends up by saying: "What do you think of that?"

Life can get away with talking about philosophy, the atom, morality and what the missus ought to be wearing even though he has to get to know how to talk her language better. That's because this is what a lot of people say about him:

"Yessir, that's about the smartest young fellow around here. He sure keeps up on things. But he isn't a smart-aleck, mind you, and there isn't a mean bone in his body. Even when he's talking about some of that deep stuff, you can see he's been studying it real hard to try to understand it himself and make it interesting. Sometimes we don't figure we'll go for some of that but a lot of times we listen and get interested in spite of ourselves.

"We figure he can speak right up to anyone, but he doesn't try to talk down to us. He's good-natured and sometimes he gives us a real belly-laugh, but he sure can get mad when people have it coming."

In short, it seems to me that *Life* must be curious, alert, erudite and moral, but it must achieve this without being holier-than-thou, a cynic, a know-it-all or a Peeping Tom. *Life* must always feel privileged to be the bearer of information or thoughts. When we do this largely as a matter of duty through the medium of a bored staff, we're through.

Maybe knowing the kind of managing editor I'd like to be would help, too. I'm proud of and sentimental about being a journalist. It comes natural to me to regard the managing editor (in this case myself) as "the old man," a newspaper term applied to M.E.s from 21 to 71. "The old man" to me is a guy who brings a strong personal flavor to editing. He has some crotchets which are the subject of wry office jokes, but all in all he is considered fairly Jovian. He rides his subordinates hard but is inclined to say nice things behind their backs. They feel that he will not pass the buck to them when he gets into trouble with the owner or other higher authority. Being "the old man" doesn't mean that one is a fatuous old do-gooder. While a certain amount of rough diamond kindliness is involved, it means that "the old man" drives with a pretty tight rein, that he blows his top promptly when some stupidity is perpetrated, that he plunges zestfully into editorial projects that interest him (which should be almost all of them).

I've been very lucky in my bosses and my ideal "old man" is composed of 41% John Billings, 40% Marvin Creager of the *Milwaukee Journal,* and 9% Happy Paulsen of the *Fargo Forum.* Both Dan and Joe let me get away with far too much for me to regard them as "old men."

Now this may be a colloquial way of expressing Joe's dictum of "full authority and responsibility under the editor-in-chief" which caused some trouble. For one thing, . . . I know an enlightened and generally reasonable employer when I see one. For another, although I think it is a good thing to have an "old man," provided I prove I am worthy of being such a character, I'm not committed to any particular mode of operation. There is more than one way of skinning a cat, and I am signed on for the duration plus six. So I think that we can somehow gear in things like supervisory committees with an M.E. who hires and fires, rides the magazine instead of letting it ride him and is in general a useful boss both to the staff and the management.

I'm certainly going to have positive and occasionally unpopular views, but I'm starting the job with humility and at least some knowledge of my own limitations. At the same time I feel reasonably confident because I think I can use my colleagues for the kinds of thing I can't do.

Most of all, though, I am approaching the job with a vast amount of good will. Please don't be embarrassed when I repeat that since the war I've developed a sincere affection and feeling of loyalty for you personally. That isn't connected particularly with your conduct as a boss, but it ain't necessarily bad for boss-employee relationships.

Here was Luce's handwritten reply:

Dear Ed—

I can't think of anything to say in acknowledgement of yours of today except that it makes me feel that I'm a very lucky guy—and that a lot of people besides me are lucky too.

Here's wishing you all the luck in the world in every way.

Yours,
Harry

Luce asked permission to quote me at a meeting of *Life* advertising managers. Their director, one Shep Spink, had walked out suddenly on the same day Thorndike had.

Luce felt the memo had "electrified" the salesmen. His conclusion: "We have a managing editor."

Billings sensed that I was "building a protective fence around the *Life* staff."

I was.

Billings's comment on my memo to Luce: "Good Thompsonese."

11

Harry Luce as He Revealed Himself

❧ Harry Luce interpreted the "Thompsonese" that John Billings sniffed at in the way I intended him to. I hesitate to identify any species of expression as "Luce-ese." Some of my contemporaries found Luce to be a dauntingly complex human being. But he tried to be not unknowable. My testimony may differ from that of others to whom the proprietor also gave a generous share of his attention. Obviously I disagree with palpable smear jobs such as that of W. A. Swanberg's *Luce and His Empire,* published in 1972.

I envy the eloquent sarcasm with which Billings scornfully dismissed the idea of there being an ethical problem for liberal-minded employees of working for the arbitrarily conservative Luce. Said he, it is "precisely the same as that of a vegetarian who is a salesman for Swift & Company. He knew what he was getting into or, if he had any sense, he would have soon found out."

I believed generally in the kind of world Luce wanted. He didn't care what political party I belonged to as long as I wasn't a proselytizing Communist, and, even then, as in the Chambers case, one might be a candidate for redemption.

The Luce reputation for sometimes being arbitrary, ungracious, and stubborn was in part deserved, but he also had an almost painful integrity and pride in his work. And when he *did* have bad ideas, one soon learned— by trial and error—which ones he could be talked out of and which could be quietly ignored and left to collapse of their own weight.

Luce was passionately American. He once admitted having "probably . . . a too romantic, too idealistic view." It was touching to hear him tell Time Inc. editorial and business executives in 1950:

> I was never disillusioned with America, but I was, from my earliest manhood, dissatisfied. . . . America was not being as great and as good as I knew she could be, as I believed with every nerve and fiber God himself intended her to be. . . . You could never guess what I have most missed having in my life . . . an American hometown. . . . An American can always explain himself by citing where he comes from—be it the sidewalks of New York, or the farmlands of Illinois, or Houston, Texas. "Where do you come from?" I would give anything if I could say, simply and casually, "Oskaloosa, Iowa."

Luce saw himself as perhaps "too much the American-in-general and not enough the American-in-particular." In another 1950 talk to staff members he noted two ideals in conflict in every American, the ideal of hero (Washington) and saint (Lincoln) on the one hand, and on the other the ideal of being a regular guy.

Casual exposure and even not-so-casual exposure to Luce would not produce the impression of a "regular guy" for most people, but the way he handled the Communist underground back in 1939 convinced me before I knew him well that he was enough of a regular guy for me.

Luce's control was basically through the managing editors of each magazine, who were entrusted with the issue-to-issue operations, although he would occasionally have direct talks with other editors. And, of course, he would sit in on discussions about subjects for editorials when he was in residence. When he was not, there could be communication by cable or phone and, in any event, we knew enough about what he didn't believe in to avoid direct contradiction of his views. We operated on the assumption that the country thought that a *Life* editorial was in Luce's own words.

Time had no editorial page, and some of the accusations about slanted reporting resulted from attempts to represent Luce's views in news coverage. From the beginning of *Time,* Luce believed there was no such thing as "objective" coverage of events. His editors agreed, sometimes perhaps too enthusiastically.

Direct communication was sporadic. Sometimes he would drop in unannounced for a chat, sometimes there would be a summons to his office (I learned to take an elevator because if I ran up the stairs to avoid delay I

With Henry R. Luce (probably mid-1950s, courtesy Time Inc.).

would arrive too out of breath to argue, if that was indicated); sometimes, too, there would be a lunch, alone or with others. Sometimes his reactions would come after the fact, with a critique of a specific issue. He was hard to please, but he was also generous in his praise when he liked an issue or a given item. And he shared or perhaps started the Time Inc. addiction to the written memo, particularly for proposing or commenting on policy matters.

The focus of Luce's attention shifted from magazine to magazine, so that some time might go by without any overt attention from him at all. He would occasionally edit specific issues of a magazine, but *Life* became increasingly difficult for him to edit. Because of its long press run, certain sections had to close two and even eight weeks in advance of the rest of an issue.

On *Time* he was accustomed to making a whirlwind appearance, throwing out a large portion of what was in progress, and starting assembly of an issue all over again. On *Life*, when I had to tell him that some of the material he wanted to change was already printed, he would grumble, "Thompson, you are just a damned technician," but resignedly go on to do what little he could. Technical factors indeed became so complicated that eventually he gave up *Life* issue-editing altogether.

Emphasis given subjects sometimes varied by magazine (the *New Yorker* had a standard headline for apparent contradictions: "Which Lucepaper do you read?"). He took a dislike to a women's fashion fad called the sack, or the bag, or whatever, and was delighted to have *Time* report that it was a flop. This contrasted with *Life*'s coverage, but I stuck with the judgment of our fashion editor, Sally Kirkland. As time went on, *Life* showed that the sack was actually being worn across the country. I don't think our photographs ever quite convinced Luce that, in this case, we (the country) hadn't been misled by the whims of Paris.

Luce's insatiable curiosity was always evident. By his example and leadership, he encouraged journalism that was provocative. The tradition of the early *Time* ("all the news a busy man has time to read") was to be irreverent and downright sassy, if superficial. As Luce and the company grew into middle age, so did a more acute sense of responsibility. The articles grew longer—not always an improvement. But he never abandoned his dedication to "raise hell and sell newspapers."

The individual editors certainly didn't agree with the boss all the time. Early in my managing editorship, Luce had an idea for something that I thought would be a serious mistake. Luce sent me a memo proposing W A R (capitalization and letter spacing were his) as a continuing theme for *Life*. At the time we were engaged in Korea, and I felt enough distaste for the philosophy that mankind is in a continuing state of combat to expose the thesis to the *Life* people who would have had to execute his idea. I provided no cues, but most of those consulted landed on the idea with all four feet. The clincher came from Robert Wallace, who wrote, "I shudder at what would happen if this document would fall into the hands of Yakov Malik [the Soviet delegate to the U.N.]."

Luce responded that "it couldn't be worse than what happened to me as a result of falling into the hands of the editors of *Life*." I regarded this as a compliment.

The editorial view of Luce as a tough and creative man of ideas obscures the fact that he was also a good businessman. He and his cofounder of *Time*, Briton Hadden, alternated as editor and business manager in that magazine's precarious early days. Luce was emphatically for making money. So was I, and I continue to be. Unless a publication is in an economically sound position, it cannot afford to achieve the high quality every good editor wants to bring to his readers.

Luce adopted standard industry devices to encourage a stable work force—health care, pensions, profit sharing, stock options, etc. In fact, the various plans were so lush that some people who were just good enough to get by, but not quite inefficient enough to be fired, were motivated to hang on. Magazines *need* turnover.

From time to time, Harry tried to become involved in personal lives as well. A continuing source of annoyance to him was his belief that too much of the salaries he paid executives was going to the government in taxes. He spent some time trying to figure out perks. Once he thought of buying a yacht but didn't encounter much enthusiasm for prescribed vacations at sea. He had a membership at an exclusive club in South Carolina and offered vacations there, without many takers. A company limousine which would pick up suburbanites was not a practical idea either—our hours were too irregular.

When he found out that *Time* managing editor Roy Alexander's wife was raising seven children with no servants, Luce was appalled. Ignoring the Alexander system in which the older children took care of the younger, Luce toyed with a plan for assigning servants to executives' families, above the normal compensation. Those in the highest salary brackets would get two full-time servants, the next bracket one and a half, and so on down to one cleaning person once or twice a week. The idea was abandoned when lawyers pointed out that the IRS would tax the salaries of the help as extra compensation for the executives.

Having worked almost full time himself in the early days, Luce, in spite of his acquiescence to industry norms, always had trouble adjusting to holidays. One Thanksgiving night, C. D. Jackson, then *Life* publisher, was at Luce's apartment to discuss a business decision. Luce ordered action the next morning. C. D. allowed that it would be difficult because no one would be at work on Friday.

Indignantly, Luce said, "I'll bet Stanley Resor [longtime head of the J. Walter Thompson ad agency] isn't having a holiday."

The Time Inc. switchboard was instructed to find Resor. A number was located, and Luce was put through. C. D. reported Luce as saying, "Oh. Oh. Oh . . . I'm sorry." Resor had been dead for several years; and on checking the next day, it turned out that the agency was indeed closed on Friday.

For years, Luce personally gave silver porringers to each employee baby, although as the company grew that custom faded out. Luce was so delighted when my younger son, Colin, decided to go to Yale that he gave him a gold wristwatch. When Colin graduated from Yale he received another Luce gold watch.

Personal contacts within the company sometimes left Harry frustrated. "It is the kiss of death," he once told me, "for anyone around here to become known as someone I like. . . . all it takes for an idea to get killed is for the word to get around that I'm for it." There was only a grain of truth in that, and I took some satisfaction in pointing out items he had suggested which did get into print.

Authorship didn't blind Luce to the possibility that some of his specific ideas were marginal. He would say in a mock pleading manner, "Ed, don't you think that you could find an issue of *Life* which wouldn't be entirely disgraced by this?"

He usually went through channels. On one occasion Dmitri Kessel, after meeting Harry and his wife, Clare, abroad, reported that the proprietor told him that some blooming fruit trees would make a good color story. Dmitri asked Luce if I knew about it. Clare burst out, "But Harry is your employer, what are you waiting for?" Luce understood and hastily interjected, "I'll try to sell it to Ed."

The editor-in-chief's insistence on high standards was demonstrated during the early, unprofitable days of *Life* ("that cost me $5 million," he

At younger son Colin's graduation from Yale, Marguerite, older son Edward T., and I celebrate with him (1957, photo by Alfred Eisenstaedt, courtesy Time Inc.).

said); *Sports Illustrated* was another dramatic example of his demand for quality despite huge losses. During the Luce era, the decision to start a magazine was by the seat of the pants, without any of the elaborate testing that's done today.

A talented *Life* writer-editor, Ernest Havemann, who was also a sports buff, was asked to prepare an appraisal of the proposed *SI*'s chances. He wrote a long memo citing the fragmented interests of sports fans (for example, a bowler isn't interested in yachting), arguing that a general magazine was a bad idea. Luce ordered the Havemann memo used in a full-page newspaper announcement ad, concluding, in effect, that even though the contra arguments were persuasive, Time Inc. was going ahead.

From the beginning, circulation was satisfactory, but the advertising establishment held back; it was ten years before *Sports Illustrated* became profitable. Any other company would have taken advantage of the strong circulation and parlayed the magazine into a cheaper product, one less expensive to produce. But Luce stuck with the original idea, even though he was not at all an informed follower of sports. I took him to his first basketball game, part of a doubleheader. We came in toward the end of a game between two Catholic colleges. As each player went to the free-throw line, he crossed himself.

"What's that?" Luce asked.

"He's asking divine help in hitting the basket."

"But what side's God on? They're all doing it."

The team that seemed comfortably ahead began passing the ball around, stalling. After that was explained, Luce said, "That team will lose. You can't just sit on the assets you have." He was right. The team that was behind caught up and won.

Except during the company's early years, Luce mostly left hiring to others. But not always. For instance, he found the comments of a former Yale football tackle and Marine Corps officer, whom he met casually at an airport, irresistible: "Mr. Luce, in *Life* you have a good picture magazine but not a great one." Luce hired the man on the spot and sent him to me for absorption into the staff. The marine knew nothing about pictures and little about journalism, but he got a full workout before he left by mutual agreement.

Luce shunned actual firing, even of old hands who felt intensely that long, loyal service entitled them to hear the news from the proprietor himself. Notable among these was Wilson Hicks, my titular superior when I came to *Life* and later, when I became managing editor, the executive editor. He always boasted that "only Luce can fire me." As it turned out, he resigned.

A special project came up for which Hicks would have been ideal— editing a book that became The *"Life" Picture History of World War II.* Hicks had organized the magazine's brilliant coverage of the war, and the subject was so good that the book made a great deal of money, only the first of a seemingly endless succession of profitable Time-Life books on the war. The project was cleared with Luce, but he didn't talk to Hicks about editing it. Wilson felt he was being shunted aside, and resigned from the company.

The not altogether exaggerated perils of *Life* at or near the top were underlined in a *Newsweek* item on the affair: "The revolving door which always seems to be open for Time Inc. executives whirled again last week and out stepped Wilson Hicks." The wording was widely attributed to Frank Norris, who had been one of a trio of *Time* managing editors before landing at *Newsweek.*

When Luce failed to evade a confrontation, he could be as brusque and irritable as his critics said he was. In one case, a senior executive who had worn out his tolerance badgered Luce at a dinner. "Now, Harry," the conversation began, "I want to talk about my past, my present, and my future."

"We'll talk only about your future," Luce snapped. "See the business people in the morning about a settlement."

Separations on grounds of policy were perhaps less abrasive but more difficult for Luce because he respected some of those with whom he differed. Even after he quit Time Inc. in a dispute about China policy, Theodore H. White, for instance, kept up his personal contacts with Luce. *Life* had been preparing a picture story comparing the art collection of Averell Harriman and that of his opponent in a New York gubernatorial election, Nelson Rockefeller. Teddy White unexpectedly submitted an article on the two candidates, which I wanted to publish along with the art. Luce asked to see it. He agreed that it was excellent and fair but said, "Please don't get in the habit of running pieces by Teddy too often. I don't want the word to get around that I have made up with him completely."

Life happily excerpted Teddy's *Making of the President* books, too. But Teddy ran into Luce's stubborn streak after he thought that indeed they had finally made up. He came to me asking if I objected to his approaching Luce with a proposal to send him back to China, where he had been a brilliant reporter before and during World War II. He would revisit the places he had known. I said, "Go ahead," and the account that follows comes from two master reporters who described with identical quotes that this is the way it went:

"No," said Luce.

"But Harry, I've changed," said Teddy.

"You, Teddy, may have changed, but I haven't. Again, no."

Teddy, of course, had changed. He became a conversational sparring partner of Harry's, and they saw a lot of each other socially. I did not hesitate at all when, after John Kennedy's assassination, Teddy called me for an assignment to go to Hyannisport to see the late president's widow, who wanted to talk. "Go," I said, and out of the interview came her characterization of the JFK years as "Camelot."

A rapprochement of sorts between Luce and John Hersey also occurred, under decidedly special circumstances. The two had split in 1945, when John, an employee of Time Inc., wrote "Hiroshima" and sold it to the

New Yorker without even mentioning it to Harry. Luce considered this treasonous and fired Hersey. As it happened, John and Dmitri Kessel had just collaborated on a Yangtze River photo essay. The material arrived in New York soon after I returned from the military. But the Hersey-Luce rift was considered so deep that editors buried Dmitri's really great photographs along with Hersey's reporting.

A dozen years later I was surprised to get a call from Hersey. He had written a short novel, *The Sand Pebble,* based on the Yangtze project. Since he had been working for *Life* and on our expense account, this time he felt conscience-bound to give us first refusal on magazine rights. His conditions were that it be published verbatim in one issue. It ran to about 50,000 words. I asked Hersey if he would let our editors experimentally cut it to about 30,000 words, which he could veto if he wished.

The answer was: "No. I wrote the book as tightly as I could. Your people are good, and if their cut version proves to be as effective as mine it will undermine my self-confidence."

Hersey did, however, agree to a compromise suggestion: we would publish excerpts from the manuscript along with Dmitri's corresponding photographs as sort of a book review. It was then that I told Luce about the plan. He, too, it turned out, wanted Dmitri's pictures used. After Hersey and our editors put the elements together, John said, "It's nice to be working with pros again." Nevertheless, the temporary truce did not work out to more Hersey writing in *Life.*

Conversations around the office were pretty much on business matters, but dinners at the Luce apartment, usually with just Luce and one staff member but sometimes with another colleague, covered a wide, haphazard range of subjects. These dinners could come on short notice when Clare was away. There would naturally be politics, but you could also expect to be quizzed about whatever was engaging Luce's ever-active curiosity—art, fashion, philosophy. The talk would resemble a high-level fraternity bull session and would invariably end on a convivial note.

Luce's streak of curiosity didn't always make him a gracious host. At an editors' luncheon he tested the amiability of our guest, Norman Vincent Peale, with a cross-examination on theological subjects. The popular preacher good-naturedly eluded the Luce probing by telling a story on himself, which he often used: "When my wife asks me why I always quote rich people to make a point, I tell her I don't know anyone but rich people." The host called off the inquisition.

A similar Luce cross-examination had Barry Goldwater on the verbal ropes as he tried to explain the difference between a republic and a democracy, supposedly his specialty. But on the other hand, Luce took delight in sparring with a genuine intellectual, John Courtney Murray, the eminent Jesuit who was official theologian at Vatican II.

It must have been tough trying to fill the job called "personal assistant to the editor-in-chief." Doing the kinds of errands required could be onerous in view of the boss's impatience with frustrating details. Consider: Luce arrived at the airport early one morning, duly furnished with tickets for a transatlantic crossing. His Pan Am flight was held up by fog. The sleepy assistant was rousted out of bed with a telephone order, "You call up Juan Trippe [who then ran Pan Am] and tell him to get his goddamned plane off the ground." A couple of personal assistants became company vice presidents. Others vanished silently.

It was common knowledge that Luce was superstitious about having thirteen at the table. When it was possible that he would show up at an office lunch, one editor was designated to hover near the door and count. If his and Luce's presence would make thirteen, the editor would quietly disappear.

Because he was so occupied with thinking and talking, Luce didn't seem to taste the food or drink served at meals. Cocktails would be ordered. He'd look around the table and say, "What's that?" It would be a martini or a Manhattan. He'd say, "I'll have one of those." The main course at his home was almost always steak, followed by ice cream.

It had been a prosperous year. The Luce limousine arrived at our suburban house with a gift—$3,000 worth of Luce's personal Time Inc. stock. His note said that 1955 had been kind of special. Luce later joked that he had been misled into thinking that the price would go down but noted, half ruefully, that it had gone up instead. In his own handwriting he had informed me, however, "Nothing can adequately express my satisfaction in our long-range partnership. But . . . I'd like to make a little sentimental gesture. . . . I hope you'll accept it as a token."

It was more than a token, and I accepted it gratefully. In later years, when the post-Luce (and post-Thompson) company did something that annoyed me, I sold other shares as a silent, ineffective protest, but I still have those first ones.

12

"Three Lousy Goddamned Managing Editors"

The mystique about being a Time Inc. managing editor was evident in various forms in the early 1950s trio of E. Roy Alexander of *Time,* Ralph Delahaye (Del) Paine Jr. of *Fortune,* and Edward K. Thompson of *Life.* Some said ours was the most virulent form of the mystique, and also its most fraternal. Harry Luce respected independence, so a generous portion of that came with the managing editors' territories.

Somewhat in contrast to the "old men" of newspapers, magazine managing editors weren't very clubbable. I certainly didn't share any of my problems with magazine editors outside of Time Inc. *Life* competed for advertising with the *Saturday Evening Post,* to be sure, but due to the *Post*'s long lead time, it wasn't competitive on topical editorial matters. *Look* under Daniel (Red) Mich gave up being a picture magazine and began using photographs for illustration rather than for their own sake, and it was a fortnightly.

Alexander, Paine, and I got along reasonably well to begin with, but what fused us into brotherhood was greed. The IRS revealed that the managing editor of the *New York Daily News* drew a salary of $133,333.33. The goal of our unofficial managing editors' union was to make that the going rate for Time Inc. managing editors.

To be sure, there were financial benefits other than salary—stock options, a profitable savings plan, free health insurance, and all that—so we weren't at poverty level. But $133,333.33 is a nice number with which to conjure, even in these inflationary times. There was a barrier to the amount that managing editors could receive in salaries—as editor-in-chief of all Time Inc. magazines, Harry Luce awarded himself relatively modest pay.

An M.E. should not get more than the boss. When I realized this situation, I tried to do something about it—on behalf of all three of us. I undertook to lecture Harry seriously on appreciation of his own real monetary worth to the magazines. Hedley Donovan, who succeeded Del as M.E. of *Fortune* and eventually Luce as editor-in-chief, called me a "Luce-baiter" in his book, *Right Times, Right Places.* He made it sound like a term of jocular approval.

Hedley rather thought that Harry did give himself a raise as a result of my admonition. The managing editors did receive raises, but, as far as I know, none of us reached the magic $133,333.33 a year. Maybe the part of Harry's take-home pay that was listed technically as salary didn't either.

In many periodical corporations, the publisher is the overall boss. At Time Inc. the managing editor, in preconglomerate days, was directly responsible to the editor-in-chief, Luce. The publisher was responsible to the president of the company. Technically, Andrew Heiskell, *Life*'s publisher, would communicate directly with President Roy Larsen, who then would talk to Luce, who in turn would talk to me. Naturally, much of the time it didn't work that way. For instance, during budget preparations, there was direct communication between M.E. and publisher. If something was going wrong, Heiskell might discuss the problem with Luce, with me, or with both of us.

Managing editors were not officers of the company, in part, we were told, so that we could not be named personally in lawsuits. Very few of those came to trial, however. Our lawyers had, to us, a frustrating tendency to settle for a modest sum—even when we were sure we were right. I have to admit, though, that it did save money, considering the expense of just entering legal proceedings.

I tried to relate directly to the approximately 300 *Life* editorial employees. I was pleased when I would hear that each thought he or she was working for me personally—more, I told myself, to foster the naturally ebullient, creative *Life* spirit than to feed my ego. I did consider my office as the court of last resort for differences of opinion.

I tended to leave my door open except when I was firing someone—an occasion not as rare as it should have been. Roy and Del had their own methods. Firing people was painful to me, but I didn't delegate it if a key employee was involved. I developed, inadvertently, a doubtful technique. I would stutter, clear my throat, and obviously be in such distress that the person I was trying to dismiss would come over, put an arm around my shoulder, and say, "Don't take it so hard, Ed."

I had sense enough to have two major assistants. One was responsible for editorial planning and one was kind of an editorial business manager. Both were available to sit in for me.

My personal concept of management resulted in my dipping into many details, right up to the point of those final decisions. Robert T. Elson, in his frank and perceptive book *The World of Time Inc.,* wrote, "Thompson would brighten perceptibly when there was any prospect of a late-breaking story turning a long day's work into a longer night's."

Elson, who served some years as my deputy, wasn't entirely happy with this kind of operation. "I'm not getting any younger, Ed," he would say, and, raising his voice, "neither are you." Nonetheless, he did report, accurately I think, that "the men and women on *Life* were convinced that they had more fun than their associates on the other magazines."

Like Elson, Maitland Edey, also my chief assistant for a time, found, as recorded in his *Great Photographic Essays from "Life,"* that "the physical effects of those marathons were brutal to everyone but Thompson." Edey had worked on *Impact* with me earlier, and later became editor of the highly successful Time-Life Books. It is fair to report that Edey also felt that I "behaved outrageously at times and felt badly afterwards. He intimidated his staff and cosseted it. He abused it but was forgiving and indulgent."

If this approach resulted in the appearance of a one-man show, a closer look would have revealed—even if I sometimes didn't agree entirely—that I tried not to sit on ideas for which others had genuine enthusiasm.

Roy Alexander pretended to believe it was more difficult to edit *Life* or *Fortune* than it was *Time*. *Time* had regular departments, most of which had to be filled every week. At *Life* and *Fortune,* the possibilities were relatively unlimited. *Time* had about the same amount of editorial space for every issue, whereas the space in *Life* went up and down, depending on the amount of advertising. Still, it took skill to expand *Time* material on a dull news week and yet come up with a readable issue and to compress the news when a lot was going on so that the readers felt they were learning everything significant for the period covered. *Life* could ignore a news story that wasn't pictorial and, if it was important enough, take care of the subject in an editorial or a text article in a later issue.

Alexander's professional background and mine were superficially similar. We both went to middle western colleges. He, too, had worked on a

Famed stripteaser Gypsy Rose Lee tries to turn the tables on me at a *Life* editors' lunch (1959, photo by Alfred Eisenstaedt, courtesy Time Inc.).

prosperous afternoon newspaper, the *St. Louis Post-Dispatch,* and we both had been part-time correspondents for *Time.* Alexander was more ingenious about taking advantage of his record as a correspondent than I was. Time Inc. checkers have an irrational respect for the written word. If Roy wanted to make an outrageous statement about St. Louis, he would write a dispatch, date it back to his stringer days, and slip it into the file. In Time Inc. a correspondent's written statement seemed to outrank what some witness, even a managing editor, remembered seeing.

Work started early each day at both the *Post-Dispatch* and the *Milwaukee Journal.* Roy could never break himself of the habit of awaking at dawn, even if he had barely got home from a night out. I always took advantage of extra sleeping time and reported to *Life* at 10 A.M.

Del Paine's rise to influence was more in what might be considered the Time Inc. tradition. He might have inherited his skill with words—his father was a prolific author of popular books and newspaper serials. And Del was a Yale graduate, with an apprenticeship as a *Time* writer.

Del's disagreements with Luce found him quietly stubborn and, in most cases, able to ride out the crisis with his position reasonably intact. Although he could react to an unwelcome Luce idea with a suggestion that maybe a new managing editor was indicated, he had too much integrity to have stayed on if he had had basic differences with Luce. Nevertheless, several times Paine engaged in effective infighting to get around a Luce decision. With this method, he several times somehow made it impossible for a man Luce had planted on *Fortune* to operate. I was glad to take one Paine victim on as a key assistant.

An attitude all three of us succeeded in maintaining was unflappability. Each staff felt it was serving on a tight ship, as near to being self-sufficient as was possible in a single company. I felt a mischievous satisfaction upon hearing one of the corporate officers quoted as saying, "Ed Thompson may be okay to work for, but it's hell having him work for you."

Without seeking the role, we were bound to become regarded, in part, as father figures. I became pretty tired of having wives call me up after a magazine outing or Christmas party and say, "My husband didn't come home last night. What did YOU do with him?" We did not invite spouses to these affairs.

The managing editors' efforts to maintain a calm, judicial appearance may have gone a little far at times, but all of us thought it completely logical for Alexander to keep the fact that he was seriously ill with ulcers a state secret. Certainly no editorial boss should admit to being worried or harassed. Alexander's condition was well concealed, and he recovered from a serious operation. When the word inevitably leaked out, the reaction was one of astonishment. A former associate, Lester Bernstein, who had moved to *Newsweek,* was shocked into uncharacteristic vulgarity: "Roy Alexander with ulcers? It's like telling me the Virgin Mary has the clap!"

The managing editors were united in our respect for the job, but we had our individual prejudices and outbursts of temper to confirm that each of us had a touch of Captain Bligh in him.

Alexander, for instance, couldn't understand that working on *Time* might not be a complete education. From time to time employees of all three magazines were tempted by the prospect of a Nieman fellowship to pursue subjects of their choice at Harvard. Editors throughout the country had come to be a little reluctant to give the required permission for a leave of absence because many of the Nieman scholars went to better jobs elsewhere. A *Time* writer with a Harvard B.A. asked Alexander for permission to apply.

"The only reasons for a Nieman fellowship," said Alexander, "are to get into the Harvard Club and work for Time Inc. You already belong to the Harvard Club and have a *Time* job. No!"

"I'm the only sadist in the company," he would sometimes brag. I don't suppose any managing editors set out to be characters. If Roy Alexander could rise up in righteous indignation and fire someone and Del Paine could physically maneuver an undesirable so that he would be out the door before he knew it, I—as noted earlier—suffered a lot of mental anguish in getting rid of people. The trouble was that transgressions were not usually as simple as getting caught with a hand in the company till or making egregious errors of fact. Usually it was just that the employee's work was average and he seemed bound for nowhere.

It was all very well to say, "This is for your own good." No one believed it, although there was one ex who embarrassed me by yelling out every time we met in public, "Hey, Ed! Thanks again for firing me. You forced me into my best job ever."

There was one minor editor who, everybody knew, needed to be fired. The everybody didn't include him. After one of my several attempts to give him the message, he emerged from my office and, when asked what had happened, said, "I get the feeling Ed wants me to do better." Although his job was reporting on the sometimes crass world of broadcast, he filled the *Life* floors with an assortment of gurus and Oriental monks, was married briefly to a beautiful model, and became a Universalist-Unitarian lay preacher. I couldn't use these qualities to advantage. Finally I said to him, "You're not going to get any more paychecks," and, at that, he said he'd come to work anyway and coach his successor.

I can remember only one instance in which I was able, with righteous indignation, to fire someone spontaneously, in hot blood. A photographer was at a polling place in California where Earl Warren, then chief justice of the Supreme Court, was voting. The photographer sneaked a stepladder up to the voting booth and took, shooting down, a photograph showing how Warren was marking a paper ballot. Deciding whether a public figure's privacy is invaded is sometimes difficult, but this was an open-and-shut case. And a simple "You're fired" over the telephone settled the matter.

I tried to operate with as few rules as possible. One that I did enforce, though, was to forbid the staff to go on junkets—trips paid for by corporations or governments. If *Life* needed an article from an area, it would pay the expenses. This rule caused some grumbling because other publications were more tolerant. I acquired a talking point when a junket plane to Indonesia crashed, killing the entire load of correspondents. I had refused to let the foreign news editor take the trip.

A planned move of Time Inc. to the suburbs brought on the managing editors' finest hour. *Time* and *Life* needed access, of course, to city-based news sources. *Life* in particular depended on objects, such as photographs and artwork, being actually in hand. The operator of a costly helicopter fleet would have become an indispensable employee if the company had moved out of New York City.

Del Paine felt that *Fortune* needed to be near the city's corporate headquarters. All three of us felt that the brisk pace metropolitan life engendered would be lost in bucolic surroundings. The overwhelming weight of corporate brass, however, seemed charmed with the campus atmosphere that publishing houses like *Reader's Digest* provided.

Sites such as a mythical Philiwell (between Philadelphia and Wilmington) were discussed, along with the possibility of a Hudson River estate. A piece of property in Westchester County was actually purchased, its zoning restrictions altered for Time Inc. purposes. A post office that could handle the vast bulk of mail was located.

My own bit of poison into the discussion pot was assuring Westchester wives, who looked forward to using the family car while the breadwinners cycled to work, that their husbands would come home to lunch and would bring colleagues home for drinks every night after work. That was a minor contribution.

Alexander, Paine, and I produced memos for collation by John Billings. Fiendishly he played on Luce's prejudices against pipe smokers and wearers of tweed sports jackets. Several times in his compilation of our arguments against a suburban headquarters, Billings wrote, "And Time Inc. will become a company of pipe smokers and tweed jackets." That was the clincher.

Unaware of the Billings contribution, the executive vice president who had negotiated the Westchester land deal gave the three M.E.s full credit for destroying the plan. After a drink or two or more one night, his indignation surfaced: "The editor-in-chief was for it, the president and chairman of the board were for it, the executive vice presidents were for it, the publishers were for it. And who killed the move? Three lousy goddamned managing editors." (Luce later helped rationalize his surrender to Billings plus three by consulting architect Eero Saarinen, who assured him that the property involved was too small for anything but a big parking lot, with no room for a country campus setting.)

Running *Life* was honestly all I wanted from Time Inc. I expressed a reluctance to move upstairs to a corporate position often enough and loud enough to be convincing. Or perhaps, as the corporate staff observed me, it became obvious that I wasn't suited for that sort of job anyway. Giving up a managing editorship, even when overdue by the traditional Time Inc. timetable, was tougher for me and Paine than it was for Alexander.

Roy reported simply, "Luce called me up to his apartment and asked me if I didn't think it was time to give the job up. I said I certainly did. I was ready." Roy subsequently served a stint of fronting as the editor of *Time,* and later happily retired altogether. He turned down an offer to run for his suburban school board, saying, "I am just too busy being retired." He claimed he once had thought he would be happy running a filling station.

Paine was moved from managing editor to publisher of *Fortune,* and the transition was audibly traumatic for him and painful for me to witness. We had adjourned to his New York apartment to wash the taste of a particularly boring office dinner out of our mouths. He had heard the news a little earlier and announced it to me with, "I've been debagged." He provided the bare details, and then his head sunk down on the table. He would raise it from time to time, repeating, "I've been debagged." I felt I had to continue the wake as long as he did.

Morning came with Paine still repeating "I've been debagged," and when his daughter came in to say goodbye before going to school, I realized I had left some work at the office that had to be done first thing. I had always vowed that if staying up socially ever made me late for a deadline I would quit drinking. I was still in formal clothing and didn't have time to go back to Grand Central Station, where I had stuffed my business suit into a locker in anticipation of going home to Larchmont after the dinner.

My secretary at the time, a composed, quiet young woman, seemed to think it gave her status to have her boss editing copy in a dinner jacket. Once the must-work was done, I went to the station, found a press-while-you-wait place, and, with a barber-shop shave, was ready for the day.

I had a certificate designed for Paine, confirming him as an honorary life member of the Managing Editors' Union. He sent me a photocopy of it at the time of my fiftieth anniversary in the business. In the meantime, he adjusted to being a publisher to the extent of making sure that every successor as M.E. met at least one businessman.

Even in the flush of our heady victory over a Time Inc. "campus" in suburbia, we members of the trio must have realized humbly that others in the trade could be meaner and tougher than we were. None of us would have wanted to emulate Lester Markel, Sunday editor of the *New York Times.* In the 1950s *Life* was paying writers a minimum of $1,500 per article. I asked Markel how he got away with paying name authors only $250 for a *Sunday Magazine* article. His reply: "Sure, some authors demand $1,500, and I tell them I'll allow $1,500, but remember, I gave you the idea. I made your lousy writing intelligible. I earned $1,250 of the $1,500 so your check will be for $250."

We may have made some people angry, but no irate subscriber ever horsewhipped any of us, in the frontier tradition, on a dusty Main Street. Roy bragged that he was the Time Inc. sadist, Del quietly savored his effective infighting, and the reader is getting to know me. When the city editor of the old *New York World,* a famous journalistic bully named Chapin, was ailing, Irvin S. Cobb, then of his staff, was said to have commented, "I trust it's nothing trivial." No one, to my knowledge, ever said that about one of our illnesses.

13

The Money Changers' Place in the Temple

⤳ The terms *church* (for editorial) and *state* (for business) did not come into common use during the 1950s, but there was then—as there had almost always been at Time Inc.—a general understanding that there was a division between the two of duties, responsibilities, and authority. Perhaps the sometimes arrogant Alexander-Paine-Thompson troika, acting as Church Militant just described, overstepped its bounds a bit.

A primary responsibility of each managing editor, in relation to his business department, was to come up with a budget for the production of a magazine that met high critical standards—and also had the capacity to generate profits. The M.E., then, was expected to spend money to make money.

For detailed figures each year, I depended to a great extent on a series of assistant managing editors who were not only my possible successors but who had financial good sense and a tolerance for dealing with minutiae. These included Sidney L. James, the first managing editor of *Sports Illustrated* and later its publisher; Bob Elson, who became *Life*'s general manager on the business side; and Philip H. Wootton Jr., a creative journalist who was in charge of big special projects.

Customarily, the assistant M.E. and I would sit down with the general manager and the publisher and come up with a figure acceptable to both sides. We then submitted the budget to Luce. This was a formality, but an exchange in 1957 was revealing. Luce said, "Ten million dollars is a lot of money, but I assume, Ed, that in an extremity you could lop a million off the top."

"I don't think that's the way to look at it," I said. "I would be delighted to cut it off the bottom, which includes charges for rent, light and heat, mandatory raises under labor contracts, etc. The top million is what gives us the flexibility to go after the kind of material that makes *Life* *Life*. It is gambling money, if you will. Sure, some gambles won't pay off, but the company gamble here would be that the chances we take would be creative."

Luce gave a grunt of acknowledgment and signed off on that budget.

There were, of course, areas in which editorial and business could be legitimately at odds. Principle might be involved, but there was no call for plain cussedness by editors or publishers.

For instance, I was willing to endure a certain amount of hyperbole by promotion writers in describing editorial content. It was the custom, for a while, to take out full-page ads in the *New York Times* and other newspapers on the day an issue reached the newsstands. The ads consisted of what were supposed to be provocative paragraphs, illustrated with small pictures from the issue. When the promotion copy was patently inaccurate due to sloppy reading of a given issue, I cringed.

Week after week during one period I remonstrated with the promotion director. He would smile equably, but again the following week there would be mistakes. Finally I ordered the picture morgue (later euphemistically called "collection") not to give any more editorial photographs to promotion. So no ads appeared at all. Heiskell, who as publisher may have been in charge of the morgue anyway, didn't say anything but finally suggested to me gently that I had made my point, so why didn't I let go? He made me feel a little foolish.

Probably everyone would have been more comfortable just believing Luce when he said: "My editors are the real promotion men." Richard Coffey, intelligent and convivial, eventually became promotion manager, and the promotion problems did not recur.

Personal relations between editorial and business people were generally cordial. Once a year, with mock formality, one ad director would phone and ask, "Do I have your permission, sir, to come up and wish you a merry Christmas?" And there was an out-and-out official session once each year when ad salesmen could fraternize with selected editorial brass at sales meetings, held at resorts with golf courses, usually beaches, game rooms— and bars.

At one favorite site, Ponte Vedra, Florida, near Jacksonville, the manager reported that the *Life* drink consumption, per capita, was by far the highest recorded by any gathering he had hosted, a statistic which at least should impress veterans of American tribal rites such as the convention.

Editors were called on at these gatherings to inspire (and amuse) the salesmen. Albert L. (Bill) Furth, number 2 to Del Paine on *Fortune,* hit high notes for this kind of performance. He conceded his magazine's articles were perhaps a little too "thorough" for salesmen dealing with companies whose businesses were being analyzed. He brought down the house with a tongue-in-cheek offer of a deal from the editors for more cooperation. He suggested that if a company would purchase a quarter-page ad, *Fortune* would describe its research as "smart" rather than "shrewd"; for a half page, the magazine would publish the wife's favorite picture of the company president; for a full page, the company's "backward" pricing policy would be described as "traditional"; for six pages, if a company had eliminated all its competition, *Fortune* would say it had brought stabilization to the industry. Bill ended with a suggestion that for twelve double-page ad spreads (one every month), the editors would agree not to mention his company at all.

Each year the message of the editorial presentation was, in essence: "We're the best goddamned editors in the world with the best goddamned photographers, the best goddamned writers, and the best goddamned you name it." This approach, delivered with a barely believable air of subtlety, was accepted as a morale booster.

My most successful contribution to convention enjoyment was achieved by arranging to circumvent a rigid rule: participants and guests were all male. *Life,* while deserving no gold stars as a bastion of women's lib, depended on female editors for significant parts of the magazine, notably Marian MacPhail, chief of research, and Dorothy Seiberling, art editor. I chose three to strike a blow for sexual equality in adland: Sally Kirkland, Mary Leatherbee, and Mary Hamman. In amused tolerance, they condescended to make a surprise appearance; they stayed at a motel instead of the Ponte Vedra clubhouse and arrived at the convention in a car with window blinds.

Sally had been recruited from *Vogue* by Joe Thorndike. She replaced an amiable editor Billings had come to rely on when he wanted "a girlie story." Sally gave *Life* respectability in the fashion world. She would get impatient with her friend Joe and resign regularly (I once went to a farewell party she gave herself). I wasn't a close friend when I took over;

I told her I felt we'd get along, but if she said to me she was quitting I would accept her resignation. I respected her professionalism, and we did get along.

Mary Leatherbee was coeditor (with Tom Prideaux) for entertainment. She had dynamic energy and a depth of backstage know-how. Her half brother was Josh Logan, the director; she had been a member of the Provincetown Players on Cape Cod and, as a pilot, had ferried airplanes from factories to military units during World War II.

Mary Hamman, a former editor of *Mademoiselle's Living,* had done some consulting for a women's section in *Fortune* that never materialized. I was looking for someone who could run a new department involved with modern living, the sometimes gracious aspects of postwar prosperity, and with other women's interests, such as food. She came for an interview, her blond hair perfectly coiffed. I couldn't make up my mind right away, but a week or so later, I phoned her to come in again and talk. This time she hadn't had a chance to visit her hairdresser, and I noticed an undyed streak of hair along the part. She agreed to fill out a standard Time Inc. employment form, and under the heading "Color of hair," she wrote "Mouse." How could any right-thinking boss resist that?

There were no rehearsals with the three women before their presentation, so I was as surprised and delighted as the salesmen. Sally regaled them with bits about the Paris showings, convincing them that *Life* was truly professional about reporting the fashions that would later be seen across the United States.

Mary L. held them with stories about stage and movie greats—her handling of difficult entertainment subjects for the magazine was high entertainment itself. Both Sally and Mary L. told me later that they had maneuvered so as not to follow Mary Hamman and be upstaged in advance.

Mary H. told the ad salesmen of an imaginary exploration for a modern living article about the upper slopes of Mount Everest. The sometimes hammy Eliot Elisofon was the imagined photographer. She described the care with which they arranged each stick of furniture in a sherpa's hut and the special attention paid to the curtains on the nonexistent windows. In her slide show she projected an exclusive view of an avalanche (pitch-black on the screen), followed by a completely white image, the first picture ever of the Abominable Snowman's belly. She said, "An anthropological scoop, gentleman. Look, he has no navel."

After the salesmen had emerged from hysterical applause, true to the traditions of the sales convention, the three stars were hustled away. Some members of the editorial delegation later met them surreptitiously for dinner.

I probably should have had the foresight to save this presentation for my final convention because editorial never elicited a similar degree of acceptance again. Editorial and business had a few shared responsibilities, notably in the selection of covers, which served both as a sales come-on for an issue and an indication of editorial matter inside. The circulation vote was usually cast by Heiskell and/or Time Inc. president Roy Larsen. I used to envy the *Saturday Evening Post,* which could simply publish a piece of Norman Rockwell folklore. Its cover said simply, "This is the *Post,*" period. At *Life* we had to have something inside to back up the specific cover—no matter how slight the story.

What makes a cover a big seller? Editors and business people agreed that, since each issue would be on coffee tables for a whole week, a cover shouldn't be too repulsive. But the criteria for selecting a cover that will sell defy anything near scientific analysis. Here are some questions, still unanswered as far as I am concerned:

• Does a provocative or beautiful photograph really attract buyers?

• Does a picture over which are printed varieties of studhorse type hawking the contents of the issue make it academic whether there is any picture or not (this practice has many current adherents)?

• If the weather is bad, does an issue sell because people want to read, or is it a bust because buyers can't get out to pick it up?

• Does good weather, which makes a stroll to the newsstand a pleasure, increase sales, or do outdoor lovers just want to forget about reading and enjoy participant sports?

The appeal of a cover to single-issue buyers became, for better or worse, of decreasing importance to *Life.* It was company policy (Larsen's) from the beginning to make subscribing more attractive than purchasing from the newsstand. Insert cards in every newsstand copy pointed out the savings to be achieved. There is an ongoing intra-industry debate about the relative values of the two types of circulation. Supporters of subscriptions cite stability; newsstand sales advocates claim demonstrable vigor (in promotion vernacular, the publication is "hot").

Posing with six glamorous women Philippe Halsman had photographed for *Life* covers, at a party given by Halsman (probably 1954, photo by Philippe Halsman, ©Halsman Estate).

For me, the letters soliciting subscriptions, like the promotion ads, also posed some problems of accuracy. I discovered that, in addition to finding out about the big projects which we were more or less committed to publish, the circulation people were polling the departmental editors for smaller items. *Life* made assignments on the possibility that a story might come off, rather than on sure things or even probabilities. Hence there were lots of unused items around, and the departmental editors would talk the direct mail authors into listing these stories in promotional materials in the hope that I would feel as if I then had to publish them.

This time, mine was the gentle voice. I asked Heiskell if there was anything he could do to enforce checking direct mail pitches for accuracy. His reply: "I promise that you will never be held accountable for anything the circulation department mentions." I waited for an irate subscriber to complain that we didn't, as promised, publish an article about Mule Day in Columbia, Tennessee. No such letter ever came in.

Although they were somewhat less threatening to the bottom line than the revenge of outraged advertisers, lawsuits were a concern. They could involve damages for libel, breach of contract, or something still not precisely defined by court decisions—the right of privacy.

In my first months as M.E. of *Life,* the midriff of a bikini-contest winner was compared with a beat-up golf ball because there appeared to be scars. Our advice: if one has had abdominal surgery, avoid the bikini. It turned out that although shadows in the photograph may have looked like scars, the bikini wearer had never had an operation. Over my early objections, the lawyers quietly settled out of court for a few thousand dollars, pointing out convincingly that the plaintiff really had a good case, and that just going to court—even if we won—would cost vastly more.

Our law firm of Cravath, Swain and Moore handled the actual court work. The chief of Time Inc. in-house lawyers was John F. Dowd, a joy to work with because he really wanted to let us say what we wanted, with a realistic appreciation of the risks involved. He might say, "Rephrase it this way and you're probably safe," or, "The most you are likely to lose if this comes to trial is X dollars. If you can afford it, go ahead."

When I thought *Life* was right, I continued to resist settling out of court, even if it made financial sense. But in one much-publicized case, it was the plaintiff, the National Football League, through its commissioner, the redoubtable Pete Rozelle, who refused to settle—mostly for public relations reasons. Marshall Smith, our sports editor, had been convinced that even in a rough contact sport, pro football players were unnecessarily brutal. A survey convinced us that the Philadelphia Eagles were even worse than most. After our article appeared, the libel suit was brought in the names of two Eagle players, but legal costs were paid by the NFL.

The key point made by the plaintiffs' attorneys was that *Life,* in sending out research queries to pro team cities, had used as a title for the project "Dirty Football." This indicated to the jury that we had made up our minds that the game was dirty before we investigated it.

Life lost, and the two players were awarded a few thousand dollars each. A fair enough verdict, I thought, but it was an expensive lesson. Our costs were somewhat enhanced because we took a group of professional witnesses to Philadelphia. They were headed by Frank Gifford, now widely known for his Monday night football telecasts. Gifford had been seriously injured when slammed against a goalpost by some Eagles.

A lawsuit of vastly more importance involved a small story, one page and two following half pages, about a play on Broadway called *The Dangerous Hours.* It was based on a real-life incident in which escaped convicts had moved in on a suburban Pennsylvania family and kept them prisoners in their own home. The family had subsequently moved to Florida, so *Life* used their former house to photograph actors from the play in the actual settings.

The family was not identified in either the play or in *Life,* but the wife became a patient in a mental hospital after the article was published. The jury was sympathetic to the claim that this was due to the shock caused by our article, an invasion of the woman's right of privacy, and by the resultant trauma of having the incident recalled.

The award was $250,000, scaled down at each stage of the several appeals which followed. These appeals culminated in a Supreme Court verdict. By that time, the plaintiffs had acquired Richard M. Nixon as an attorney. Harold Medina, son of a famous federal judge, represented *Life* throughout.

The verdict finally was in *Life*'s favor, but the cost of litigating was far in excess of the original $250,000 award. The end to the lengthy litigation, however, at least indicated that the right of privacy is not unlimited. If the original claim had been confirmed, the courts and press lawyers generally would have been swamped with nuisance suits in wholesale lots. I had to be satisfied with this somewhat Pyrrhic victory.

14

Windsor, Winston, and the Viscount of Alamein

～❧ It is ridiculous for an editor to think that he is going to be buddies with a big-name author whose writing he may purchase for publication. Editors rarely move in the same social circles as the Royal Family, the Tory Party, or the High Command, whose landings in the 1940s and 1950s at *Life* added to the income tax receipts of the British Treasury and culturally enriched American readers. A cat can look at a king, however, and the fact that the Great Ones in some ways had feet of clay should surprise no one.

The man who tried to be at one with the ink-stained wretches of journalism was the former king-emperor, Edward VIII. *Time* originally scooped the British press by revealing Wallis Simpson's affair with the monarch. When, after his abdication, he became the Duke of Windsor, he decided to speak out. *Life* was ready, and so was Charles J. V. Murphy. The Duke wanted an American to help him write his book, and his attention had been called to a short book Murphy had coauthored, *The Lives of Winston Churchill.*

Theoretically, Murphy and the Duke shared the same language, so getting the details of a glamorous royal life might have sounded easy. It was in fact like pulling teeth, partly because of the leisurely life to which the Duke was accustomed. In ghosting *A King's Story,* Murphy rose from his lace-curtain Irish background to become more royal than the former king. There were many frustrations reflected in cables back and forth in which the "author" was called discreetly "our friend." In conversation I'm afraid there was less respect. On occasion Edward was sometimes "the little man" and sometimes "the little king."

Personally, I would have been happier with an "as told to" in the byline, but the first section of the Duke's memoirs appeared before I took over as managing editor. So, if the American equivalent of the English shopgirl readership liked to read royal prose, they were going to get it, albeit by Murphy.

Shopgirl or secretarial appeal could be assured, after a fashion, even in the Time & Life Building. When the Duke was visiting, word would get around and my outer office would be jammed with people from all over the building who just happened to want to consult my secretary.

Whatever the Duke may have thought about Charlie, he truly thought that he was writing his book himself (although sentences such as "Christmas at Sandringham was Dickens in a Cartier setting" must have given him pause). He did indeed try personally to write and fit captions for the illustrations that accompanied the articles—and performed almost competently. A fringe benefit was that he so charmed the *Life* copy room that a left-wing cell was temporarily immobilized.

The Duke continued to consider himself a part of our organization. Years later, when we were doing a small story on the garden he had designed around his French mill, I heard a substitute secretary outside my office yell into the phone, "That's what you say!" and slam down the receiver. She came in and reported, "There's some kook who says he's the Duke of Windsor." A few minutes later he got through and said, "Ed, you'd better have your phone checked. There's a lot of noise on it. I was cut off."

No matter how one judges the way we obtained the information, the golden young manhood of the Prince of Wales and the abdication of King Edward VIII were very much worth our while to record. The Windsor installments pushed sales up 10 percent—25 percent in Canada.

My friend Charlie was essentially accurate in his own later book, *The Windsor Story,* cowritten with J. Bryan III, in which he identifies most of the quotations from *A King's Story* as the Duke's own words. After the collaboration was finished, they certainly had become so.

I have two autographed copies of *A King's Story,* one from the Duke and one from Murphy. Each believed, accurately, that he was the author.

There could have been no question about the authorship of that other Briton, Sir Winston Churchill. I owed the arrangement to publish his memoirs of the war years to the efforts of my colleagues and predecessors. Luce led *Life*'s attempt to land Churchill, and Dan Longwell ingeniously added various devices to butter up the author. We had bought the rights to publish a couple of Churchill's wartime speeches in the Commons, to which he may or may not have had legal title. We had also paid for and reproduced some of his paintings. He gave one of his originals to Luce, adding some sheep on request to a landscape that seemed a little empty. (Incidentally, I never saw this work hanging in any of the Luce collections of excellent art.)

Churchill, as we were to continue to realize over the years, had his eye on the best deal from a tax standpoint and did not sell directly to *Life*. He disposed of the property, as a package, to Lord Camrose, who then owned the *London Daily Telegraph*. *Life* became, along with the *New York Times,* a sort of subcontractor for U.S. rights.

Editing included making selections to publish a mere fraction of his hundreds of thousands of words. Getting agreements on what survived was an exercise in international diplomacy. Luce delivered himself of a generality or two, and Longwell composed a section-by-section critique of the first volume. Churchill, who had every reason to be sensitive about his prose, took these observations with equanimity, possibly because he was not going to pay much attention to them.

A detailed and sometimes less than adulatory analysis by Jay Gold, *Life*'s assistant articles editor, gave us a scare, however. It was intended for office use only, but somehow it got to the author. The latter found the judgments "intelligent," or pretended to, and from then on would elaborately and equally sarcastically express the hope that he was "adhering to the Gold standard."

There was some technical difficulty in sharing Churchill's memoirs with the *New York Times,* but Gold solved this along with *Times* Assistant Managing Editor Theodore Bernstein, who also was adept with words. For roughly half a week, the *Times* would be ahead of *Life* and vice versa for the other half. *Life* was the exclusive purveyor of Churchill for the non-*Times* part of the country.

For each volume of *The War Years* we felt we could sustain interest for, at the most, a half-dozen installments of around 6,000 words each. Just fitting the essence of the books into manageable elements of a magazine issue was a formidable job, for which I was fortunate to have skills such as Gold's. There was also the presentation to consider, though. This involved creative visual concepts about which the author, his book publishers, and the *Times* did not have to worry. In addition to news photographs and paintings of the events described, Longwell, Thorndike, and I were concerned with establishing an understanding of this thoroughly British character for American readers. It seemed fair enough to recall the Duke of Marlborough, a Churchill ancestor about whom Winston had produced eloquent writing. It was also apropos to publish portraits of other great prime ministers.

I worked directly on volumes 2–6. As the project went on, even the author seemed to be flagging, relying more and more on documents salvaged from the records. Churchill had an industrious staff for assembling his "minutes" (memos), and he would more and more just stitch them together with a sentence or two here and there. The scantily documented early sections of the memoirs, when the author was relying on his memory without worrying about checkable facts, tended to be livelier.

Some of his "minutes," as recorded in the memoirs, must have driven military commanders up the wall. The British did not embrace the American concept that a field commander is in charge until he is relieved altogether. Thus, Churchill himself would direct that the defense guns at Singapore be positioned at slightly different angles, which turned out to be irrelevant because the Japanese captured them from the rear. Indisputably, though, he did know more about political consequences than the generals did.

Churchill worked in bed a great deal of the time. When he was up he usually wore his "siren suit," a Royal Air Force coverall which was a holdover from the Battle of Britain.

I learned from Churchill's physician, Lord Moran, when I signed him up for a condensation of his diaries, that his patient habitually slept naked. In 1949 we got an intimate view of our own, albeit clothed, when Churchill visited the United States for an important speech at the Massachusetts Institute of Technology. Jay Gold was invited to his New York hotel room and found Churchill working in bed with a burning candle and a scotch and water without ice. The candle was for relighting his cigar, which tended to last all morning. He took only an occasional sip at the drink.

I was mildly astounded at a staff dinner given by Luce during Churchill's visit. We knew that caviar was one of Churchill's weaknesses, so there was a mountain of it between the paws of an ice sculpture of the British lion. Churchill found a full-size dinner plate, thrust it into the pile, and came out with at least a foothill. He shoved the grains into his mouth with his hand.

By way of conversation I allowed that my elder son was a graduate of M.I.T. "Oh, yes, M.I.T.," Churchill said. "Fellow from there came to see me one morning. Said he was dean of humanities. Didn't know what that is, but I offered him a scotch anyway. He took it. Good man." At the dinner

Churchill proved that he liked martinis as well as scotch; his after-dinner drink was cognac.

Quite often strangers come up to me and ask, "Do you know you look like Churchill?" I suppose it is my cigar (smaller and cheaper than his) and my round face (Churchill's comment on his own appearance: "All babies look like me").

Was the cultivation of Churchill and providing all those graphic block-busters worth it? It was. It solidified *Life*'s reputation as the recorder of great events—whether they attracted any new readers or not. As an added bonus, we found we could land other desirable books and notable personalities by promising "the Churchill treatment."

Life acquired American serialization rights to the memoirs of Field Marshal Bernard Montgomery, Viscount of Alamein, by a somewhat unorthodox sequence of events. He made a brief visit to the United States shortly after the end of the war and had only a breakfast date open for the usual Time Inc. salute to visiting dignitaries. Luce used his ultra-exclusive Lynx Club for a suitable background. Monty refrained for once from peppery digs at his American wartime colleagues. He came out four-square for postwar Allied unity.

Luce wound up the rather unfestive occasion by announcing that our guest was going to receive a present that his fellow Britons could not have—the domestic, not the overseas, edition of *Life*. The point was that the flimsy airmailed version had no ads. Goods-hungry Europeans would have liked to revel vicariously in the lush food, appliance, and automobile ads in the domestic *Life*. I had received the U.S. edition at SHAEF, and copies were stolen immediately unless I destroyed the covers and camouflaged the magazines as contents of my wastebasket.

Recently demobbed as a lieutenant colonel, I was designated as a temporary aide for the Montgomery limousine ride from breakfast to the SS *Caronia,* which was taking him home. As the sirens and sweeping lights of the New York police escort led us toward the docks, he turned to me and asked, "This *Time* and that *Life*—which is the big one and which is the little one?"

Receiving the U.S. edition put the Viscount on the domestic promotion list, so he was duly apprised that *Life* had contracted for the serialization of General Omar Bradley's memoirs. Sensing accurately that the commander of the other army group in the Allied Expeditionary Forces would not admire him extravagantly, Monty launched a cabled rocket at *Life* demanding space for his version. Thus, it wasn't difficult to arrange for the serialization of his book. We were able to extract enough characteristic Montgomery barbs to make some good reading.

A group of Time Inc. editors joined those whom Montgomery favored with inquisitorial attention. He had become, by his account, a confidant of Eisenhower. Montgomery had tried to snub his supreme commander during the war, but was now giving him advice on how to win points in U.S. politics—an area where almost any other observer would have conceded that Ike was an instinctive master.

As host at a luncheon, Luce undertook to introduce each of us individually. When he got to me, he said, "Now, Ed Thompson is from North Dakota . . ."

Montgomery: "North Dakota? North Dakota? Never heard of it."

Luce: "To paraphrase Daniel Webster's description of New Hampshire in the Dartmouth College case, it is a small state but there are those who love her . . ."

Montgomery (pointing to each editor in turn): "What was the legal issue in the Dartmouth case? What was the legal issue? What was the legal . . ."

The bony finger and the accusing eyes intimidated me so that I couldn't even choke out that it had something to do with the ownership of Indian tribal lands. The others in the room knew the details more precisely, but they, too, failed to respond before the moving finger moved on.

The prosecutor kept chortling, "Didn't even know the legal issue," as an embarrassed Luce changed the subject, leaving the field marshal triumphant on another battlefield.

15

Sweating Out an Unpleasant Era

◯ Though the war was well over, the early 1950s were still full of danger, thanks to the Soviet Union. Most Time Inc.-ers were deeply anticommunist. But many of them also shared the admiration of much of the country for Alger Hiss as the prototype of young idealists who devote themselves to serving the nation. For them it was thus a time of consternation when fellow employee Whittaker Chambers accused Hiss of being a Soviet agent. And, despite a superficial sharing of beliefs, *Life* and Time Inc. found the way Wisconsin senator Joseph McCarthy practiced his brand of anticommunism distasteful.

It has occurred to me that if I had been properly curious, I would have examined Communism more thoroughly while I was younger. Hadn't Lincoln Steffens, the journalistic muckraker, visited the USSR and pronounced, "I have seen the future and it works"? I allowed myself to be assured, by former Party members and fellow travelers, that I had been intelligent and spared myself a lot of pain. I did wonder when men like Theodore White and Roger Butterfield felt they had to quit Time Inc. because of differences with Luce over the Chinese variety of Communism.

At first, my relations with Chambers were confined to occasions when, as assistant managing editor, I closed an issue in which one of his articles in *Life*'s series "Western Man" was scheduled. As did many others, I found him evasive and perhaps a little patronizing, surly, and arrogant.

On one occasion Chambers's copy failed to appear, and *Life*'s copy editor, Joe Kastner, couldn't locate him. Kastner and Columbia University professor Jacques Barzun, our history adviser, prepared to devise a substitute piece of text, but the next morning Chambers's copy finally started coming. I fumed at what I considered sloppiness.

When I raised hell with Chambers, he implied that Kastner hadn't been precise to him about the deadline. Although Chambers was silent about it, a look at the Associated Press teleprinter would have revealed that he had been testifying that very day to a congressional committee about Alger Hiss. It should be noted that Chambers—when his sweeping textual generalizations drove the cultured Barzun up the wall—would agree to compromise.

Impressions of Chambers emerged from anecdotes by acquaintances who admired him for his eloquence and erudition. A *Fortune* editor described how, at a social lunch, Chambers would position himself with his back to a wall so that he could be surveying the room for possible assailants, a holdover from the days when he was a Communist courier.

As publicly revealed, Chambers's personality was compared unfavorably to that of the personable Hiss. The many, many Hiss supporters just couldn't believe Chambers.

During the original hearings, Marguerite and I had a party at home for members of the Ultra intelligence group with whom I had served in Europe. Many of them had been dedicated New Deal lawyers. Just as the party was gathering some steam, someone asked me, "What do you think of Chambers and Hiss?"

My answer was that I thought they probably were both liars (in the subsequent Hiss trial for perjury, Chambers admitted seven lies under questioning). Suddenly the room was quiet. Almost without exception the guests eased themselves out of the apartment amid perfunctory thanks for the party. The unemptied drinks were just an indication of how the Chambers-Hiss affair would affect some of my friends.

Chambers had appropriately submitted his resignation from Time Inc., but Luce at first just kept it in a desk drawer without accepting it. He believed in the possibility of Christian redemption for Communists and other sinners. Then it developed that Chambers had actually been a spy for a foreign country, the USSR. That made an important difference, and Luce accepted the resignation.

The first Hiss perjury trial, in which he was charged with lying under oath about his membership in the Communist Party, ended in a hung jury (eight of the jurors voted for conviction) toward the end of *Life*'s editorial week. I had only three and a half pages left open for a story but concluded that the readers had been getting the substance of the testimony, and that the second trial much later would be repetitious from a news standpoint. Our reporter, James Bell, had heard all 735,250 words of testimony and had seemingly total recall. We—the editors and Bell—had less than two days to get all this into about 3,500 words. We chopped away far into the second night, and a rereading today indicates that our work provided a coherent account.

The second trial, which resulted in the conviction of Hiss, revealed that we had focused on the salient facts in the earlier testimony: possession of an identifiable Woodstock typewriter in the first three months of 1938 and proof, as accepted by the second jury, that Hiss had copied classified documents for Chambers, a Soviet spy.

Before the second trial, I got a call from a guest who had been at our Ultra party inviting me to lunch "so I can pump you." He explained that he, a lawyer, was part of an informal save-Hiss committee and said, "Tell me the name of the insane asylum in which Whittaker Chambers spent some time."

I said I didn't know anything about any such period, and if I did I wouldn't tell him. He said mildly, "I didn't think you would, but it was worth a try."

Also between the trials, Alistair Cooke, the host of cultural TV documentaries, was a guest at a *Life* editors' lunch. His book *A Generation on Trial* had just been published, and he announced triumphantly his analysis of Chambers, saying that he was a modern Titus Oates, the "litigious paranoiac" of seventeenth-century England. Oates became notorious for perjured accusations against nobility and royalty—he accused the queen of high treason—and his testimony sent many Jesuits and other Roman Catholics to their deaths. Cooke based his belief that Hiss would be acquitted on the erroneous assumption that the typewriter evidence would be refuted. He bridled when I mentioned "litigious paranoiac" at a later meeting.

My Ultra friend was more gracious. He had started his career as Harlan Stone's law clerk and sent me a note saying, "I should have remembered that the Chief Justice told me never to anticipate a verdict until the jury is in."

I sensed that Luce was annoyed at me for not getting serialization rights to *Witness,* Chambers's autobiography. I had been told that the bidding was still open, but the literary agent, it turned out, had sold the rights to the *Saturday Evening Post.* Frankly, I wasn't too chagrined at first because I was still embarrassed by Chambers's previous employment by Time Inc. It turned out that Luce had tentatively planned to serialize *Witness* in *Time,* not *Life.*

When I eventually read the book I was moved by the intensely human account of this little fat boy, the butt of the nastiest practical jokes, and his tortured life. I was rather relieved that my counterparts at the *Post* had failed to notice the best parts and had simply reprinted the account of the House committee hearings and the trials—every newspaper had had those at the time.

The Senator Joseph McCarthy technique of setting one citizen against another might have seemed a different matter. Time Inc. generally and I in particular underestimated the effectiveness with which the senator could induce Americans to look under their own and their neighbors' beds for Reds. McCarthy's opening gun, promising to name card-carrying Party members in the State Department, seemed ridiculous at first, and an argument was made that any attention paid to it would just give him the publicity he was obviously seeking. If he didn't get it, maybe he would just go away. He didn't.

McCarthy also took in stride the ridicule attempted about the antics of his two amateur gumshoes, Roy Cohn and David Schine, who were ham-handedly looking for clues about American Communists in Europe.

Life did not shrink from editorially advising Robert A. Taft to be wary about accepting McCarthy support for his presidential campaign, and in 1952 we all winced inwardly when *Life*'s candidate, Eisenhower, received the senator—who had criticized the former commander—on his campaign train in McCarthy's home state of Wisconsin.

A distressing number of witnesses before McCarthy's Senate committee were taking refuge in the Fifth Amendment rather than answering the question "Are you now or have you ever been a member of the Communist Party?" Scholarly books were being examined for traces of Communist propaganda.

The witch hunt deposited an unexpected victim into my Larchmont home. A *Life* photographer, graduate of a top university, confessed that he had read subversive material and offered to atone by spying on suspected Communists on the staff. Naturally, I declined. He became somewhat violent, and the neighbors called the local police.

After a short period of confinement, he went home to his own psychiatrist. He then went to Washington and tried to surrender to the guards at the FBI building. The FBI told us that this was not at all an uncommon occurrence. Such was the state of the country in the McCarthy era. The relatively happy ending was that the photographer responded to psychiatric treatment and settled into a placid life running a photographic supply store.

In March 1954, *Life* finally pulled up its socks and published a hard-hitting, nine-page lead article calling the senator "reckless" and "irresponsible." We barely beat out Edward R. Murrow, who came out the next week with his justly memorable treatment along the same lines. I am certainly not downplaying what Murrow did. It was more courageous in the then generally timid world of television to air such material than it was to publish it in print.

As *Life* noted, a Gallup poll at this time showed that 50 percent of the country approved of McCarthy and less than 30 percent disapproved. With practically no success, McCarthy went to Time Inc. advertisers and demanded that they withdraw their business from our magazines.

McCarthy bulled on, in his thick-skinned way, but it was more significant than I thought at the time that he objected to nothing in the *Time* cover story about him by James McConaughy, our Washington bureau chief, except the revelation that the presumably good Catholic ate meat on Fridays. In 1954, as chairman of the Senate Government Operations Committee, McCarthy proceeded to take on the U.S. Army, focusing on a brigadier general and the Secretary of the Army. Horrors: a dental major, whom he accused of being a Communist, had been promoted.

Providence intervened in the form of an upright, skillful Boston attorney: Joseph Welch, special counsel for the Army. He scored decisively where frontal attacks had fallen short. He caused McCarthy, under questioning, to make a fool of himself and, having impaled him, twisted the knife with, "Have you no decency, sir?"

Life reported Welch's resounding successes in photographs and words. The culmination was an article written by Welch. He later gave his literary counsel at *Life,* Ernest Havemann, a gold railroad-type pocket watch with a leather fob he had made by hand.

In Massachusetts, support for McCarthy and his tactics continued even after his power base in Wisconsin began to erode. Jeff Wiley was *Time-Life* bureau chief in Boston at the time; he was one of several bureau chiefs who were allowed to stay in one place long enough to get to know their territory well. I was in Massachusetts on one of my periodic pulse-feeling trips, and Wiley sent me to Mike Ward, who would have become political boss of Boston if he hadn't been in ill health. Ward was convincing in arguing that McCarthy could run for any office in Massachusetts and win.

Ward's views on McCarthy and religion are noteworthy. He said, "No Catholic will say this out loud to an outsider. The Al Smith campaign in

1928 caused deep scars. Now, for the first time since then, the voters are being influenced by religion instead of party. Their priests have been ranting for years about atheistic Communists, but no one thought there was much danger. Now, a fellow Catholic, McCarthy, steps up and convinces them that the menace is closer than they thought. They note that McCarthy is the only Republican Catholic senator, and they note that he is being attacked with the same things that were said about Al Smith. He has become a hero. They are convinced that Joe is being persecuted because he is a Catholic. There isn't much logic in this, but they are also convinced that, although the Democrats voiced most of the anti-McCarthy sentiment, the Republicans are letting him down because of his faith."

Ward's analysis was credible, but McCarthy's continued excesses propelled him toward censure in the Senate and a belated exit from the scene. John F. Kennedy's victory in 1960 should have quieted Catholic worries about discrimination.

McCarthyism as a word is firmly in the language. The *Random House Unabridged Dictionary* definition is "the practice of making accusations of disloyalty, esp. of pro-Communist activity, in many instances unsupported by proof or based on slight, doubtful, or irrelevant evidence." The possibility of political demagoguery hasn't receded enough to guarantee that this country won't have to face in the future another McCarthy or another Hiss-Chambers type of confrontation. Diligent hate-mongers could still stir up intolerance, the West versus Muslims, for example.

Certainly one editor—who feels unclean just from being in touch, however gingerly, with McCarthyism—could be relied on to man the barricades against a revival.

16

Splendors of the World *Life* Lived In

For major news stories the weekly *Life* had an organization that was flexible and opportunistic. We tried to provide a powerful *Life* spin through analyses by the shapers of great events themselves. But in addition, substantial parts of the magazine were devoted to the great series—conceived, delivered, nurtured, and fine-tuned in-house. They were unmistakably only *Life*'s, and they went far toward counteracting the unpleasant situations thrust on us by such as McCarthy, Hiss, and Chambers.

The conception of the series "The World We Live In"—the champion of them all in terms of critical success, demonstrably popular and profitable—was deceptively casual. A chance comment by Andrew Heiskell stimulated my thinking about how the magazine could get credit for the care and imagination we lavished on making thought-provoking subjects into understandable but still accurate fare for a mass audience. "This is the kind of thing," Heiskell said about one now forgotten story, "that only *Life* could do."

Later, while examining rough sketches our science editor, Kenneth MacLeish, was showing me for a proposed single article on the birth of the earth, I asked myself why we couldn't go from there to a series on what happened after the birth. We could. The very enormity of the project and the way in which it would be presented would provide continuity of interest through a couple of years. In all, three dozen or so individuals, on staff or under contract, combined to produce 13 installments, and we listed more than 250 outside experts who advised on individual items.

In the formative stages of the project in 1951, I told Heiskell that I didn't expect the series would add any circulation and that the cost would be high, but that I thought *Life* should do it. We were off.

Luce was engrossed in reviving the two-party system but nodded agreement, perhaps absentmindedly. I explained that a sizable part of the staff might be tied up on this series, that I thought it would have a broader appeal than "Western Man" (also a prestige item), that we were constructing the individual installments as chapters in a book so that one could be published with a minimum of extra work, that we were attempting to surprise the readers with unfamiliar aspects of familiar sights, that we weren't trying to startle scientists with facts they already knew.

I had been the titular boss of three brilliant science editors. I had had the combative Gerard Piel ("No one but an idiot can fail to understand what I write") because he refused to work with anyone else. There was Denis Flanagan, who later joined Piel when he took over *Scientific American.* Denis was just as stubborn as Gerry and expressed his prejudices with eloquent silences. Then there was Ken MacLeish, a superb all-around journalist. The son of poet Archibald MacLeish, he scared his friends by driving fast cars and motorcycles and by flying airplanes (he was a navy dirigible pilot during World War II) and making incredibly deep ocean dives. Ken had the assistance of Ralph Graves (later the last managing editor of the weekly *Life* and editorial director of Time Inc.) in preparing the original prospectus for the series. Philip Wootton, who also had a good grasp of the editorial use of science, was editor of special projects. He represented me in riding herd on the numerous details of closings, although, as with all *Life* material, I read every word of copy. The installments were published one every two months in 1952, 1953, and 1954.

Art Director Charles Tudor furnished vastly more than the usual control of design. He had to take the raw research gathered for each installment, decide where to use photographers and which subjects needed diagrams or full-fledged paintings, and combine these into layouts of more than twenty pages each, with the use of foldouts when extra space was required. Although I tended to be quite intrusive when layouts were made, I had complete faith in Charlie's direction of this vital phase, after seeing very preliminary sketches.

Bob Elson, in his *The World of Time Inc.,* accurately sensed a "telepathic communication" between my mumbles and Charlie's grunts and shrugs. Tudor field-marshaled the production and assemblage of graphic material, from the microscopic to the almost infinite. For instance, more than fifty varieties of tiny plankton were painted for a double-page spread, while a panorama of the woolly mammoth and its contemporary mammals required a three-page foldout. Three pages, tipped sideways, were needed to show a profile of a rain forest, from its floor to its canopy of emergents, 160 feet high.

I had specified to Luce that the "writing would be of a high order." It became so, but not in the way we had anticipated.

Members of the staff nominated authors for individual installments. Rachel Carson was a natural for the sea, William Beebe to report from under it. We would have liked Roy Chapman Andrews or T. E. Lawrence for the desert, Edward Ullman or A. B. Guthrie for mountains. We had the temerity to wonder if Fred Hoyle was "solid enough" for our astronomy. We thought of adapting already written fictional material, such as that of Conrad, Melville, and Francis *(The Oregon Trail)* Parkman, for some articles.

As planning got underway, however, it became obvious that the graphic material was going to dictate the form of the series and that we needed one writer who would follow through on the whole thing. Outside writers couldn't be expected to mesh their work into *Life* layouts, and we didn't want the quality of writing to vary from installment to installment. As each subject was blocked out by Tudor with the artist and/or photographer, moreover, arbitrary decisions had to be made as to how much room would be left for descriptive text material next to each picture. There was room, of course, for the writer to wax lyrical at the beginning and end of each article, but someone accustomed to *Life*'s ways was better for exactly fitting the intermediate sections.

I chose Lincoln Barnett, who carried off the general textblocks for the series and subsequent book brilliantly. Barnett, who had started as a journeyman writer of short textblocks for the magazine fresh from being a reporter on the *New York Herald Tribune,* graduated into signed articles for *Life,* then took time off to write *The Universe and Dr. Einstein* on his own. The book was a great critical success and was eventually translated into twenty languages.

Barnett's dedication to whatever subject he tackled was immense—and fatiguing. After the Einstein book, he used his own time, almost two years of it, to answer personally every letter of comment that came in. Sometimes his zeal seemed excessive to workaday editors who had to get issues out on time, but he had a bland answer: "But I'm a slow reader."

Even with a general outline agreed upon and many details planned, it took a year before the first installment of "The World We Live In" appeared—December 8, 1952. The writers, illustrators, and editors themselves had to understand what they were saying. They had to distill this information into intelligible form. If you're excessively technical you don't get readers. If you oversimplify you alienate the consulting experts for future use.

Each of the installments took one assistant editor and several reporters an average of eight months to complete. They produced research on a huge variety of topics, including the comparative sizes and shapes of, say, the hatchet fish (one inch) and the giant squid, to guide the artists in giving explicit form to the sweeping generalities in which Barnett would luxuriate.

From the land, with spectacular renderings of the birth of mountains, the work of water, wind, and ice on the terrain, we went to the air—from its creation by exhalations from the molten interior of the infant earth to such manifestations as the aurora borealis, shown in rare photographs by J R Eyerman in an explanation of weather.

The wonders dazzled the staff as well as the readers. The emergence of earth from barren waste into its observed evolutionary development evoked vast pageants of images. There were the creatures of the sea, down to the stygian darkness, the reptiles, the dinosaurs, the emergence of mammals. There were the swamps, the coral reefs, the deserts, and the arctic barrens. There were flowers and the rain forest.

Consider one relatively simple chapter—the familiar woodland. Finding a proper woods wasn't easy. Virtually all of the virgin deciduous forests in the then forty-eight states had been cut down. Fortunately we found one small tract of sixty-five acres in New Jersey that had been kept intact by the same family since 1700.

The site was within commuting distance of New York, so Gjon Mili set aside parts of all four seasons to record the year. He had made photographic history with the use of high-speed stroboscopic photography, and his instinct for effective lighting served him as well when he used the natural variety as when he used electronic flashes that would stop action at 1/30,000 of a second.

Gjon had the patience to stalk the baby raccoons, skunk, and deer of early spring, as well as to record the freshness of the foliage and flowers. His photographs then reflected the fullness of summer and the many hues of autumn. He found the grown animals preparing for winter. The same white oak stretched toward the sky of all seasons.

Photography provided half of the sights in the twenty-page article. Artist Walter Linsenmeier complemented the photographs with meticulously constructed panoramas of the animals and birds, the stream dwellers, the underground creatures, and the winged insects of the forest. Linsenmeier thus painted more than 150 individual portraits against his detailed backgrounds. Barnett added the poetry of Frost, Emerson, and Wordsworth to his own sensitive observations.

The *Life* army swept to a triumphant end of the operation with the last installment—earth's place in the universe. The expensive project, which had been undertaken three years earlier just because this seemed to be the kind of thing *Life* should do, had proved to be a financial as well as a critical success. Every issue with a detail from "The World We Live In" on the cover showed newsstand sales substantially above average, and many sold out.

The assumption that the United States was turning more to self-improvement, a culture binge if you will, turned out to be accurate. *Life* had more substance than some cynical editors would have thought acceptable. It really was okay to make readers work a bit—although, of course, one shouldn't push one's acceptance and try to get too far ahead of them.

The book toward which the series was precisely structured was also a smashing success—650,000 copies sold, mostly by mail order. In all, I thought it acceptable, with scores of others, to feel a quiet pride.

Similar series followed, but only "The World's Great Religions" produced anything near a comparable impact. This series was planned to appear throughout 1955. Sections dealt with Hinduism, Buddhism, the philosophy of China, Islam, and Judaism and would come to a climax with a double-sized special issue on Christianity in December.

Because of the holiday season, liquor advertisements normally accounted for a large percentage of our commercial space in that issue. Over the years liquor ads were a subject of some controversy. As a quid pro quo, it had been suggested once that in order to get an interview with Pope Pius XII we omit liquor and women's underclothing ads from the issue involved. We didn't get the interview, but for the Christmas of 1955, Harry Dole, a truly star salesman, successfully persuaded all but one of the liquor advertisers to withdraw voluntarily from the issue. The sole holdout was a kosher wine producer, which claimed its product was sacramental. We arbitrarily threw out that half-page ad.

The power to eliminate certain ads was only part of my control of that issue. Harry Luce was spending most of his time in Rome, where his wife,

Clare Boothe Luce, was U.S. ambassador, but as the Christianity issue took form I tried conscientiously to keep him informed. He tut-tutted at the idea of a revival session involving inmates of a southern jail, saying, "although I suppose that kind of thing happens." As we approached the peak of work on the article, he cabled to tell me to "close the rest of the issue as you see fit."

If I hadn't had all kinds of theological counsel from experts throughout the series, I would have been scared by the idea of Luce—a leading Protestant layman, a pillar in the Madison Avenue Presbyterian Church, and husband of the most conspicuous Catholic convert in the country—trusting a subject about which he cared deeply to me, a mostly Christmas-only worshipper. As it was, we were very fortunate to have an impeccably knowledgeable, if voluble, son of an Episcopalian bishop, Sam Welles, as editor for the whole series. The only problem with Sam was in choosing from the cornucopia of story ideas he and his staff proposed.

"The World's Great Religions" became a book, as did the other series. The adaptations were handled by *Life*'s staff, but it soon became obvious that books needed a division of their own. Time-Life Books took over. I was past the period when I grabbed everything. I was not, by nature, really an empire builder. I was devoted to *Life,* the weekly magazine, which fully engaged my abilities—and probably then some. If I had been an athlete, I suppose I would have been playing "within myself," not straining much beyond my capacities.

17

HST and Libel? "I'm Going to Tell the Truth about Those S.O.B.'s"

❧ Two figures marched along Third Avenue in Manhattan at the standard army drill-manual cadence: "Hup! Two! Three! Four!" One was the former president of the United States, Harry S. Truman; the other was the managing editor of *Life*, which had just bought publication rights to the Truman memoirs. Departure had been from the Waldorf Astoria.

It was just after 7 A.M., the usual hour for the Truman morning walk, but a most unusual hour for me, a night person. I had been challenged by my author, however, and had spent the night in the city so as not to be late for the exercise which he guaranteed would extend my life to 100 years "if you keep it up." Truman didn't make it to 100 himself. Since I had only one more of those walks—again with Truman, later, in Kansas City—I may have forfeited *my* chances.

The circumstances were unusual only for the guest walker. Street cleaners would call, "Hi, Mr. President." Taxi drivers would slow down and yell, "Give 'em hell, Harry." He would respond with a smile and a half wave of the hand. We had a full complement of reporters and photographers along.

The photographers were most agile, running backward ahead of us, and I found myself with the former president in almost every daily paper in the country. The photograph showed us both laughing, and later I got a Truman autograph saying, "I wonder just exactly what we were laughing at." I knew. One of the cameramen had backed into a trash can outside a Third Avenue restaurant and covered himself with garbage.

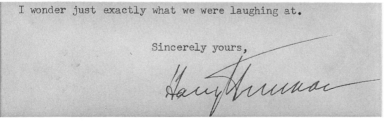

I wonder just exactly what we were laughing at.

Sincerely yours,

Harry Truman

Walking with former president Truman in New York (1953, photo by Walter Sanders, courtesy Time Inc.).

By any reasoning, the Truman memoirs were valuable. Truman had surprised his critics and doubters, conspicuous among them being Time Inc., by being a very good president. His major decisions, such as support for the Marshall Plan, establishment of the Truman doctrine in Greece, and the way he responded to the invasion of South Korea, had been unmistakably statesmanlike. His way of communicating with the people was pithy, to the point, and wholly American. Dealing with him proved to be generally enjoyable. His signing with *Life*—since it had opposed him editorially in 1948 and since he thought Luce's wife had insulted Mrs. Truman—seemed surprising at first.

Collier's was part of a syndicate which made one of the two leading bids. It had been the only national publication which consistently supported the New Deal. As 1952 approached, however, it not only deserted the Democratic Party but supported the most conservative Republican, Robert A. Taft. In Truman's code it was worse to turn traitor than to have been in opposition all along. He spotted the name in the syndicate bid and simply said, "*Collier's,* shit."

Thus, when Andrew Heiskell and I were invited to the White House, we were assured that, barring unexpected developments, we would get the contract. It was January 10, 1953. I had been in the White House before only on a short tourist visit and a couple of times to witness FDR's not-so-playful spanking of recalcitrant reporters by directing them to sit in the corner with dunce caps.

We crossed the street from the office of John Snyder, the secretary of the treasury. Clearance had been phoned ahead, so we were just waved along to the private elevator, where a white-haired black usher said the president and Mrs. Truman were in the subbasement. "I don't know what they doing."

Snyder killed time by showing us the first floor, and by the time we reached the second-floor study, the president was waiting. He said, "I don't know what we're going to do with that durn stuff in the basement. . . . If I'd've known it was so much trouble to move I wouldn't have given up the job."

In the mistaken notion that an interjection was needed to keep the conversation going, I suggested an auction. This reminded the president of a durable enemy whose name would come up from time to time thereafter.

"That's what that son of a bitch Chester Arthur did. He cleaned all the priceless antiques out of the White House and had them auctioned downtown. Only brought $6,000. Replaced them with stuffy Victorian furniture."

Margaret Truman stuck her head into the room a couple of times, and there was time out for introductions. Then, as later, it was hard to keep him on the subject at hand.

"Oh, yes, I know all about memoirs. I started with U. S. Grant . . ."

There were more interruptions to show us his library. ("That's a proclamation by Napoleon. . . . I've read every durn one of these.") Then he made a reference to the Rock Island Railroad and to "those old robbers, Jay Gould and Vanderbilt." Next he mentioned the manuscript of Churchill's Westminster College, Missouri, Iron Curtain speech, which *Life* had bought for the college, and a senator who tried to make some money from a Truman letter: "He sold a private letter I sent him. He got $50, and I made him go out to the open market and buy it back for $125."

As we tried to stick to routine clauses in the contract, he would dangle his wrists over the edge of his chair, bored, but then he would perk up and contribute comments such as "I always go over Margaret's contracts and try to get everything in. We've been glad we did."

We approached the possibility of his not being able to complete the book, and he waved aside our attempt to be delicate. "Of course, I may get hit by a truck or someone may shoot me."

On the matter of routinely indemnifying the publisher against suits, he said, "I'm not going to libel anyone. I'm going to tell the truth about those sons of bitches."

Although he had a group of politicians waiting for him, the president acted as our operator for the self-service elevator. As we walked out Snyder said, "You've got to keep him working if you expect to get the book." He was prophetic.

Setting a total price was easy enough. We proposed to buy all rights as a package to keep his income tax as low as possible. We would sell book rights (to Doubleday), newspaper rights (to the *New York Times* and *St. Louis Post-Dispatch*), and waive the TV and movie rights back to the author if and when he wanted them. We had been given to understand that, as a matter of pride, Truman wanted to get more than Eisenhower did for *Crusade in Europe:* $500,000. This had been syndicated by the *New York Herald Tribune,* from which *Life* had bought magazine rights, so we specified an amount above $500,000. That was satisfactory.

Judge Sam Rosenman, who was a good speechwriter for both FDR and HST, was Truman's attorney and turned out to be no tax expert. If the author had received the whole sum in one year, as Rosenman suggested, most of it would have gone to taxes, so, perhaps irregularly, we had our firm—Cravath, Swain and Moore—advise the president. For his protection we undertook to obtain for him the maximum take-home pay. Eisenhower's Department of the Treasury—relations were amicable at the beginning—agreed to an arrangement that would permit payment over a number of years.

It was not until later that Congress established pensions for former presidents, and Truman told me, while on a walk in Kansas City, that, until the *Life* payments started coming in, his only income was $90 a month as a retired army officer. The amount was figured on length of service, but "the Veterans Administration wouldn't even give me credit for seven years as commander in chief of the Armed Forces."

Judging from our first conversation, I thought that if he would write in the simple, lucid, and colorful way he talked, we would have no problem. Trying to maintain this tone, along with the difficulty of keeping him at work, were to be headaches throughout the project.

At first no copy came out of his office in Kansas City in spite of my periodic trips to protect the investment. We had promised delivery of a manuscript to Doubleday for 1955 publication. I didn't really worry during 1953. The president deserved some time to unwind after seven years of heavy responsibility. My trips to Kansas City and Independence produced only disjointed bits of opinion, including:

John Foster Dulles, President Eisenhower's secretary of state, was to Truman a "durned old snollygaster." Truman said, "I call him that because he's two-faced. He tells you one thing and then goes out and knifes you."

FDR's elder sons had worked against Truman's nomination in 1948. "I didn't have enough glamor for them." In time he stopped calling President Eisenhower by name, instead referring to him as "Glamor Boy."

He was proud that he had confounded the Library of Congress with a quotation by the Duke of Wellington which he had read in a privately printed book the library didn't have.

Jefferson, John Marshall, and Henry Clay had had the same law teacher. "Too bad they had to poison that old man at the age of 75." (I never could get that old man's name out of Truman.)

A couple of times his staff successfully diverted my concern about the lack of visible progress by showing me little notes or unmailed letters. They said these would get into the narrative. There was a draft of a chiding letter to Adlai Stevenson from 1952, for instance. It had never been sent.

A great admirer of former vice president Alben Barkley, Truman had carefully copied some of Barkley's gamey jokes into notebooks. Truman told one, illustrating a political point:

"There was this good-looking young fellow campaigning along a ridge in North Carolina. He left his Model T and climbed up to a house. A pretty widow lady answered the door, and he said, 'I'm running for sheriff, and I'd appreciate your vote.' She asked him in and volunteered that not only would she vote for him, but she'd go along the ridge and get all her kinfolk to vote for him too. She just happened to have some country ham frying and after supper there was a cloudburst. She said, 'You can't go out in this, but I have a trundle bed just under mine so you just stay over.' He then took alarm and said, 'What have you got in that barn out there?' 'Hay, why?' The candidate put a coat over his head, bolted out the door and slept in the hayloft that night, away from temptation. When he woke up the sun was out and the widow was noisily beating a bull in the barnyard. He was shirking his duty to a cow. 'Get up there you so-and-so,' the widow yelled between blows of her broom, 'You ain't runnin' for sheriff of this county.'"

Truman also had a scrapbook full of jokes about Calvin Coolidge.

This was all fun, but I was becoming increasingly worried about what writing for publication was actually being done. On my trips to Kansas City, I was greeted blandly. The former president would invite me to lunch at the Muehlebach Hotel with whomever of his friends happened to be in town. A table of bottles would be rolled out. The Truman libation before lunch was two tumblers of the hotel's special brand of bourbon. He didn't gulp, but the glasses would empty as if the contents were being absorbed by osmosis. Although we had a private room, the president scrupulously ordered only the businessman's lunch (sample entree: braised oxtails for ninety cents). He thought he was paying, but the manager of the hotel confided that Truman was never billed and didn't notice the omission. The liquor seemed to have no effect.

I had recommended strongly that, to preserve the tone of Truman's conversation, extensive interviews be undertaken. In February 1954 I got to read 100,000 or so words of transcripts. There were touches of Trumanisms here and there, but no attempt had been made to organize the material, and only thirty-five pages were in what might be called editable first-draft form.

What should have been more apparent, perhaps, was that we were dealing with a man who was not inclined to be very introspective and whose patently great decisions were made on the basis of his common sense and his strength of character.

A good editor works with what he has, and although he may have an optimistic faith that the Lord will provide, he must arrange that all available assistance be marshaled. There are various obstacles which work against getting the most out of memoirs. One is an author's faith in the brilliance and clarity of observations he has had time to rewrite into stiff bureaucratese.

Although a good staff is indispensable to a president, a great man sometimes has a few assistants who are less than helpful. Truman had two who proved, from whatever motives, to be roadblocks. One was William Hillman, a former Hearst newspaperman who had produced a rather superficial Truman book, *Mr. President,* mostly pictures but with some HST quotes. Bill seemed content to fill out his career as part of a Truman entourage.

The other was David Noyes, an advertising man who had served as a speechwriter for Truman during the 1948 campaign and now had been brought back to help with the book. I am convinced that Noyes wanted to protect Truman from those he suspected of wanting to denigrate him.

People who tried to work on the memoirs, including several college history and journalism teachers, came to refer to Hillman and Noyes as "the boys," and these two pretty well insulated the author from everyone else. This shield became more and more evident as the work proceeded toward a deadline.

The author himself made a show of insisting on being the final authority on the manuscript, as he should have, but he rarely changed more than a word or two and left the final versions to "the boys." He seemed to suffer me with more tolerance than the other outsiders and would say, "Now I want you to get your money's worth." I may have neutralized Hillman, but subsequent developments showed that Noyes had remained suspicious.

Doubleday planned to come out with the first volume shortly after our serialization in the fall of 1955 and the second early in 1956. We had available a skillful editor and the most talented of rewrite men, Ernest Havemann. Like me, he admired Truman.

The boys and the president seemed glad to have extra help, so Havemann took on the job. He labored patiently with whatever material he could get his hands on, and prepared drafts which were rejected with suspicion when submitted through Noyes and/or Hillman. The visiting professors, who tackled specific sections, had the same experience, and all left unhappily.

Thanks to a long, close relationship with Havemann, I was sure that he could not have done anything to become persona non grata, so it must have been *Life* itself which was suspect. By that time I was resigned to trying to salvage a creditable serialization by judicious excerpting and by using our graphic resources to dignify and generally dress up the presentation.

With my agreement Doubleday's editor-in-chief, Ken McCormick, dispatched an able editor, Hawthorne Daniel, to Kansas City, replacing Havemann. Daniel did not have the *Life* stigma, but just as I had antagonized Noyes and Hillman by warning against a "scissors and pastepot job," Daniel gave offense by using the word *cut* in reference to bringing the material down by about 70 percent to book size. "No one is going to 'cut' this material," he was told. Like Havemann, he found that volume 1 had not been "written" at all. The text he encountered was "lacking in continuity and mixed in subject matter." With saintlike patience, however, Daniel produced a manuscript for an autumn closing. He tactfully substituted the word *condense* for *cut*.

Photographer Eliot Elisofon produced a poetic version of what the president had seen on his early morning walks in Washington. We used everything Truman wrote on his memories of his childhood and his early political career as a picture-shooting script. We provided a photographic background of Jackson County, Missouri, his home. We wanted the overall impression to be as Trumanesque as possible. His little homilies on such as the desirability of political organizations and the nature of the vice presidency we highlighted in boxes.

We wanted him to have his say even when it made us wince. Thus we included his words about the "kept press" in 1948 without remonstrance, even though he must have included the Luce publications in that category. Truman's controversial nature was one of the reasons he titillated the public.

Life had, of course, sounded out Douglas MacArthur on his memoirs. We were assured that General MacArthur would never ever put his name on an account of his career. But when the time approached for the dismissal of MacArthur to be described in the Truman narrative, surprise! It turned out that the Big General himself did want to sign one article. This literary confrontation would be a journalistic coup, and we asked him to proceed. However, when a request came from a MacArthur aide for a look at what the former president was going to say, I refused it. The general managed to get it anyway, through the *New York Times,* which wasn't so scrupulous.

The MacArthur article arrived, and as a matter of courtesy and out of a sense of fair play, I then sent it to Truman. I wasn't asking his permission. Technically, we had the right to put anything we thought appropriate into an issue along with the comparable Truman installment. I would have preferred to have MacArthur's version follow Truman's by an issue, to insure two sellout issues instead of one, but MacArthur made release of his article contingent on being in the same issue. It seemed a reasonable price to pay.

Truman himself wasn't ruffled—at least at first. He read MacArthur and phoned me, cheerily: "Go ahead and run it. When a hot air balloon is punctured a certain amount of gas has to escape." A slightly less colorful confirming letter followed.

I then received a "more in sorrow than in anger" letter from Dave Noyes, who had not been consulted on this matter by Truman. "I had reason to hope you would keep this one 'clean.' . . . even during my active days of huckstering . . . I avoided involvement in quackery."

I answered that we *had* kept it clean and that we had kept the author informed about what we were doing. I never again heard from Noyes. He may have convinced Truman that we were guilty of quackery—whatever that meant in this context. In any case, while Truman had inscribed the first volume of the memoirs to me "with kindest regards and great appreciation," the second, which appeared after the MacArthur article, had only a signature.

My relations with the former president ended on a friendly note, however. He was volubly grateful for a scrapbook of *Life* photographs we had made up for him on Margaret's wedding to Clifton Daniel. And we had behaved with generosity in waiving our technical rights back to him so he could narrate a television series.

My personal contacts with the former president did convince me that I was sufficiently a part of the Truman family to remonstrate gently with Bess Truman about her favorite television entertainment. She let me know that it was outrageous to imply that the results of professional wrestling were fixed.

18

Reminiscences by MacArthur: "Ah . . . When Knighthood Was in Flower"

~~ The bigger-than-life image that General Douglas MacArthur projected was not an exaggeration. It started to form when he was commanding the World War I Rainbow Division in France while Truman was a National Guard artillery captain.

The MacArthur career, spanning more than sixty years, was an American saga. It was very much part of *Life*'s franchise to record it as such. Clare Luce had written a full-length article on MacArthur as commander of the Philippine army, which appeared in *Life* just before Pearl Harbor. Luce himself, although he may have subscribed pragmatically to FDR's Europe-first strategy in the war, in his heart agreed with MacArthur on the importance of the Pacific and Asia—which was only natural considering his family's missionary background.

The general had a way of speaking to people that came to be called "the MacArthur treatment." Those who heard his pet discourse emerged with a kind of glassy look and an inability to convey precisely what he had said. Everyone agreed that he started out by declaiming, "War is obsolete!" After that, hypnosis seemed to take over.

I don't think anyone produced a direct quotation that the general would never ever write his memoirs, but that was the implication when Major General Charles Willoughby, his intelligence officer, wrote a book and when Major General Courtney Whitney, a former Manila businessman and the general's permanent aide, proposed that we buy serial rights to one *he* would write. We accepted.

We were led to believe that General Whitney's work would be the closest anyone would ever get to an authentic MacArthur memoir. Whitney had taken a small apartment on the same floor of the Waldorf Astoria Towers as his general's palatial suite. Whitney's writing couldn't be all that bad, could it? The price was not exorbitant, and his source was close at hand.

When I saw the first installment of what Whitney had written, however, I knew we were in for trouble. Whitney resisted any suggestion of editorial assistance. I didn't think I could approach General MacArthur directly, even if I could have slipped past Whitney's guard. My impression was that MacArthur was a resolutely remote figure.

While I was still at the Pentagon during the war, I had asked a young brigadier general temporarily there from the Pacific if MacArthur was as reclusive as he seemed. "Look," he said, "he was chief of staff and had four stars before most of us were even second lieutenants. He has no one around him of anywhere near his own generation. He's lonesome."

Even Dwight Eisenhower was a generation younger. After his retirement as U.S. high commissioner to Occupied Germany, General Lucius Clay, at a private dinner I attended, gave this version of why MacArthur was cool toward Eisenhower: "In 1937, MacArthur, retired, was employed by the Philippine government at a reported $100,000 a year to build up its army and prepare a constitution for the independence the U.S. had promised. Ike, a temporary captain, was on loan as MacArthur's assistant at $10,000 a year, which was a pretty desirable stipend for a regular army officer in those days. Some Young Turks in the Philippine government heard that Ike was doing most of the drafting on the proposed new constitution and suggested that Ike replace MacArthur. This would save money. Ike got wind of the idea and immediately quashed it. MacArthur heard about it, too, and couldn't believe this could have been considered without some encouragement from Ike."

I did hear of one true contemporary, though, who was perhaps the only man in the United States who could call the general by his first name. He was General Robert Wood, retired chairman of Sears Roebuck, who had been a second lieutenant in Panama with Second Lieutenant Douglas MacArthur. With credentials arranged by mutual acquaintances, I flew to Chicago to see General Wood. As I came in his office door he greeted me with, "Don't tell me your problem. I'll tell you. Courtney Whitney is an idiot. Douglas is a great man, but he has a weakness for surrounding himself with incompetents."

With Wood's quiet support, I got Charlie Murphy installed as Whitney's "assistant." Despite Wood's characterization, Whitney was acute enough to realize that Murphy was imperiously in the process of taking him over—just as he had the Duke of Windsor. Whitney protested successfully.

Charlie was replaced by A. B. C. (Cal) Whipple, a tactful, facile editor. Cal negotiated Whitney's manuscript into four barely respectable excerpts, which we ran in 1955. I had to spend more time than I should have in the author's apartment soothing ruffled feelings.

We rarely saw the Big General, but comments written on the Whitney-Whipple manuscript we could identify as being in MacArthur's hand. Cal absorbed enough MacArthuriana to parody one of the general's communiqués in a memo to me: "By the Grace of God Almighty and despite superior enemy forces I have accomplished the impossible . . . with my Army, my Navy and my Air Force . . . while at the same time overcoming the obstacles thrown in my path by Washington, with no other resources than those of Courtney Whitney."

Cal was entitled to blow off steam privately—we were all embarrassed by what, despite Cal's work, was a mediocre product.

One day in 1962, completely unexpectedly, General Whitney arrived in Luce's office with a cardboard box. In it, written in longhand on legal-length, yellow, lined paper were MacArthur's own reminiscences—so labeled because he refused to allow them to be called either history or memoirs.

This time it was not a matter of buying on faith. The product was there. I had no difficulty recommending what Luce obviously wanted—that we buy it. No bargaining was necessary. It had been conveyed to us that MacArthur had a definite sum in mind for all rights—magazine, book, movie, and television. It was $1 million, and when, on cue, we offered it, he said simply, "That will be very satisfactory."

There wasn't much editing involved, in the normally accepted use of the word. If you have genuine MacArthur prose, you find that purple becomes the color of choice. You don't try to change its rolling, sonorous, majestic quality.

Our real task was a straightforward adaptation of selective choice passages from the manuscript plus appropriately grand illustrative material; Gene Farmer, a former correspondent and foreign editor with a grasp of history, had the right combination of admiration, diplomacy, and editorial judgment to produce the *Life* serialization, which ran in 1964. My role was more that of a project manager and a wall off of which the general himself could bounce his verbal comments.

The brigadier general mentioned earlier was undoubtedly right about the scarcity of suitable companions for the general. I must have been acceptable. I spent a lot of time in his Waldorf Towers living room, surrounded by massive Oriental screens and listening to what usually were monologues— stories about his father, Lieutenant General Arthur MacArthur, and about historic battles. I became genuinely fond of my elderly friend, and I seemed to have some influence with him.

For instance, he was adamant about not having an index or a table of contents for the book. *Life* didn't need them, but, on behalf of McGraw-Hill, the book publisher, I had to overcome the author's conviction that "book reviewers don't really read much. They look up a couple of items that catch the eye and base their conclusions on them. I'm not going to help those so-and-sos. I'm going to force them to read this book." He may have had a point, but I convinced him that genuine scholars had to be able to have points of reference.

If the general could be brought around to the understanding of himself as a historian, it was harder to convince him that he might be considered a plagiarist. We had been horrified to find out, too late, that Whitney, in his MacArthur book, had duplicated a passage from the earlier book by General Willoughby. The scene was a hill near Seoul, already in enemy hands and burning. The defeated Korean troops were streaming by on each side, and MacArthur was already planning how, eventually, to snatch victory from defeat. Whitney's words were exactly like Willoughby's, and here they were again in MacArthur's manuscript.

"Plagiarism? Nonsense. I wrote them and just made them available to both Willoughby and Court. The words indisputably belong to me."

Of course, they did start out as his words. But after careful explanations, he seemed to understand that his ideological enemies, of whom he was always conscious, might find the apparent duplications a target. He reluctantly accepted some minimal changes. That hill was still there, to be sure. Seoul was still burning in its "agony of destruction," and there was "no whimpering, no hysteria" among the fleeing refugees. Still, the passage sounded a little different in his version and no charge of plagiarism was ever voiced.

Then there was a movie agent, who was absolutely awed by being admitted to the Presence for a short talk. MacArthur dismayed him by saying that it was his strong preference that the film rights not be sold until ten years after he died. The agent later had a hot idea and asked me to pass it on. John Wayne had his own production company and wanted the title role. At first there was no answer from the general, implying assent, but then later he said: "I have looked up this man, and he is a ruffian. He will not play me." We never did sell the movie rights.

Mostly, my sessions with the general would go on from around noon until we would break for a late lunch. He never offered to call Waldorf room service. Once I had to say, "General, today I am under higher orders than yours. It's my birthday, and my wife is on the ground floor waiting to take me to lunch."

"That's quite all right. May I ask what birthday?"

I mumbled, "Fifty-six."

"Oh, I wouldn't think you were a day over thirty-five."

I waved my cigar and said, "These will do me in."

"Well, if you wait for cigars to kill you, you'll live to be a hundred."

Compared to Truman's promise of 100 years if I kept up those morning walks, I preferred cigars as a specific for longevity.

At first, MacArthur's trembling hands, as he tried to locate his pipe with a lighted match, made me nervous, but I got so I didn't notice it. He neutralized the palsy when speaking in public with a tight grip on the edges of the podium. In conversation he frequently acknowledged that he was mortal, but one came to believe it only slowly.

The Japanese unwittingly contributed to the liveliness of MacArthur's narrative. They burned his records at Manila covering the time before their capture of that city, so he had to rely substantially on the colorful items which remained in his durable memory.

As MacArthur remembered them, all his commanders were skillful, daring, and resourceful. All his former enemies praised him, and even I gained some luster by association with him. In an autograph on a portrait, he wrote that I had "brilliantly guided this project past many pitfalls." We hadn't yet passed all of them when he wrote that.

The fact is that MacArthur did all the things he wrote about and did them in superlative style. His almost boyish satisfactions were disarming at times. Once we had to use an illustrator to re-create items in his story. He took a look at an unpretentious sketch showing him as a young officer killing two Filipino guerrillas. He turned to Farmer and said, "Ah, Gene, when knighthood was in flower, eh?"

Douglas MacArthur (early 1960s).

The general anticipated his own death by autographing flyleaves of his book, as well as the portrait, in advance. He also read every word of testimony before Wilbur Mills's Ways and Means Committee, which was considering a Kennedy tax proposal. The bill that finally passed had a provision by which a one-shot contractor, a MacArthur—or a Sonny Liston—could set a date on which to accept a large single payment and have it spread over several years for income tax purposes. MacArthur hit the exact year which would turn out to be the most advantageous for him and his estate. In that connection I have a handwritten note asking that Courtney get $100,000 of his million.

The general milked his final bows a bit. His "Old soldiers never die, they just fade away" speech moved not only Congress but a whole nation. A graduation speech he quoted to end the book will live with a whole West Point generation: "I want you to know that when I cross the river my last conscious thoughts will be of the Corps—and the Corps—and the Corps." He left me with a permanent personal memory, too. Although he had been ill, he walked me, as usual, to the door of his apartment, holding my arm. "I've looked that old devil, Death, in the eye a hundred times," he said, "but this time I think he's got me." It was the last time I saw him alive.

The general had gone over suggestions for his burial place as meticulously as he had followed the income tax hearings. A restored old southern courthouse in Norfolk was to be his memorial. Despite his sincere regard for his father, he chose not to join him in Arlington.

Mrs. MacArthur was a wonder. When insisting that she be allowed to accompany him on his wartime submarine escape to Australia, he had said of her, "We drink from the same cup." To every mourner at the large "private" ceremony, Mrs. MacArthur said, "Thank you, thank you," and had a little personal message for each one. When I happened to be taking her in to dinner in Norfolk, she waved aside my concern over the strain it must be with the comment, "The General would have wanted me to do it this way."

After the last ceremony at the memorial I slipped out of the rotunda, along with General George Kenney, MacArthur's air commander in the Pacific, in order to spare Mrs. MacArthur two more handshakes. Kenney told how he had lectured his boss after Washington had ordered MacArthur not to engage the Chinese across the Yalu River: "'General, commanders are for winning wars. If you hadn't gone to that trade school up on the Hudson where they teach you all about that sacred duty you would have gone ahead and should have.' MacArthur told me: 'As long as I wear this uniform' (he pointed) 'I will obey orders.'"

19

Politics as a Great Game—
for Editors and Readers

᠁ Although presidential politics do not produce Nobel Prize–winning writing, they do, in print, produce some rich examples of Americana. One condition is that there should be some genuine suspense about who will win. Another is that journalistic coverage should get below the surface of what, particularly on TV, amounts to saturation coverage of a staged "set-piece" show.

The year 1952 provided ideal opportunities for *Life*-type coverage. Two attractive presidential candidates eventually emerged. The TV coverage of the Republican convention in Chicago was so boring that the *Chicago Tribune* station used convention time to run old movies and outdrew its competition. *Life* had the troops to record all kinds of on- and off-the-floor events and the time to analyze the mass of material and select for publication only the items that added up to what contributed to a thrilling contest.

Partly because of my goof in the Truman-Dewey campaign of 1948, when I allowed a caption to run calling Dewey "the next President," I was going to lean over backward to give both sides exposure in *Life*.

Truman definitely was not a candidate, so the Democratic contest was wide open. The conventional wisdom was that Robert A. Taft controlled the Republican nominating process, but there were hoarse, audible whispers of "Taft can't win!"

The entry of Dwight D. Eisenhower into competitive politics was not unexpected, even though he may well have thought that he could just wait for a spontaneous summons. The general concluded that he was closer to being a Republican than anything else, a belief not shared by some diehard conservatives.

As the campaign year developed, the front-runners were proceeding by different routes. Estes Kefauver, riding on the publicity of his televised Senate committee investigation of organized crime, was winning primaries, but the Democratic Party bosses were against him—perhaps because of his investigations. The Keef's twenty-hour-a-day campaigning also called attention to his weakness as a national candidate. Noting that he spoke at a rate of about ten words a minute, *Life* writer Robert Wallace characterized his appearance as that of a splendidly prosperous undertaker and speculated that people "might not vote for Old Coonskin if they thought he was going to bury them." Estes was cheerful enough, however, in thrusting the hand with which he offered compulsive shakes toward our photographer for a frontispiece to the Wallace article.

Bob Taft may have deserved his chance at the office he had sought for so long. He was an exemplary senator. He had earned his nickname, Mr. Republican. His organization, however, had ridden mercilessly over regional party conventions, and this became an issue in the finals at Chicago.

Life was developing all the film and producing all the text and layouts in Chicago, where the text was then edited and checked and sent directly to the nearby Donnelley printing plant. Normally, my direction of the staff was scarcely visible, but here I indulged myself in some direct control by stationing myself in the front row of the mezzanine press section with binoculars, dropping notes directing photographers to lively looking floor areas (the FCC wouldn't let us use walkie-talkies).

Viewers of both parties' conventions had been given a *Life* preview of Chicago. There was a photographic essay on the Taft family in Cincinnati and one on Adlai Stevenson at home, still undecided about running. Eisenhower, as a civilian, was appraised in a large article. If we couldn't get enthusiastic about the Keef, we at least cast a vote for his wife, Nancy. A double-page diagram showed television viewers a plan of the convention floor so that they could follow what was going on.

The key question about the Republican convention was whether Taft's establishment strength would prevail in seating delegates from state conventions (Eisenhower was running ahead in states where there were direct primaries). There was a showdown in Texas, where the Taft organization had its way—temporarily. *Life* showed dramatically how delegates were pressured by the establishment forces, with a picture of J. Carroll Reese of

Tennessee in action on the floor. Viewers of the 1948 national convention, which he had chaired, may remember the spectacle of his tongue darting rapidly in and out like an anteater's.

In the meantime the Eisenhower Texans allowed sarcastically that the precinct conventions by which Taft delegates (twenty-two versus sixteen for Ike) were designated "could have been held in phone booths." But, said conservative Henry Zweifel at the Texas convention, "I'd rather lose with Taft than win with Eisenhower."

The bitterness from Texas continued in Chicago, with early convention proceedings punctuated by scuffles and punches thrown imprecisely by delegates who wouldn't have lasted ten seconds on a hockey rink. The question still was which of the disputed delegations from Texas and three other states would be seated.

The Taft people allowed fuel to be added to the so-called moral issue of "phone booth" selection by having the proceedings of the credentials committee closed to the press. Just to show that it could be done, Francis Miller of *Life,* using a camera concealed in his necktie, photographed the session—it didn't look all that sinister in the picture we ran. But the fact that the picture was forbidden did call attention to the attempt at secrecy. The lame duck committee dutifully voted to seat the Taft delegates, although an appeal to the floor of the convention was still to come.

For the convention itself, *Life* assigned fourteen photographers accompanied by reporters because, with the possibility of an early deadlock, no one could know what pictures would turn out to be significant. Three full-color cover photographs—of Taft, Eisenhower, and Earl Warren, the most likely compromise choice—were engraved and made ready to slap on the presses once the nominee was selected. Against the possibility of a prolonged deadlock there was an alternate cover and a story on the USS *United States,* with a three-page color foldout, which could have been moved up into the lead position. The ship had set a new transatlantic speed record.

The *Life* staff roamed the hotel rooms and corridors, the caucus rooms and convention halls, watched recognizable representatives of the candidates, kept an eye on private dining rooms in the Stockyards Inn next to the convention auditorium, and even located conferences in hotel kitchens. Much of our coverage of wheeler dealers turned out to be, as expected, useless.

Eisenhower's very professional chief of operations, Herb Brownell, stayed mostly hidden. But Ike had a now-you-see-'em-now-you-don't pair of movers and shakers—Governors Arthur Summerfield of Michigan and John Fine of Pennsylvania.

The key to the nomination was a vote on the credentials of the disputed delegations, and Pennsylvania was crucial. *Life* reporters and photographers observed at least seven Fine-Summerfield meetings. Fine was particularly elusive, and at one point a harassed convention big shot grabbed photographer Alfred Eisenstaedt by the shoulders and implored, "You must tell us where he is!" The Fine-Summerfield actions were recorded in a sequence of eighteen photographs.

Eisenhower did capture Pennsylvania, and it remained only for the favorite sons to switch to him on the second ballot. The appropriate cover picture of the winner started rolling off the presses.

Laying out a late-closing story is hectic and satisfying. The photographers had exposed 35,000 frames, mostly of 35mm film. Of these, the negative editors selected 2,000 for enlargement. With most of the issue already on press, there were only 16 pages open. One of these was for the table of contents and photographic credits, which can't be closed until the issue is complete. Another page had to be reserved for the editorial, which, naturally, was to be on the convention results. That left 14 pages.

What was intimidating was not so much the mountain of prints (we used 56 of the 2,000) but the eyes of the photographers boring into my back. When more than one photographer was involved in a story, I never looked to see who took each picture as I made layouts.

To meet the press deadline, I had to make arbitrary advance decisions about placing subject matter. Out of fourteen pages, two were set aside for the victorious candidates; two were devoted to the victory of the Eisenhower forces on the disputed delegates. Two went to the mechanics of television coverage. Two more recorded the significant operations of the Fine-Summerfield team, something TV viewers didn't see. Two pages were needed to wind up the narrative, with the elusive Herb Brownell surfacing at last to pass on the decision that Richard Nixon was the choice for vice president. Two pages seemed necessary to introduce Mamie Eisenhower and Pat Nixon. That left just two pages for the spectacle of the convention and the participation of such notables as Herbert Hoover, Tom Dewey, and MacArthur.

In the same issue as the Republican convention was a photographic essay, mostly by Cornell Capa, on Adlai Stevenson in his elegant home, trying to decide whether to run. Readers got a look at his distinguished forebears, too.

The technical plan for covering the Democratic convention pretty much duplicated that of its predecessor. The conflict this time involved a Young Turk movement spearheaded by Franklin Roosevelt Jr. to require a loyalty pledge aimed at preventing southern delegates from bolting the eventual candidate. The pledge had no support from the potentially victorious Stevenson forces, and Estes Kefauver alienated support he might have obtained from the South by agreeing to it.

The suspense continued to be provided by Stevenson himself—until an obviously spontaneous demonstration after his speech to the convention as host governor brought the rueful admission, "I guess I'm stuck." Eisenhower's popularity made it imperative that the Democrats have a strong candidate, a point emphasized by Truman, who had some doubts about Stevenson.

Despite the television coverage, both *Life* convention issues were virtual sellouts on the newsstands. The campaign was lively and ideally adapted to photo coverage. Harry Truman was characteristically "pouring it on" for Stevenson. Adlai's literate wit kept the opposition off balance with light jabs, if not haymakers. Eisenhower projected his extrovert personality successfully. His manifest sincerity on issues of governmental responsibility and his ability to impart a sense of personal involvement were both evident to enthusiastic crowds.

Then came a hitch in what otherwise would have been a triumphal march to victory. The existence of a fund for Nixon's personal expenses, contributed by friends, became known. The Democrats characterized it as slush, and the question for several days was whether Eisenhower should dump his vice presidential candidate from the ticket.

Nixon went on TV with an emotional appeal to the public to believe in his honesty, citing the facts that his wife wore a cloth coat and that they did receive a spaniel pup named Checkers, a gift which Nixon said he would not return. The response to the telecast was overwhelmingly pro-Nixon and, whether it was this positive response or that his running mate had proved himself "clean as a hound's tooth" (a figure of speech Eisenhower appropriated from Theodore Roosevelt), the ticket remained intact.

During the campaign, *Life* duly recorded such details as the engaging hole in the sole of Stevenson's shoe and our not-so-trivial chagrin over Joe McCarthy's reelection in Wisconsin, where Eisenhower had injudiciously received him. Stevenson had some troubles of his own, including an inadvertent admission that there was a "mess in Washington," which infuriated Truman. I later saw an unmailed letter Truman had kept in his desk which said, "Dear Governor: I have come to the conclusion that you are embarrassed by having the President of the United States in your corner in this campaign."

Direct from President
Eisenhower's inaugural ball,
I lay out a lead article with
Assistant Art Editor Mike Phillips
(1953, photo by Frank Scherschel,
courtesy Time Inc.).

If there was a clincher to Eisenhower's overwhelmingly successful campaign, it was probably his pledge "I shall go to Korea," which was reassuring to a war-weary electorate.

Luce's Republican friends told him that despite conspicuous partisanship in editorials, *Life*'s graphic but evenhanded presentation had the most to do with Eisenhower's success. I was happier with the fact that Democrats generally, including my overwhelmingly pro-Stevenson staff, thought we had kept our noses clean. At one point Luce had wondered whether maybe Eisenhower was "too good to be true," and he wondered about his intellectual depth. But now Luce believed that the new president owed him something.

From the Willkie campaign on, Luce, personally, was a political presence. In late 1952 he mused, "The only job I would really want would be secretary of state, but I would sincerely advise the president not to offer it to me." John Foster Dulles had a firm lock on that job—he had been the Republican foreign policy spokesman during those lean years.

Luce felt strongly that his support of Ike warranted a major ambassadorship for his wife, Clare Boothe Luce. She got one—Italy—and distinguished herself with a settlement of the Trieste problem. As a kind of shadow ambassador, Harry himself was a plus, particularly with Italian businessmen and the press, but his absence for long periods put the managing editors pretty much on our own.

On the editorial page, *Life* settled down to being pro-Republican. Even there Luce sometimes found himself in opposition to Republican foreign policy, although he approved of Eisenhower's domestic views.

Nixon's presence in the Republican hierarchy worried me, if not Luce and some others at Time Inc. If the vice presidency could have been considered just a haven where Alexander Throttlebottoms could be stashed away, Nixon would have been no problem, but Eisenhower's actuarial expectations, due to two serious illnesses, weren't all that favorable.

Eventually, it seemed to me, *Life*'s readers ought to be able to make a judgment on the controversial character of the vice president, who was the proverbial heartbeat away from the top job. At nobody's suggestion but my own, I asked a star staff writer, Robert Coughlan, to investigate the pros and cons about Nixon. As a policy question, of course, I had to show Luce the result, which was skillfully done in the form of an imaginary debate, "resolved," etc. Luce was inclined to temporize a bit and suggested that I check the manuscript with James Keogh of *Time*. Jim was already an avowed Nixon partisan and had written a book which was unabashedly favorable, so I told Luce, "I respect Jim, but he is the last person I would consult on this subject."

Luce admitted that Coughlan had done well but fussed a bit about the timing. He finally registered his *nihil obstat,* and the article ran just before the 1956 Republican convention. There was not much likelihood that the renomination of the winning ticket was in danger. Still, the voters had a chance to consider the subject during the replay of the contest with Stevenson. I had made at least a gesture at sustaining tranquillity with my own editorial conscience.

Nixon, on his own, narrowly lost to Kennedy in 1960. He still had something to say and said it in his *Six Crises.* He was always most plausible in small, private groups. And so he was when James Shepley, his friend and later president of Time Inc., and I negotiated magazine rights for the book.

Nixon volunteered to us convincing reasons why he shouldn't run for governor of California:

1) His specialty was foreign affairs, and he shouldn't waste time, if he won, wrestling with California's disastrous financial condition.

2) The California legislature was "venal," and Sacramento was a "hick town."

3) Adlai got renominated without running for anything between elections, didn't he?

Nixon didn't follow his early reasoning. He ran for governor in 1962, lost, and issued his famous sour grapes statement: "You won't have Dick Nixon to kick around anymore."

The first parts of the book manuscript were promising. An accomplished Doubleday editor, Alvin Moscow, who was far superior to the average run of ghostwriters, put the first five crises into publishable form. He worked under what I thought was a cruel atmosphere, in an office without air conditioning during a hot summer above the Nixon Bel Air garage. The sixth crisis, the 1960 campaign, the author thought he should do by himself, so he disappeared into the mountains.

My last trip to Bel Air, with Doubleday's chief editor, Ken McCormick, was to go over part six. This one section, to my dismay, seemed book length all by itself, and I spent most of a day reading and taking notes. In the late afternoon, having finished a little before Ken, I started on a walk to clear my head. I do not consider myself charismatic to dogs, but Checkers followed me. When I returned she wasn't there, and I was dismayed over possibly losing the most famous dog in America. She returned on her own, though, and I faced the unpleasant job of a critique.

The length was much more Doubleday's problem than mine, but other people's excess verbiage does bother an editor. I kept saying things like, "But Dick, no one cares what happened at every airport." (Actually, *Life* had published a notable picture of Nixon glancing anxiously at his wristwatch at an airport while absentmindedly shaking someone's hand.) As I talked from my notes, McCormick was frowning, but afterward he said tolerantly, "Most of what you said made sense, but remember, Ed, a 600-page book sells better than one of 500 pages."

In any event, *Life* could select what it wanted for serialization. Mc-Cormick went back to see Nixon the next morning and then reported, "You had a terrible effect on our man. If you think he has a five o'clock shadow, you should see him after he has stayed up all night and not shaved. He was working on your corrections."

There was some hidden dynamite in the Nixon treatment of the Bay of Pigs operation. The text of the book said that Kennedy had been briefed during the campaign on intervention plans. Kennedy, the president, obtained a prepublication copy while *Life* was putting to press the installment with that section of the book in it. Kennedy denied that his CIA briefing in July

1960 had included a reference to U.S. operations in Cuba, and Allen Dulles, then director of the CIA, backed him up. The telephone wires in and out of my office hummed for a few days.

In one exchange with Nixon, I said, "*Life* can't call the president a liar."

"But I know he was briefed," Nixon said.

"Dick, you're a lawyer, and you know that you have only hearsay evidence. The only two people at the briefing were President Kennedy and Dulles, and they both say you are wrong."

I talked to Dulles more than half a dozen times and to his successor, John McCone, several times, too. I finally got a wording of the passage in *Life* that satisfied Kennedy, and I told Nixon what we were going to do. We were *not* going to use his statement that Kennedy had been fully briefed on Cuba. He let it go at that, and in the second and subsequent printings of *Six Crises* he had a footnote, without changing the text of the book itself, acknowledging the White House statement. Later he autographed my copy of the book "with special gratitude" for my "support" in the "Second Battle of the Bay of Pigs."

Life could have been accused of being memoir-ridden, but I did turn down the two volumes of Eisenhower's presidency. Luce remonstrated, saying, "Don't we always run presidential memoirs?"

I replied that we should "spare the readers from boredom." Luce countered by asking me to indicate a few of the "least boring" passages. I did my best and didn't hear another word from him about the matter.

20

From Hemingway: "Wonderful . . .
I Hope You Feel Good about It Too"

A cartoonist for the old *New York Herald Tribune,* H. T. Webster, had a number of regular features in that paper. One was "Moments You Would Like to Have Last Forever." That was how I felt about Ernest Hemingway's reaction to the way *Life* handled *The Old Man and the Sea.*

Ernest Hemingway was a literary hero from the late 1920s on. He and *Life* were not complete strangers—he had written captions for clips from the Loyalist documentary *The Spanish Earth* during the civil war, but I didn't meet him until a month or so before D-Day in wartime London, when I ran into him at that party.

Our paths did not cross again for eight years, although I suppose I proved myself somewhat of a peeping Tom looking at pictures Bob Capa took while he and his girlfriend, Pinky, were hamming it up with Ernest while he was recovering from his skull fracture in a London hospital. A couple of the pictures showed Pinky parting the back of Hemingway's hospital gown, revealing that he had a very small rear end for such a big man. In later years Hemingway laughed when I told this story.

At *Life* in 1952 some squabbling developed as to who could take credit for finding *The Old Man.* One might say that it came in over the transom. A volunteer agent, Leland Hayward, the film producer, had shown it to *Ladies' Home Journal.* It was rejected, and, unaccountably, the *Journal* failed to tip off its sister magazine, the *Saturday Evening Post.* Hayward then brought the manuscript to Sidney James, assistant managing editor of *Life.* Sid knew Hayward from his days in Los Angeles as chief of the *Time-Life* bureau.

Sid gave it to me without comment. I took it home, read it overnight, and, without consulting anyone else, simply said, "Buy it." The price tag was $30,000. There was a stipulation that not a single word could be cut out or changed.

The book was not divisible into installments. Art director Tudor selected a creative and sensitive illustrator, Noel Sickles. We sent Alfred Eisenstaedt to photograph the author in Cuba. Hemingway adopted a boisterous, somewhat frightening attitude to begin with. At one point he pretended he was going to throw Alfred off the pier. Another time he noticed the diminutive Eisenstaedt shrinking from the hordes of mangy and snarling cats, both domesticated and stray, which infested the Hemingway *Finca Vigia.*

"Alfred," he said, glowering, "you do not like cats?"

"But Papa," insisted Alfred, "I love cats." Privately he conceded that he was repelled by these, but only because of their number and condition.

Hemingway wanted to wear only swimming trunks for the photographs. "My body," he said, "women love my body." He listed some glamorous examples. Alfred jollied him into a thin, yellow sports shirt, and the result was the frontispiece for *Life*'s presentation. Alfred took another close-up for the cover of the issue, Labor Day, 1952, which didn't have many ads; thus I had room to publish the entire 30,000-word text as promised. We fitted the book exactly by reducing and/or enlarging the size of illustrations.

Hemingway autographed copies of the issue for me and the others connected with its publication and sent me a handwritten letter in the script with which I was to become familiar. Sometimes his lines were reasonably horizontal, but frequently they slanted down from left to right. "Please let me thank you," he wrote, "for the wonderful job you did. . . . I wanted to tell you how much I appreciated it and how happy I am. . . . usually there is always something wrong that spoils a thing for you if you want it perfect. But there was nothing wrong with your work. . . . I hope you feel good about it too."

Naturally, I felt good. But I reminded Hemingway, a baseball fan, that when the great second baseman Rogers Hornsby became a manager he was criticized for not praising well-executed plays. "That's what they hired out for," Hornsby would say. I also said that the best thing all of us involved in the presentation could do was restrain ourselves from lousing up a fine thing.

There was controversy within the book business as to whether Hemingway was ruining sales of the book itself by allowing every word of it to

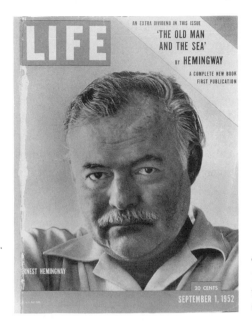

The *Life* cover for September 1, 1952, a close-up of Hemingway taken by Alfred Eisenstaedt (*Life,* ©Time Inc.).

appear in *Life* before its publication as a book. What a bargain at a twenty-cent newsstand price! Nonetheless, the book became a best-seller, though it never rose to the top of the list. At least the magazine publication didn't prevent Hemingway from getting the Nobel Prize for literature.

As I and my successors found out, no other Hemingway manuscripts were floating around. There were reports several years later, though—a few people whose judgment I respected had seen excerpts—that a manuscript dealing with the Paris of the 1920s, vintage Hemingway, existed. I wanted that very badly.

Feelers put out through another Hemingway friend, Will Lang, *Life*'s Paris correspondent, revealed in 1959 that, yes, we might get the manuscript, but first Ernest wanted to report for *Life* on the bullfighting competition between the great Dominguín, who had come out of retirement, and the newest star, Ordoñez. I do not like bullfights. I secretly—though vainly—always want the bull to win. But this matchup was probably news, and the fact that Hemingway was doing the reporting would make it so. He went to Spain under contract to *Life*. We hoped for a manuscript by early fall.

The title of what turned out to be a series was "The Dangerous Summer," and our summer was certainly a long one. The report, originally discussed at three or four thousand words, was also contracted for at $30,000.

Hemingway talked of it as an appendix for a reissue of his classic *Death in the Afternoon*. In August 1959 Hemingway hinted that he might prefer to do a shorter article, and he was annoyed because someone at *Life* had complained about his expenses. These, witnesses reported, were high because, in character, he was always buying drinks for the house. By March 8, 1960, however, he had written 6,500 words, "which is a lot of words for me," he pointed out. Then, voilà, by March 31, he was up to 63,562 words (counted by Ernest himself), and by early June the total was 108,746! And he wanted to go back to Spain to gather more material for an ender! This bounty of words overwhelmed me.

Hemingway was touchy about each of his words—he considered them golden, so cutting even a few was a major diplomatic negotiation. Hindsight suggests that Hemingway was fiercer in defense of doubtful material than when he knew they were dealing with his best.

We had some inconclusive talks over drinks when Hemingway was in New York. He selected the bar at the Hotel Barclay and drank only twelve-year-old House of Lords scotch. He explained that hardly any bartender, even in boondock saloons, dared to adulterate that. His size and beard made him pretty easy to recognize, but he pretended that he didn't want to be. "When a guy asks me, 'Aren't you Ernest Hemingway?'" he said, "I answer, 'No, I know him and hate that son of a bitch.'"

Hemingway did realize that what he had produced was more than we had contracted for and offered, I don't know how sincerely, to let us out of the deal. He didn't suggest that he reimburse us for the expenses, however. And he wrote me that, in view of our interest, he had "stalled all other offers" on the Paris book.

The massive bullfighting manuscript had bits of good Hemingway in it, and some that was not so good. His descriptions of how Spain looked after his long self-exile ("I wouldn't go back while friends of mine were in jail") was vivid and evocative. He did have a good time there. There were descriptions of how his party "ate and drank well." He attracted the admiration of touring American girls. He played softball with his friend, A. E. Hotchner, who "had a good pair of hands."

Hemingway fussed about the practice of shortening the horns of the bulls for the current fights. This upset the bulls' instinctive grasp of the exact location of their tormentors. He dwelt lengthily on the technical details of the matador's trade, and his descriptions of one encounter after another seemed pretty repetitious, approaching the boring.

To cut the verbiage down to something almost acceptable, I imposed on the good nature, skill, and loyalty of Ralph Graves, then the articles editor, by asking him to cut it during his vacation. Ralph got the 100,000-odd words down to a respectable length, but when this version hit Hemingway's *finca*, there was an explosion. In a phone call to me during an electrical storm it was hard to tell Hemingway's invective from the thunder.

In his book *Papa Hemingway,* Hotchner says I displayed "great coolness under fire." I don't give myself that much credit, though, because the resulting compromise contained several thousand words that Hemingway forced back in. A notation to my secretary during this period said that I thought the project might eventually be known as "Thompson's Folly." The work never did become an appendix to *Death in the Afternoon.*

I don't know why, in 1961, Hemingway shot himself, and neither did Hotch, who had spent a lot of time with him. There was an incidence of suicide in the Hemingway family, and I have a wild guess that discouragement with his own writing had something to do with it. Some colleagues, perhaps soundly, doubted my judgment about accepting less than grade-A Hemingway, even with *A Moveable Feast* as a prize.

I had a good relationship with Hemingway's widow, Mary, who had been a *Time* London correspondent before she and Ernest met during World War II. She had some questions about whether it was in acceptable taste for her, as a widow, to rush into print too early with *A Feast.* Eventually Mary and the wise Hemingway lawyer, Alfred Rice, agreed to *Life*'s purchase of the serialization rights. It was everything it had been predicted to be. David Scherman did a masterful job of adapting part of it for the magazine, and it was published in 1964.

Sticking with Ernest through "The Dangerous Summer" and afterward did pay off, but, due to the tragedy of his death, I didn't feel as happy and triumphant as I might have about getting *A Feast* later.

21

Three Weeks of *Life,*
Lucky Breaks and All

❧ The memorable special projects—Hemingway, MacArthur, Truman, et al.—were personally exciting and punctuated dramatically my days at *Life*. But whether there was such a feature on tap or not, the magazine still had to be created every week. Thus I now invite readers to look over my shoulder during three frenetic weeks when three pretty typical consecutive issues were shaped, reshaped, and then shaped again.

The year is 1956. Publication dates are October 29, November 5, and November 12. I have been managing editor for eight years, and as always I will yes or no each proposed article and decide how many pages will be devoted to it.

In those days an issue was built around three anchors: a lead story for the news section, a pictorial essay, and a major text article, the last two having what we considered "lasting value." In the prosperous autumn of 1956, each issue ran more than 200 pages and contained as many as 30 items, most of them with pictures. The number of editorial pages varied with advertising sales but was always at least 51 percent of the total.

Six million copies had to be printed, so the components of each issue were produced in installments. Work on full-color pages started as long as nine weeks before publication, whereas the news section closed five or six days ahead of printing. I would be sending to the printer pages of at least three different issues all at the same time.

These staggered deadlines would be complicated enough if one were operating in a stable, predictable world, but the editors had to react to the unexpected—which we actually hoped for—if *Life* was to be as good as it could be.

One anchor for the October 29 and succeeding issues had been in preparation for two years: a serialization of excerpts from Winston Churchill's *A History of the English-Speaking Peoples.* The manuscript was vintage Churchill prose, much of it written in the 1930s while he was at the height of his literary powers. (From then until he returned to government in 1939, he could accurately list his occupation as "writer.")

Paring down the 500,000-word manuscript into installments that would fit into *Life*'s editorial space called for considerably more than just hacking away at the words. I assigned Emmet John Hughes, a brilliant journalist, to the editor-cum-diplomat handling of the Great Man and his copy. Emmet had been my articles editor, then had gone on leave to write speeches for Dwight D. Eisenhower (he is credited with the "I shall go to Korea" statement in the 1952 presidential campaign). Emmet was back on *Life* and available for a trip to Sicily to visit with Churchill, who was on a holiday with the Luces.

The author had to be persuaded to write a preface that would make the centuries-old events relevant to twentieth-century Americans. He responded to Hughes's diplomacy with eight pages, winding up with: "It is in the hope that contemplation of the trials and tribulations of our forefathers may not only fortify the English-speaking people of today, but also play some small part in uniting the whole world, that I present this account."

Hughes and I agreed that, to keep the installments within the bounds of space and the narrative clear, we needed brief "bridges" to connect the best passages and give the reader a full measure of Churchillian eloquence. Hughes wrote a few and submitted them to the author. He liked them and gave Hughes carte blanche to treat the rest of his volumes similarly.

Churchill bit off a vast amount of English history in the October 29 installment: the reign of Henry VIII, which included the exploration of the New World, the basic concept of the navy which later ruled the waves, and the Protestant Reformation.

Churchill's Henry was many notches above the bibulous, lecherous boor depicted by the movies' Charles Laughton. Originally destined for the church, Henry was a student and theologian. He was pictured in *Life* in his prime in a rich, full-length portrait, a fine figure of a man, complete with sables and jewels.

Pictorial essays were inserted along with the Churchill text. Assignments were given to Gjon Mili and Dmitri Kessel. Because Mili was from Albania and Kessel the Ukraine, an office wag called the subject "the English-Spicking Pipples." Both were highly literate journalists, however. Mili captured the atmosphere of the era, for instance, with moving photographs of Hampton Court Palace and the dark, sinister Tower of London, scene of hundreds of executions, including those of two of Henry's wives.

The pictorial showed the British navy of the day, also in color, in spectacular contemporary paintings. It displayed portraits of six of the wives, none of whom looked as sexy as Henry. A painting of Anne Boleyn was to be the cover.

A traditional lead article for the issue would have been that year's presidential contest. James McConaughy, *Time-Life* Washington bureau chief, had been assigned to write an analysis for someplace else in the issue. He concluded that the real contest was for a congressional majority. Personally visiting twenty-two states and drawing on the reports of thirty other correspondents, McConaughy correctly anticipated the probability that Eisenhower would face a hostile Congress. No surprises, so no lead here.

One potential new voice on the Supreme Court was more than worth noting. It was that of a relatively obscure nominee to become an associate justice, William J. Brennan Jr. A Roman Catholic and a Democrat, Brennan told the *Life* reporter—in support of the only cause with which he was identified publicly, court reform—that "delayed justice is bad justice." If *Life* didn't anticipate that Brennan would become the forceful and articulate leader of the Court's liberal justices, neither did the president who nominated him. Eisenhower was said to have expressed rueful surprise later.

Of interest to all parents was the decision that a polio vaccine taken by mouth instead of by the Salk injection method was considered safe enough to test on babies.

Parents of movie-struck girls would read that director Otto Preminger, after considering 3,000 candidates, came up with a seventeen-year-old Iowa girl, Jean Seberg, to play Shaw's Saint Joan.

On the lighter side: a photographer was reflected in the eyes of an owl; two workmen on stilts plastered a Cleveland ceiling; Frank Lloyd Wright proposed a 528-story "stratosphere scraper," with no takers; a young Elvis Presley, in court, warily eyed two filling-station attendants he had socked.

By late in the closing week I had considered scores of items, and of the thousands of photographs submitted I had seen several hundred. Members of the picture staff and departmental editors did preliminary weeding, but

I wasn't always satisfied and would demand to see rejects and sometimes even the 35mm contact prints.

Editors devoutly hope that the Lord will provide important, exciting, spontaneous events, but He doesn't always deliver, so lesser providers have to prepare something. For that final week in October, Tuesday through Saturday, the best potential was a seasonal phenomenon. The country was in the grip of football fever, nowhere more virulent than in Texas. That state had 100,000 players in uniform each weekend, and on this one, two undefeated national-class college teams, Texas A&M and Texas Christian, would meet. Four top staff photographers were in Texas. They covered a peewee game with anxious mothers watching from the sidelines. High school cheerleaders, bare legs flashing, would be candidates later for the gyrations of the famous Dallas Cowboy troupe. Other tribal rites, such as a fifty-two-band halftime entertainment at the University of Houston and a flame-lit "Indian" village at McMurry College, were photographed in color.

The last pictures of the big game itself would arrive in New York on Saturday night for layout and shipment to *Life*'s printer in Chicago, R. R. Donnelley. A heavy rain didn't faze the zealots who jammed the stands.

But while the *Life* teams were smothering Texas, something else happened in the Pacific, between Honolulu and San Francisco.

An airplane went down. Years before, *Life* had found that pictures of crash wreckage had become repetitious. A flight mishap had to have some special aspect if *Life* were to report it. And there was something decidedly special about Pan Am Flight 943, en route to San Francisco with twenty-four passengers and a crew of seven.

During the night an engine had roared out of control. In the tenseness of the next five hours, the crew arranged with a Coast Guard weather ship for a ditching. The sea was relatively calm, and Coast Guardsmen sprayed foam on the water to provide a runway of sorts, on which the pilot managed to safely down the plane. Passengers and crew were then transferred to the Coast Guard's *Pontchartrain.* A potential disaster with a happy ending, this event had the elements of a great story. But how to get at the narrative? Obviously, no staff photographers or reporters had been on the plane.

We assumed that there would be those on board articulate enough to re-create their experiences. And it was as good a bet that, as tourists, some would have cameras. If we were willing to bid, sight unseen, we could buy film. Cash in the hand was worth more than all the promises our rivals could make. We also heard that the Coast Guard had photographed the planned crash landing.

Richard Pollard, *Life*'s San Francisco bureau chief, was one of a large crowd of newspeople crammed onto the pier on Friday waiting for the *Pontchartrain* to arrive with Flight 943's passengers and crew. In the waiting crowd were a couple of writers who would later be famous. One was Alex Haley, Coast Guard public relations officer and the future author of *Roots.* He was helpful. The other, Cornelius Ryan (author of *The Longest Day* and *A Bridge Too Far,* also best-sellers and hit movies), understandably was not. Ryan headed a task force from *Collier's,* a wobbling competitor, which wanted to buy up exclusive pictures and assemble the narrative for a later article.

Life's contingent was tougher and more professional. Pollard knew the territory. He had colleagues and friends to make up a task force. We wired the necessary cash for bargaining to San Francisco. A writer, Herbert Brean, flew out from New York. Pollard persuaded the Coast Guard to radio the *Pontchartrain* that *Life* would be at the dock prepared to buy passengers' film. *Collier's* made a deal with a Coast Guard photographer for his film, but the official ruling was that this was government property and should go into a pool for all users—including the Associated Press, local newspapers, and *Life*.

The passengers, however, were individual entrepreneurs. Pollard had arranged with a public relations friend who was meeting the *Pont* beyond the Golden Gate to scout the plane passengers for those most likely to have usable pictures. His friend walked down the gangplank behind a French doctor, pointing at the man's head, and also indicated a Dutchman, Hendrick Braat. Pollard held up five $100 bills to the Frenchman, Marcel Touze, felt a shove from behind and a voice calling him an s.o.b. He thought it was Ryan's. The *Life* cash deal was made.

In the meantime, a *Life* photographer followed the Dutchman to a hotel. He bought Braat's film for $500 cash and another $500 in a check. Philip Kunhardt, who later became managing editor of the monthly *Life,* had come up from the Los Angeles bureau to help Pollard. Kunhardt followed the Coast Guard film to the Associated Press office, where a few pictures were handed out to everyone. For second rights, he paid cash to the Coast Guard photographer, William Simpson, and dispatched the film to the *Life* lab to get prints of those pictures not selected by the pool and better reproductions of those that had been sent out over the wire.

Amateurs generally shoot in color, so there was a problem getting Eastman Kodak to process film on Friday afternoon before shutting down for the weekend. It was then 11:10 A.M., but Kodak promised to develop Touze's Kodachrome if the rolls arrived in Palo Alto, thirty-five miles away, before noon. A $10 tip to a messenger got it there.

The developed film had to be on the last plane to New York by 9 P.M. Kodak had it ready at 4:10 P.M. A former *Life* reporter who lived nearby agreed to be a messenger. She bundled her three-month-old son, who had never been outside the house before, into her car and took off. She had $1.60 in her purse, and the Kodak bill was $1.55. She had enough gas to reach the airport.

The Dutchman had shot in Agfacolor, a German film. It would take a couple of weeks to get it processed in a German lab. A local color-lab man thought that by using Ansco black-and-white developer (also German) he could get acceptable black-and-white negatives. He did.

The air express package with the Touze color pictures, the task force deduced, contained a possible cover photograph. There were also the Coast Guard black-and-whites of the crippled plane overhead, the ditching and rescue, and the later sinking of the plane, as well as Braat's shot of the *Pontchartrain* from the plane window and of 943's captain emerging as the last to leave the plane. A passing airliner had photographed the downed plane, with *Pontchartrain* nearby, from above.

Photographers waiting at the pier had taken pictures of the arrivals and joyful reunions, including a stunning exclusive shot by an Oakland freelance photographer, Lonnie Wilson. It showed an exuberant husband running away from the gangplank, carrying his weeping wife. This became the final full page for the article.

We had all the makings of a complete story except pictures of the inside of the cabin during the tense hours before dawn. The task force had heard that a seabee on board, Albert Spear, might have something, but he had checked out of his hotel, presumably for the airport, leaving a message: "If any of those bastards are looking for me they can see my lawyer." The air express package was on board before Kunhardt and Pollard found Spear at the airport. He had had his roll of film developed and said that it wasn't any good. Kunhardt held the negatives up to the light, however, and saw the shapes of passengers waiting for the ditching. These included a fuzzy image of three-year-old twins in life jackets being held by their parents.

Ruby Dami is carried away by her husband after surviving the Pacific Ocean ditching of an airplane and being rescued at sea in October 1956. This photo, by Lonnie Wilson, was the *Life* article's closing page.

Getting this to New York involved finding a passenger who would carry it. A late boarder running for the plane turned out to be a golfing partner of Pollard's. He was wearing an official tie of the Princeton Stage Club, Kunhardt's. Identification was set for the *Life* messenger who picked up the film at the airport in New York.

At 9:10 P.M. Pollard and Kunhardt went to the airport bar and ordered two double Gibsons each. Brean wrote almost all night and filed his passenger interviews by teletype at 5 A.M. Saturday before going to bed—temporarily.

Now, the scene shifts to New York, on Saturday, for the closing. A preliminary view of the photographs and of Brean's text, which would complement each other in an integrated article, indicated that the running text would end most dramatically with the arrival of the passengers on board the *Pontchartrain,* to waiting blankets and coffee. I woke Brean by phone, suggested a rewrite of the ending, and asked him to insert all the extra detail he had. He complied and then went back to sleep.

So now, what about Anne Boleyn? It would have been possible to stop the cover presses earlier, but we didn't know if we had a suitable cover for the rescue at sea article. It turned out we did, so an assistant art director flew to Chicago with one of Touze's transparencies. It showed a yellow life raft pulling away from the jagged plane wreckage under a blue sky on a bluer Pacific. It was engraved in color in the then record time of fourteen hours.

Anne Boleyn had already been printed on 1.5 million covers; the substitute went on the other 4.5 million. The Boleyn covers would be sent to subscribers, since one function of a cover is to attract newsstand buyers. It was too bad to deprive some subscribers of the rescue cover, so all of *Life*'s readers saw the rescue picture when it was subsequently reprinted in the "Letters" section.

Anticipating the Flight 943 lead, I had arranged to move the Texas football article farther back into the issue, eliminating some of the less colorful parts. Shifting around stories in yet-to-be-printed forms was often necessary.

The payments for the pictures may have been chintzy even for those noninflationary days. Touze got $1,200, Braat $1,000, Spear $300, William Simpson $345, and Lonnie Wilson $310. There were no complaints, even though Touze and Braat lost the pictures of Oriental pagodas, taken earlier, on their rolls of film.

During a normal *Life* weekend—Sunday and Monday—I managed to get a morning's sleep but had to spend the rest of the two days on the phone.

We knew the journalistic pot was simmering in Poland and Hungary, and suddenly it came to a very visible boil. What we didn't anticipate was "a little war" involving the Suez Canal and four countries: Egypt, Israel, Britain, and France.

What was happening in those autumn weeks of 1956 was more than enough to rivet the attention of the world—and of *Life*—even though we didn't dare dream of the developments to come. I couldn't have continuous contact with the forces behind the Iron Curtain as I had had with our people in San Francisco after the plane was ditched. Success would depend on properly selected correspondents and photographers already at or near the action.

For the November 5 issue, the Churchill installment, which had gone to press weeks before, recorded the glorious reign of Elizabeth I. She presided over the early exploration of America and the defeat of the Spanish Armada. Dmitri Kessel captured, in color photographs, the grandeur of what remained of the Elizabethan landscape and of its stately halls.

Along the border between Israel and Jordan, correspondent Keith Wheeler and photographer James Burke recorded the problems of a U.N. peacekeeping mission. They were given no hint of a major Israeli thrust against Egypt toward the Suez Canal, which was to be coordinated with a French and British attack within a week.

When I came back to the office Tuesday morning, Poland was conceding that bloody riots against the regime had started. I sent *Life*'s foreign editor, Gene Farmer, flying to Western Europe to write a report on what was happening—or what might occur. Khrushchev's concession to Tito of Yugoslavia that there could be more than one way to pursue what he called socialism made the satellite countries—Poland, Hungary, and others—think about freedom.

Bureau chiefs, photographers, and reporters abroad didn't have to be prodded. They were preparing to move, along with freelancers lined up as reinforcements.

Subsurface Communism had operated in its mysterious way. It was apparent that Khrushchev had failed to prop up the stooges who constituted the Polish government. They had to accept as Communist Party boss Wladyslaw Gomulka, who had spent a prison term imposed by the Party for Tito-like conduct.

Freedom had made gains that were convincing enough to entice young Hungarians to start demonstrations. These broke out into open rebellion. The trigger was a massacre by AVOs, Hungarian security police, of eighty-five protesters who had asked that Soviet emblems be removed from an AVO headquarters. Because of Iron Curtain restrictions, no staff photographers had been in either Warsaw or Budapest. In Poland the feeling was anti-Russian, but not effectively anti-Communist. In Hungary it was both, which made a difference in the way *Life* could report the two events.

On the Tuesday before the November 5 issue closed, I didn't know what we might be able to get from abroad for the kind of lead article we needed. We would start by assembling a *Life*-type background analysis. In historical pictures and words, we put together Poland's history of struggles against oppression by Prussia, Russia, Austria, Nazi Germany, and finally the Soviets. We found evidence of deep religious faith and yearnings toward westernization. Similarly, *Life* recalled Hungary's past, from its Magyar beginnings in the ninth century through Hapsburg rule to independence after World War I, a brief Communist rule, its own dictatorship, and subjugation by the Nazis and then by the USSR.

Despite the profound changes in Poland, the government did not lift controls on the media. We had to scrounge around among obscure agencies for the kind of photographs *Life* needed. For Hungary, however, we could assemble task forces from Paris, Bonn, and Vienna.

A managing editor should never get hard-boiled enough to shrug off the risks that other people are taking. You can tell yourself that these risks were included in the terms of enlistment for reporting, and that almost everyone on an enterprising staff considers foreign service a plum. I had been lucky through the years, but even one casualty would be too many— even indirectly it could be my fault. That is why I would stay up to any hour waiting for shipments from a combat zone. If someone had risked his neck, the least I could sacrifice was a little sleep to see what he had produced.

No staff material could be expected in time for the November 5 issue, but from an outfit called the Central Photographic Agency in Poland we got a photograph showing a quarter of a million Poles hailing Gomulka's return, which we could use as a double-page spread. The Polish people were unrealistically hopeful that Gomulka would loosen Communist restraints.

In Hungary, the Keystone Press Agency collected early evidence of the chaos. It included photographs of trampled barricades and Russian tanks facing off against the rebels.

All these events combined to make the lead article, which underlined the ominous potential of what was happening. An editorial admitted that the United States could not answer Hungarian cries for help. Unquestionably, the events in Central Europe were more compelling than the predictable end of a presidential campaign, so *that* possible lead story was also moved back into the issue.

Among the items in preparation at this time for future issues were a three-part reconstruction of Pearl Harbor on the fifteenth anniversary of the attack, by Walter Lord, and a double-sized special issue on the American woman. For a staff with more than its share of males, this latter was perhaps a presumptuous idea.

For the November 5 issue we signed off with a nod to a fading way of life: a maharaja gave himself an extravagant farewell festival as he sank his 300-pound bulk into the invisibility of the salaried Indian civil service.

Tuesday, the start of the five-day period during which the November 12 issue had to be closed, arrived with no definite news of the Hungarian task forces but with a major new complication. Israel, under the pretext of cleaning out guerrilla bases on its border with Egypt, sent forces lunging toward the Suez Canal. Within forty-eight hours, France and Britain had attempted to join in—with air strikes and a not very efficient paratroop drop from Cyprus.

New *Life* task forces started for the Middle East, some members coming from New York and London. A cartographer in New York began work on a relief map of the Israeli offensive, and we started a search for any independently taken photographs of the early action.

Details from Hungary began to come in. The senior correspondent in the area, James Bell, who had been coordinating *Time* and *Life* coverage from Vienna, complained that things were dull in that command post. But it was almost too dangerously exciting on the firing line. The photographers and reporters who went into Hungary found that a lack of visas in so chaotic a situation did not make much difference.

An unorganized battle provides opportunities for realistic journalism, since carefully controlled public relations tours are impossible. Obviously the chaos provides more chances for getting hurt, too. By Wednesday, the first task force was out of Hungary and promising that they had sensational pictures of the three days during which the rebels had seized temporary control.

No firm decisions as to the relative value of the Hungarian and Suez material had to be made before the shipments came in—there was time enough between planes in Paris to process the film. In the meantime there was much more than enough to keep the New York staff working up to and perhaps beyond capacity. The foreign news writers and researchers were bolstered by loans of staff members from other departments. The executives who served all departments, such as the picture editor and the art and research directors, gave most of their attention to the overseas events.

I usually paid more attention to layouts than was needed. In selecting pictures, I relied a lot on instinct. My judgment turned out to be less than impeccable 5 or 10 percent of the time, but the results weren't any worse than if I had laboriously thought through each problem as if it were the first time it had occurred. My initials on every piece of copy meant that I had read every word that went into the magazine, too.

There were 216 pages in the November 12 issue, and only about a score of them were still unclosed on the Friday and Saturday of the final week.

In that issue, Churchill wrote about the beheading of Charles I and emigration to North America. Cecil B. deMille towered over the movie scene with *The Ten Commandments,* and Rosalind Russell started her reign over Broadway in *Auntie Mame.* Excerpts from a posthumous book by Fred

Allen provided laughs out of vaudeville memories. A boyish Elvis Presley was host to Natalie Wood in Memphis, and an RCA-Victor advertisement offered an Elvis "Perfect for Parties" record at an introductory price of a quarter.

Among the news stories I had to squeeze in was an event planned months before, a visit by Princess Margaret to Tanganyika and Kenya. We had expected it to be colorful and it was. Mark Kauffman, a superb news photographer, complained that covering the princess had put him into the wrong part of Africa during the Suez crisis. His photographs had already been engraved in full color. The story, in some other week, could have been a lead, but, like Texas football of two weeks before, it had to be pushed back.

By midweek, details of the courageous coverage of the days during which the Hungarian rebels were in control began to come out of Vienna. Three photographer-reporter task forces had entered Hungary.

Everywhere the rebels were eager to help the American newsmen—too eager to be concerned about safety. They wanted to show the United States what they were accomplishing. Russian tanks, those that had not been seized by the rebels, had withdrawn, but only to regroup. The visible targets for the revolutionists' rage were the AVOs, the Moscow-trained secret police who had brutalized the country.

Only one staff photographer, Michael Rougier, had been available to go into Hungary. He was teamed with reporter John Mulliken. A talented independent photographer, Erich Lessing, who was better known for beautiful art subjects than for grim military action, was working alone. Timothy Foote teamed up with John Sadovy, a fashion photographer who had covered combat with the British army in World War II.

Foote and Sadovy found themselves in the most perilous situation—the middle of a square with only some skinny trees behind which to seek shelter. Foote was shot in the hand and was evacuated to a first-aid station without Sadovy realizing that the reporter was no longer beside him.

Sadovy was only three feet away from the entrance to the besieged AVO headquarters, which had just fallen to the rebels. Young AVO officers were facing the rebels who were about to become their executioners. "Nothing I saw [in World War II] could compare with this," Sadovy wrote. As the officers pleaded for their lives, Sadovy took four pictures in needle-sharp focus. The smash of the bullets was shown in excruciating detail ("I could see the impact of the bullets on the men's clothes"), and then the AVOs crumpled to the ground.

Members of the Soviet-trained Hungarian secret police as they are shot by rebels in front of their headquarters in November 1956 (photo by John Sadovy, courtesy Time Inc.).

Sadovy followed the rebels as they strung up a Red colonel by his heels; he recorded a woman spitting on the corpse. "My knees were beginning to give in," he wrote in a cable afterward, "as if I were carrying a weight I couldn't carry any more."

His photographs had a comparable effect when spread out, in print form, on my layout table. I have seen the pictures taken by all the great combat photographers, but nothing with the impact of these.

Rougier and Lessing, along with other photographers, including Rolf Gillhausen of the German magazine *Stern,* had produced pictures which would otherwise have seemed unique. There were too many memorable pictures to be squeezed into the ten pages still available when the packets arrived on Friday. Later, *Life* published a 50-cent, 100-page book on Hungary, with all profits going to the International Rescue Committee.

There was no question about making the Hungarian revolution the lead article in the issue. All hands agreed with Tim Foote's cable to me:

"Violence, bravery, hatred of oppressors. You're getting a story *Life* was made for."

Highly poignant events of a different sort occurred at the United Nations, where the United States found it necessary to repudiate our closest allies, Britain and France. For the Eisenhower administration this meant the risk of losing what political folklore, at least, recognized as a Jewish vote, and the election was the following Tuesday. Prime Minister Anthony Eden hadn't told the United States, or indeed all of his own cabinet, about the plans to attack Egypt. At the U.N., Secretary of State John Foster Dulles guided a cease-fire and peacekeeping-force resolution through the General Assembly. It took all night. Dulles, frequently considered inflexible and haughty, had followed his religious conscience and worked with Third World and uncommitted delegations against our erstwhile friends to win a sad victory.

Walter Sanders, as always a sensitive and compassionate photographer, caught Dulles as he emerged on his way to a hospital. The photograph was not perfectly exposed. Parts of it were not sharp. The clock on the wall showed 3:30 A.M. The face under the homburg was haggard. The picture told enough.

The job of managing editor of *Life* was the most fulfilling I had had up to this time, but no one in such a position at Time Inc. lasted more than ten years. I thought it only fair to tell Luce that I was beginning to consider what options I would have in the future.

He wrote in reply: "I hate to think about what you're thinking about. . . . here we are and here let us stay until the Big Umpire unmistakably blows the whistle." I did not assume from this that Luce was decreeing my lifetime tenure as managing editor of *Life*.

22

A Stellar Group, Stomp-outs Included

꩜ In an organization that includes many gifted individuals there are, inevitably, clashes of personality. They can be boss versus employee, or among rival employees. Group journalism, as practiced at Time Inc., can have an inhibiting effect on creativity or what the individual perceives as his creativity. Bitching about this was very acceptable, given the characters of those pleading each side of the cases.

Here is Alfred Eisenstaedt photographing a story on the great pianist, Rachmaninoff: "Play," says Alfred.

Rachmaninoff runs off a few scales and asks an impassive Eisenstaedt, "Why aren't you taking pictures?"

"Oh, I just wanted to get in the mood."

But Alfred's ego never prevented him from taking an assignment or caused him to complain about a layout. He never adopted a holier-than-thou attitude.

There were examples of walkouts, though. When Ralph McAllister Ingersoll started *PM,* he offered Margaret Bourke-White a job. Maggie hesitated. Although tempted by her approval of *PM*'s left-liberal politics, she went on a *Life* assignment in Turkey but then indicated her acceptance of the *PM* offer by air expressing a pair of red curled-toe Turkish slippers to Ingersoll from Istanbul. Since she was on assignment, I considered her behavior unacceptable, but her departure was, at worst, in low dudgeon. *PM* ran out of projects for such a high-powered employee and assigned her to photograph a mother bird hatching and raising her chicks near the newspaper's door. She quit and talked Luce into taking her back. I wasn't managing editor yet, and I would have been harder to mollify than was Luce. But this kind of behavior, like Eisenstaedt's, was part of being Bourke-White—no hypocrisy.

Two other resignations, if judged by emotional intensity, were in super high dudgeon. They were those of photographers David Douglas Duncan and W. Eugene Smith. They came with accusatory sermons on ethics.

Dave Duncan usually seemed amiable enough, but, underneath, he never gave up his conviction that he had no need for reporters, editors, or writers. This was supportable on occasion. Duncan produced superb photographs. Normally, I was able to just roll with his temperament, although once I burst out with this cable to Korea: "Possibly someday a system can be worked out whereby the photographer can take pictures, shuttle in to lay them out and then write the textblocks and captions. . . . until that happy day we have the archaic system of having editors."

I was worried about the morale of other equally brave and dedicated photographers, who, understandably, thought Duncan was trying to take unfair advantage by flying home to lobby for his product. I certainly was not stuffy about requiring a formal assignment when he suddenly took off to accompany "my marines" back from the Yalu River disaster in Korea. The pictures he sent back of the haunting faces among the half-frozen troops showed Duncan at his most effective.

I trusted Duncan when he was reporting what he had observed personally, so I refused to fire him—as Luce suggested—after a U.S. diplomat protested his written account of low French morale in Indochina, long before U.S. involvement. I arranged a dinner for Duncan with Luce in Rome and got the following cable the next morning: "Encounter with Duncan ended satisfactorily. He has not—repeat not—yet fired me. Harry."

Luce's amused tolerance got us over that Duncan crisis—and Duncan proved to be correct about the French. He was naive, however, on general political questions—specifically, in 1956 he disagreed with better-qualified political reporters who questioned the fiscal honesty of the Afghan royal family. Duncan always identified with his sources. When I used text by a seasoned observer as counterpoint to his Afghan pictures, Dave angrily quit.

He summoned a press conference in Cairo to call his erstwhile *Life* colleagues all kinds of names. He signed up with *Collier's* and bought Crowell-Collier stock with the avowed purpose of running Time Inc. out of business. He seemed surprised when he showed up later at the *Life* office and found some individual resentment.

To achieve his aim of being self-sufficient, Duncan produced his own books. He would write, make layouts of his photos, execute contracts with printers, and then check bookstores to see that his volumes were well displayed.

Luce's relationship with Duncan continued friendly up to a point. Duncan breakfasted regularly at a Schrafft's near Rockefeller Center. One morning Luce came in and sat down beside him. Duncan told him about his current involvement with Picasso (the subject of several Duncan books thereafter). Luce thought that was okay, but said he was a little doubtful about one period in Picasso's professional life.

Duncan leaped up from the counter, dashed over to the *Sports Illustrated* office, where he had left a set of pictures on Picasso's bullfight ceramics, and snatched them away from the managing editor, Sid James, exclaiming: "I won't sell to anyone whose boss feels that way about Picasso!" I think the pictures were part of a larger set Curtis Publishing owned anyway.

One could spar with Duncan about ethics reasonably good-naturedly, but Gene Smith's attitudes in this area led to a deadly serious confrontation—ethical truth seeker versus venal boss.

Gene was working for Ziff-Davis publications early in World War II but found that he couldn't get near any action, so he joined the staff of *Life*. In the combat he covered he came to believe his mission was to make a statement against war itself. Smith watchers found he was using prescription drugs heavily, and he was scaring his colleagues and bosses with the chances he was taking. He talked about showing an American advance from the viewpoint of the enemy—out in front. Looking back over his war pictures, though, the most notable were about life—a GI saving a tiny naked newborn baby on Saipan—not death.

Unsurprisingly, Gene was wounded because he stood up while photographing soldiers in a mortar barrage. A substantial part of his jaw was shot away, and *Life*, as it should have, picked up all his medical expenses.

I feared another Smith statement against war might be fatal to him, so I said no to his demand to be sent to Korea. "You can't prevent me from committing suicide if I want to," he said.

"No, but you can't do it on a *Life* expense account," I told him. "No Korea."

Suicide was a frequent threat of Smith's. His father had shot himself to death in 1936. At tense moments Gene would phone someone and say that he was in a window poised to jump. This was scary, but he never did jump.

My first important postwar Smith project was his "Country Doctor," in 1948. Kenneth MacLeish, our science and medicine editor, sensed that, in an era of increasing specialization, the country doctor might be becoming a vanishing species. Correspondents throughout the United States were solicited for names of doctors for such a story. After investigation, MacLeish and Smith selected Robert Ceriani, a rural Coloradoan, as their subject. Somewhat like Gene, the doctor was intense, worked grueling hours, and was compassionate. No one had to suggest what individual pictures Smith should take; he knew instinctively.

Art Director Charles Tudor and I laid out this story. Gene and I argued a bit about using the exhausted doctor with his cigarette and a cup of coffee as a full-page picture to end the essay, but I prevailed. I never heard a complaint thereafter. Dr. Ceriani became famous. At his retirement almost forty years later, he was the subject of national press and TV coverage, all because of the *Life* story.

As was the case with the doctor, Smith's "Spanish Village" essay would not have been possible without advance work by *Life*'s correspondents. We wanted to have some kind of look at the closed society that was Franco Spain. An excuse came when Spain requested surplus grain from the United States. Will Lang, in Paris, wangled permission for a "nonpolitical" story by Gene on the need for bread in some unspecified town.

Gene went in with only a driver and an interpreter. After many days of driving, he found the village of Delirosa. He made a token gesture to the official excuse for the incursion by taking a picture of a girl carrying loaves on her head. Although he said he was avoiding a political statement, Gene conveyed a strong impression of stern governmental control with his portrait of a trio of Franco's Civil Guards. What gave the essay universality was a two-page photograph of a grieving family around the coffin of a husband and father.

I must admit that *Life* was not the ideal employer for the kind of statements Gene eventually felt he wanted to make. Still, *Life* was the only game around in which photographs could be displayed effectively, and it provided his everyday subsistence. When his erratic behavior in a New York park attracted police attention, *Life* paid for his care at the Payne Whitney psychiatric facility.

The trigger for Gene's resignation from the staff was his Albert Schweitzer essay in 1956. I was cool to the idea because the subject had become a kind of cliché. Gene wanted so badly to portray the doctor that I agreed he

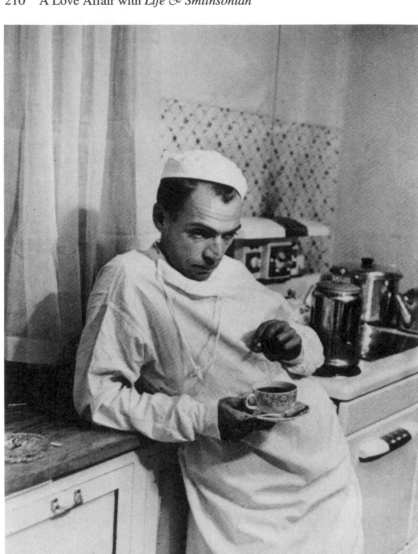

W. Eugene Smith's "Country Doctor," Robert Ceriani, exhausted after a day's work in rural Colorado. Smith's essay ran in *Life* in 1948 (©Time Inc.).

should have a chance. Schweitzer did not turn out to be the father figure for whom I think Gene yearned. He was autocratic and an obstructionist.

Schweitzer, upon receiving a written Smith threat to leave, gave Gene more leeway, and the focus shifted more to the leper colony and the village around it. By this time Gene no longer trusted the excellent *Life* photo lab to make prints. He was taking weeks of night and day work, and finally produced his prints only after we heard rumors that *Look* was scheduling a Schweitzer story.

None of the layouts we made satisfied Gene, so I decided we couldn't go on pasting up photostats forever. He later said, "I would have preferred silence to what appeared." He did not demand silence at the time. I had told Smith that we would give the essay twelve pages. We didn't often have twelve pages of space available, though, and one week, when I was away, my deputy found ten pages and used them for the Schweitzer essay. The dropping of two pages was an insult to Smith, and he resigned immediately.

Apart from this fairly typical reaction, the real problem was that he had come to think, he said, that Schweitzer should have been only the departure point for thirty to sixty pages, or perhaps an entire issue, on Smith's yet-to-be-photographed Africa. He wrote to me, "I believe it to be my misfortune that you were not present," but that was nonsense. I was convinced that he was about ready to leave the magazine anyway. He assured me, "I have outgrown the concept of the *Life* essay."

His next three years—on a freelance project on Pittsburgh—showed, he hoped, that, like Duncan, he didn't need editors, reporters, art directors, and other support troops. It was to be his "revenge" on *Life*.

For all his intransigence, though, there was no question that all of us at *Life* wanted more Smith essays. We were anxious, as in Matthew 19:13, to "rejoice" more of that sheep than of "the ninety and nine which went not astray."

The ninety and nine included many other distinguished photo essayists, which was fortunate since *Life* published fifty-one issues a year (for the last two weeks of the year we produced a special single issue). Like the earliest *Life* photographers, they were also masters, in their own ways, of conveying what was intensely human about individuals. For instance:

• Leonard McCombe created intimate studies of the career girl, Gwyned Filling, and many others who turned out to be not-so-ordinary human beings.

• Henri Cartier-Bresson, the French genius of "the decisive moment," selected his own projects but would sell his work to *Life*.

Life's entire photographic staff in 1960, with guess-who in front as mascot (photo by William J. Sumits). *Front row:* James Whitmore, Paul Schutzer, Walter Sanders, Michael Rougier, Nina Leen, Peter Stackpole, Alfred Eisenstaedt (stepping on my head), Margaret Bourke-White, Thomas McAvoy, Carl Mydans, Al Fenn, Ralph Morse, Francis Miller. *Middle row:* Grey Villet, Hank Walker, Dmitri Kessel, N. R. Farbman, Yale Joel, John Dominis, Gordon Parks, James Burke, Andreas Feininger, Fritz Goro, Allan Grant, Eliot Elisofon, Frank Scherschel. *Back row:* Edward Clark, Loomis Dean, Joe Scherschel, Stan Wayman, Robert Kelley, J R Eyerman, Ralph Crane, Leonard McCombe, Howard Sochurek, Wallace Kirkland, Mark Kauffman, George Silk.

• Philippe Halsman, a master at suggesting (and photographing) cover subjects—from handsome, sexy women like Eva Gabor to international statesmen and business tycoons.

• Mark Kauffman could cover spot news with the brassiest of the tabloid photographers, but could also relate to every family with his documentary of a housewife or to every military recruit with his new marines and their fearsome drill instructor.

• The multitalented Gordon Parks combined eloquent writing and photography in unforgettable character studies, such those on "Red," a Harlem gang leader, and Flavio, the Brazilian slum boy.

• Cornell Capa, a photographer technically superior to his brother, Robert, brought sensitive understanding to subjects as widely different as an aged mother living with her son's family, a group of missionaries in South America, and Adlai Stevenson. Cornell went on to found the International Center for Photography and become a major influence in all fields of camera work.

• Eliot Elisofon was equally at home with native Africans and their art and a professional fight manager. A pioneer in the use of four-color, with Kessel and Mili, Eliot was consultant on color for the movie *Toulouse-Lautrec*.

• If people made fascinating essay subjects, so did superior photographs of, say, moods. A virtuoso in the use of equipment, Andreas Feininger could capture the claustrophobic feelings that gridlock arouses by depicting city traffic, foreshortened so the vehicles seemed plastered together.

• Kosti Ruohomaa, in contrast, made readers shudder in the bone-chilling stillness of a Maine winter.

• George Silk used imagination, in concept and in choice of lenses, to make flowing poetry out of the sweaty world of track and field. A New Zealander who photographed combat in World War II, he was a committed naturalist and also turned the world of birds into photographic poetry.

Photographers Frank Scherschel, Eliot Elisofon, Alfred Eisenstaedt, Dmitri Kessel and I test the strength of a gift rocking chair at my fiftieth birthday bash (1957, courtesy Time Inc.).

• Nina Leen warmly conveyed her affection for animals with her photographs of all kinds of creatures—she even made bats lovable. She had a pixyish sense of humor, but I don't believe she was laughing in her essay on ghosts. She believed.

Like other humans, photographers can be jealous, but, to their credit, they generally admired without reservation Gene Smith at his best. So did I, despite irritations at times. And certainly, the managing editors who followed me, George Hunt and Ralph Graves, also tried to rehabilitate him—with little success, however.

23

Under the Pole and Out in Space

 Time Inc.'s flagship magazine, *Time,* started with anonymous writing, but *Life* almost from the start had at least one signed article on an important subject every week. Preferring bylines, a number of *Time* writers found their way to *Life,* including Paul O'Neil, a star. O'Neil described his discontent with *Time* this way:

> The theory of group journalism is highly overrated. . . . the brigades of editors, researchers, advisers and assorted double-domes, who are popularly believed to be helping the writer, are actually just riding around on his back, shooting at parakeets, waving at friends, and plucking fruit from overhanging branches, while he churns unsteadily through the swamps of fact and rumor with his big, dirty feet sinking in up to the knee at every step.

At *Life* Paul got as many bylined articles as he could handle. One was on a piece in 1958, when it seemed that *Life* was about to be scooped on the kind of story in which it liked to specialize. The crew of the nuclear submarine *Nautilus* startled the world that fall by passing under the North Pole. It was a secret mission. No publication had any representatives aboard. But we found out, after the announcement, that the *Saturday Evening Post* had a prior contract with the skipper, William Anderson, for a general article on underseas nuclear operations. Now he would be pressed to tell the story of the historic polar mission for the *Post.*

Our September 1 issue just happened to have a twelve-page photographic essay on submarines already being printed. It had been in preparation for a year. Five photographers, two of whom had worked outside submarines in aqualungs, and two reporters had been involved. The pictures showed

215

Polaris missiles bursting out of the water, a mine exploding, and a record transatlantic crossing by the submarine *Skate,* a newer sister ship of the *Nautilus.*

The navy required Commander Anderson to be available to the press, so we were able to photograph him in the sub's tower for a *Life* cover. We gathered narratives of the voyage from crew members riding on a train and at a *Life* party in London. We provided blind dates at the party for sailors who wanted them. Of the clean-cut crew, a British observer noted that it looked as if "Washington had built them to specification."

The *Nautilus* sailors were serious and professional. A frieze of their intent faces, photographed by one of the crew at an Anderson briefing during the under-ice voyage, was spread across two pages to start the *Life* story O'Neil fashioned into a coherent narrative from all the individual accounts by the task force and from additional material gathered in Washington.

The historic voyage had been so well planned that the crew seemed to consider it almost routine. Whatever feelings of danger there might have been were minimized by fathometers that indicated whenever the overhead ice, which looked like "beautiful moving clouds" to the naked eye, was too close to the submarine.

Space for the O'Neil article was cleared next to the preprinted color essay. Fortuitously, it looked as if we had planned the combination in advance, and the issue was a virtual sellout.

The *Nautilus* was definitely in Jules Verne territory. *Life* would later ascend into another Verneland for a lot more than just one issue. I was determined that the magazine would be firmly identified with space. Robert Hutchings Goddard had started experimenting with rockets in 1909. Ten years later he suggested a rocket trip to the moon. Goddard's experiments were ridiculed by some and then neglected by his fellow Americans. The Germans, however, used his ideas to produce the V-2 missile, though too late in World War II to avoid defeat.

The United States and the Soviet Union, each with a contingent of German scientists, were both working on rocketry when the Soviet *Sputnik* shocked America into an accelerated program to explore space, including manned probes. Manned! That was the aspect of the story to which readers would relate, much better than to machines. It seemed likely that once the space program escaped from earth's confines, it would forever be a standard against which other meaningful and dramatic achievements would be appraised. We would be hearing "If we can put a man on the moon, we can . . ." (fill in the rest of the sentence for yourself) ad infinitum.

The astronauts, when they became a reality, were the subject of an intricate and long-running debate over whether it makes sense to send men into space when most of the information can be obtained through instruments. Nonetheless, the program was going ahead, and *Life* was committed to making intelligible as much of the information that came out of the space projects as possible. Naturally, we—and a lot of other publications—wanted the story of human participation in the space adventure exclusively.

The hitch, for all of us, was that the astronauts were government employees. How could their story be anyone's exclusive? Here enter Walt Bonney, the resourceful director of NASA public relations. There was no question, he said, that the media generally was entitled to all information NASA released. But, he argued, an individual's thoughts were his own, and the wives didn't work for the government. Besides, all the first astronauts were to be selected from the armed services and would have no income other than salaries and flight pay. Their new duties were risky, to say the least, and deserved extra remuneration. Thus, he concluded, personal accounts could be contracted for under certain circumstances.

I went to Washington in 1959 for the announcement of the names of the first group of seven astronauts. They had been selected from all over the country, so seven *Life* teams, consisting of a photographer and a reporter each, were alerted. Since a long wait for these reports was likely, I moved my "office" to a Washington key club, where the long-distance calls came in. We wanted to do an article about the husbands and wives together. There was a momentary scare when we heard that one of the seven was about to be divorced. The couple got back together in a hurry—temporarily. It may not have been spelled out, but the impression was firm that NASA wanted a "clean" image for the group.

There were formidable obstacles to getting significant mileage from a contract. At the press conference for the introduction of the seven astronauts, I sat next to a possible rival bidder, Clay Blair of the *Saturday Evening Post.* A reporter asked the seven which one was ready to go into space immediately. The resulting photograph showed six single hands up. John Glenn, characteristically, put up both of his.

Through Bonney, the group arranged that day for a lawyer, Leo De Orsey, to represent them. He was a former chief counsel for CBS and had briefly been president of the Washington Redskins football team. He had the kind of worldly wisdom the seven needed.

Other media representatives scraped around to figure out some way of using the new astronauts. TV chose not to bid (possibly because NASA would not allow implicit endorsement of a specific product). The daily newspapers and wire services were leery of the possible price and decided to be content with the official releases. Blair pleaded with the *Post* editor, Ben Hibbs, but Hibbs felt his long lead time made a deal impractical. *National Geographic* had an even longer lead time and declined to bid. Almost by default, because we could close within a couple of days after each flight, *Life* got the contract.

NASA's and *Life*'s detractors called this "checkbook journalism." But how was it different from our expenditures to snatch the *Nautilus* story away from the *Post?* I heard no criticism at all about that. Purists, led by the *New York Times,* never did accept the legitimacy of the astronaut contracts, although the *Times* happily shared with *Life* the cost of buying the Churchill and Truman "personal stories" of their contributions to history.

For Project Mercury, which involved the original seven astronauts, *Life* paid half a million dollars, in installments, with each man sharing equally. Lump sums were agreed to for each of the succeeding projects, with the totals higher but with each active astronaut receiving a smaller share because their ranks grew.

From the outset it was obvious that satisfactory results depended on the goodwill of the individual astronauts. Characteristically, then, things started off at Langley Field, the first training site, with a *Life* party for the group, the staff of NASA technicians who were being assembled, and the magazine staff members who were assigned to the project. We found out that the astronauts were by no means teetotalers.

What we didn't realize then was that we would be compelled, at the risk of boring readers, to stretch out accounts of the training for the next couple of years. During this period, I got one peremptory demand from an excitable foreign subcontractor that I go down personally and fling the spacecraft off the launchpad.

We got to know each astronaut perhaps better than we wanted to. We became the recipients of unwanted confidences and some backbiting rivalry among the seven—and their wives. We considered such information privileged then. Most of it seems trivial now. The astronauts managed to retain the public belief throughout the program that theirs was a team effort by all-American players.

Members of the *Life* staff spent time with each astronaut and his wife. At Cape Canaveral *Life* provided a rented house for the astronauts and their families, to guard their privacy. One photographer, Ralph Morse, worked so closely with all concerned that he came to be called the "eighth astronaut."

Several writers took turns covering the activities of the wives. Notable was Dora Jane Hamblin, who had the task of attending exercise classes and bowling with the women. (She got her revenge with rather unflattering portraits of some of them in an uninhibited book, *That Was the "Life."*)

Before, during, and after a flight, the activity became intense. We could not keep exclusivity because our photographs went into a pool. But the quality of our reproduction was so much better and the pages of the magazine provided room for so many extra pictures that we didn't feel we were much hurt by the fact that a few of the color pictures were published elsewhere before we could print them.

Getting something distinctive out of the "personal story" of the astronaut himself was a catch-as-catch-can proposition for the writer assigned. As a kind of amanuensis for an individual astronaut, the writer had to combine what had been released publicly with whatever else he could snatch in pressured interviews. Then the result had to be shown to the astronaut to be sure he was saying what he wanted to say. After that, according to policy, a NASA official had to review the text. NASA was excessively concerned with the image of its employees, so there is no doubt that the public got something less than completely candid impressions of the men involved.

Some of the deletions were downright silly. The reviewing officer on a Walter Schirra flight, for instance, objected decisively to a rather poetic description of a shining icicle of urine floating by the window during waste dumping. Was all-American Wally expected to go for days without having to relieve himself?

Admittedly the *Life* contract was something of a problem for NASA. On the plus side it allowed the enforcement of a measure of personal and family privacy from the rest of the media. (John Glenn was so private that he once denied access to his house and family to no less than Vice President Johnson.) *Life* did its job effectively enough so that a mention of the magazine at a general press conference usually elicited a chorus of jealous boos.

By this time Harry Batten, the wise, strictly ethical chairman of the N. W. Ayer advertising agency, had replaced De Orsey, who had died, as legal representative of all the astronauts. I think De Orsey's services were without fee. I know Batten's were.

There were always doubts about the legitimacy of our arrangement for coverage of the astronauts. When John F. Kennedy became president in 1961, he appointed a new administrator for the program, James E. Webb, who greeted me with, "Why can't I just declare this contract to be contrary to the public interest and cancel it?"

Of course, Webb could have. Kennedy had designated the vice president to keep an eye on space, so as a precautionary measure I tackled LBJ on behalf of getting the contract extended. His comment was, "Those are mighty fine boys. Had 'em down to my ranch."

I worked on Press Secretary Pierre Salinger, to whom I had given cheap cigars before the Kennedy nomination in Los Angeles. Having by this time graduated to what looked like big Havanas, Pierre was noncommittal. He never offered me one of those.

I got a secondhand message from the vice president's office. "Pretend you are an astronaut and describe the benefits of the contract." That was easy: money and a measure of privacy.

In the meantime, Glenn had been invited to visit the Kennedys at Hyannisport. Glenn may have been more persuasive than I was. At any rate Salinger told me grumpily, "You win. The boss will let the contract stand, but I want you to know that I was against it."

Then there was another threat. As a second batch of astronauts entered the program, Marshall Field Educational Enterprises came in with a monetary offer I didn't feel I could top. It proposed to let *Life,* in a new role as a subcontractor, operate much as before. But this proposal was withdrawn when Bailey Howard, the supersalesman who ran Field Educational, found out what he should have known all along—that he couldn't, according to NASA rules, put astronauts on television sponsoring World Book Encyclopedias.

So *Life* again won a contract, and, to my surprise, I found that my second memo to the vice president's office, verbatim but not attributed, was handed out to the press.

The number of astronauts was growing. I got to know the second and third batches a little but couldn't keep up with the fourth and later generations. John Young, the quietly humorous commander of the first space shuttle, was the last practicing astronaut I really knew.

I was determined to hang on to the contract, at least through the landing on the moon. There was a voice or two, even at *Life,* questioning it—correctly—on the ground that the literary quality of the accounts left something to be desired.

Although the slices of the *Life* pie got smaller and smaller for the later astronauts, most of the early astronauts were able to buy houses near the

Houston Space Center. I christened this settlement Togethersville, but my sarcasm was wasted. Their neighborhood persisted, more or less as a unit. One wife, however, agreed with my distrust of communal living: "I can stand most of the men," she said, "but those women!"

Life's pampering practices got a little strained the day of John Glenn's triumphal parade in New York. His whole entourage wanted to attend *How to Succeed in Business without Really Trying,* which had been sold out for months. Mary Leatherbee of *Life*'s entertainment department rallied the theater into calling up all the known ticket holders and getting enough of them to give up their seats for that night.

After a bristly beginning, Jim Webb became a friend. Every once in a while he would phone to compare notes on some of the understandably inflated egos of the new-age heroes. One call came about a prospective scandal that NASA, sticking with its desire to present the astronauts as squeaky clean, wanted to prevent. Webb started with, "Ed, how do you stop a book?"

I explained that, although a libel suit could be brought after publication, there was really no way to stop a book except to somehow buy off the author in advance. The book was supposedly entitled "The Astronauts' Mascot"; the author was rumored to be an attractive girl who had expressed her intention—in a Cocoa Beach, Florida, bar in the hearing of two *Life* people, among others—to sleep with all seven of the first astronauts. Webb's operatives uncovered some evidence that she had succeeded with at least two of the seven.

I agreed to ask around for the manuscript. One book editor, a friend, said that although he didn't have it he would pay me double the agent's fee if I could get hold of it. Finally, I phoned Washington to report failure in my search. I then discovered that a young NASA public relations man, above and beyond the call of duty, had gone to Cocoa Beach, picked up the girl in a bar, and, after some drinks, asked, "How about that book you're writing . . ."

"Book?" she replied. "There isn't any book. I can't write an English sentence."

Human cupidity was bound to crop up from time to time. To retain whatever exclusivity *Life* had, I refused to waive the provisions of the contract so that one astronaut could pick up $50,000 from a *Saturday Evening Post* article to retire a private debt. I said we would go to court to prevent him from getting out of our contract, and he asked, "It would hurt my image if I appeared to be a welsher, wouldn't it?"

"Yup."

To Ed Thompson —
With thanks for making the steps
up to this one a little more
pleasant than they might have been. —

Neil [signature]

Apollo 11

This photograph of man's first landing on the moon was a gift to me from Neil Armstrong (1969, NASA photo).

He decided to leave his public image untarnished.

NASA eventually came around to letting up on its pressure to maintain a front of unalloyed marital bliss among its charges, so a few divorce suits appeared—some of them overdue.

It was easy to become genuinely fond of some individuals in the space program. And, in turn, there were thoughtful gifts to me, souvenirs such as seared heat shields, coins that had been in space, and autographed pictures.

I was particularly touched by an unsolicited gift from Neil Armstrong, who was certainly not demonstrative by nature, after his return from the moon. He gave me a copy of the photograph of the first human foot being put down on the moon's surface, with the handwritten inscription "To Ed Thompson—with thanks for making the steps up to this one a little more pleasant than they might have been." Neil's modest choice for a further career after space was university teaching.

There was nothing in particular about the backgrounds of the astronauts that indicated later successes in other fields except perhaps that the selection process also gave an important place to qualities of leadership. Frank Borman became president of Eastern Airlines. John Glenn, Jake Garn, and Harrison Schmitt won seats in the U.S. Senate, and Tom Stafford was promoted to a four-star Air Force general in charge of spending two-thirds of that service's budget.

Mike Collins, who wrote an excellent book on the astronaut program, *Carrying the Fire,* became director of the Smithsonian Institution's Air & Space Museum. He brought in his spectacular building early and under budget. To Washington's bureaucracy, that may have been the major miracle of the space program.

24

Light on the Chilling "Riddle Wrapped in a Mystery inside an Enigma"

The events in Hungary and Poland described in Chapter 21 are prophetic today, but those tentative moves toward liberty were preceded by many individual acts of bravery—daring defections from Communism. Shedding light on Churchill's "riddle wrapped in a mystery inside an enigma" was what journalism was all about. *Life* addressed the riddle, in part, with the frightening memoirs of defectors.

Now that millions of Eastern Europeans are adjusting to liberty, if hardly prosperity, it is difficult to appreciate the terror under which those behind the Iron Curtain lived. The arm of Stalin's vengeance was long. A dissident would "fall" from a window. A familiar face would disappear from a holiday lineup on top of Lenin's tomb.

Details of specific incidents, when they leaked out, were usually grim. Take the case of a barking dog that disturbed Stalin's sleep. "Shoot it," the dictator ordered.

No barking the next day.

"The dog won't bother you again," his guards reported, explaining that it was a seeing-eye dog for a blind old Bolshevik who had fought in the original Communist Revolution. It had been moved out of earshot. Stalin insisted that the dog and master be brought back. They stood before him, and Stalin barked at the guards, "Follow orders!"

They led the miscreants away. Two shots were heard, and then neither man nor dog was seen again.

That anecdote is from *The Secret History of Stalin Crimes,* by Alexander Orlov, serialized in *Life* in 1953. What would have happened to Orlov, also an old Bolshevik, if he hadn't escaped? The Orlovs could grasp it, too vividly, which was why they hid for fourteen years before taking a chance on surfacing. Having lived on the charity of relatives, they needed money.

Orlov had held the highest rank of any of *Life*'s defector authors. He had served with the NKVD (predecessor of the KGB) and was an associate of Andrei Vyshinsky, the prosecutor for the notorious purge trials. During the Spanish civil war, the NKVD sent Orlov to Spain as an "adviser" to the Loyalists, but he was widely accepted as the de facto commander of the antifascist troops.

As the liberal elements which were part of the Loyalist forces (e.g., members of the Abraham Lincoln Brigade) chafed under Russian control, Orlov came to be regarded as the villain-in-residence. His methods for enforcing Stalinist power seemed appropriately ruthless. He was blamed for diverting the Loyalists' chief asset (an estimated $600 million in gold bullion) to the USSR for "safekeeping" in a one-way trip.

Orlov disappeared from Spain well before the Franco victory. He had realized, according to his account, that he was about to be purged. Picking up his wife and daughter near the French border, he headed for the American Embassy in Paris, only to find it closed for the July Fourth holiday. He then switched to the Canadians, who guided him to a ship just about to sail from Cherbourg.

By the time Orlov reappeared, ever so warily, he was almost forgotten. His daughter had died. He could visit her grave only surreptitiously. Word that he wanted to sell his story came to John Billings through a roving editor of *Reader's Digest,* William L. White (William Allen White's son). But was White saying that he was the real, long-missing Orlov? I went down to the Wall Street area to confront him in the tiny office of an obscure lawyer. *Harper's* editor John Fisher, who knew Orlov, agreed to rule on the identification. It promised to be a dramatic moment, although it seemed unlikely to me that the mild-mannered little man I met, while waiting for Fisher, could be the notorious Orlov. Fisher came in and said, "Hello, Alex," and all doubt was removed.

Association with Orlov had tense moments, for he considered himself to be a prime target for assassination by the Soviet secret police. Mrs. Orlov always accompanied him, and both of them were continually looking around for possible pursuers. Orlov made one visit to the *Life* offices but then chose to believe Whittaker Chambers's old charge that the place was infiltrated with Communists who would probably put the finger on him. He never came back. (Chambers himself, fellow writers on *Time* reported, had kept a loaded pistol in his desk.)

Maitland Edey, my assistant managing editor, worked on the manuscript Orlov had been assembling. Meetings took place in "safe" locations. Once, Mait asked Orlov to his club but made a small error in giving him the street number—the author didn't show up. When Mait emerged, he found Orlov scrunched into a nearby doorway, hiding.

Mait struggled to shape the material into installments. Orlov was unjustifiably proud of his English. He retained the inverted sentence structure of Russian in the bulk of the manuscript, so quite a lot of rearranging was necessary in the interests of clarity.

For a final review, Edey invited the Orlovs to his home on Long Island. Orlov read. Stung by the changes, he announced that the result would not do in any way. Edey said he was going to bed and told Orlov to re-revise the copy—he had all night. Not long after, Orlov was heard going to his bedroom. In the morning he announced that he had decided the Edey version conveyed the essential meaning after all.

There was criticism from left-wing sources of the decision to publish the charges that Stalin had murdered many old colleagues and had either driven his wife to suicide or killed her, but later, in his famous denunciation of Stalin before the Party congress, Khrushchev produced much the same script. Orlov claimed that Khrushchev had lifted whole paragraphs verbatim from the Russian-language version of his book. A Russian diplomat who defected in the late 1980s read the English version of the book in my home and agreed with Orlov.

Intelligent though he was, Orlov had a difficult time adjusting to life in America. This was even more true of other defectors who came our way. The standard procedure was for the U.S. debriefers to wring every possible bit of information out of them and then turn them loose in what was, of course, a strange environment. The CIA was compassionate enough to try to expose the defector to a chance of earning a nest egg through sale of his material to a publication.

Peter Deriabin was perhaps an extreme case. A Siberian by birth, Deriabin was a double agent who came completely over to the West. He was a diabetic and shouldn't have tasted alcohol, but in his disoriented existence he became a heavy drinker. His *Life* editor, Frank Gibney, served in fact as his keeper. Deriabin's drinking brought on diabetic seizures, and Gibney was likely to get a call at any hour: "Fronkie, come for me. I'm on floor of bar. I can't move." Frank would get him to a hospital. In the book that resulted from Gibney's editing, the wry inscription to me was "from Frank, Ted [Deriabin's nickname] and the other members of the Siberian Temperance Society."

The prime example of an Iron Curtain country that split openly with the Soviet Union and Stalin, although to be sure not with Communism itself, was Yugoslavia, ruled by the indomitable Marshal Tito. The world held its breath to see if Soviet tanks would roll. They didn't, and Tito got away with it.

In 1952, *Life* persuaded Tito to tell who he was, how he got that way, and how he was going to dodge Soviet bullets if need be. The project required a whole team: his public affairs spokesman, Vladimir Dedijer; John Phillips, a *Life* photographer who covered Tito's partisans behind the German lines in World War II; and Robert Coughlan, the versatile writer/editor from *Life*'s staff.

The narration of a single incident might go like this: Tito would tell Vlado, who would put it into his Slavic-type English words and sentences. Coughlan would render it into understandable English. Vlado would react, with Coughlan watching the spot where the top of his skull should have been. Thanks to a World War II artillery shell, there was no bone on the top of Vlado's head. If he merely scrawled furiously on the copy, the situation could be handled. If his hair started wiggling, look out. Vlado had a violent temper, although he was sentimental and cried easily, too. Phillips would be called in to negotiate between Coughlan and Vlado, and a compromise eventually would be effected.

But no matter who did what, the title of the article was "Tito Speaks," so Tito had to be shown what he was saying. In Belgrade this could be done immediately, but at one period Vlado was temporarily assigned to the Yugoslav embassy in Paris. Then, every few thousand words or so, he would climb on the Orient Express to go get the boss's reactions.

Coughlan, a marvel of patience and ingenuity, never actually met Tito, but when he cabled me that he had obtained the clearance of enough material to insure that we had a publishable text, I believed him and only then made a definite bid.

After the series went to press—both on the same day and without the other knowing about it—John Phillips sent me a memo saying the Tito project would have failed without Bob, and Bob Coughlan sent me one saying the same thing about John.

Tito was a hard-boiled Communist, but it was for nationalistic, patriotic reasons that he resisted Stalin's attempt to rule Yugoslavia. Vlado had his own stubborn brand of honesty and was heartbroken when he was purged from the party. But he survived into the post-Tito era to become a book publisher. His firm issued a volume of Phillips's Yugoslav pictures.

We had to let the Yugoslavian dictator praise his own type of Communism. Anyway, any leader who could make "Buckle Down Winsocki" (a satire on an American football fight song from the Broadway musical *Best Foot Forward*) part of his band's repertoire on state occasions couldn't have been all bad.

In 1963, we were told that the daughter of a famous Russian from an earlier period was alive and had written a book. The prospective publishers, Robert Speller & Sons, wanted to sell magazine publication rights. The author claimed to be the Grand Duchess Anastasia, whom most historians believed had surely been executed by the Bolsheviks in 1918 along with Czar Nicholas and the rest of the royal family.

A legend that Anastasia might be alive had brought out earlier claimants to her identity, one being Anna Anderson, who lived in Germany. Her story was the subject of a 1955 movie starring Ingrid Bergman, but Anderson was suspect, not the least because she was reluctant to speak Russian.

This latest Anastasia, under the name of Eugenia Smith, had lived obscurely in Illinois for forty years. She did speak Russian, and her grasp of palace details, supported strongly by a test administered by one Cleve Backster, a polygraph professional, had convinced the Spellers of her authenticity. They were willing to let *Life* make further tests. If true, her story would be a journalistic sensation.

Loudon Wainwright, later to write his own version of the *Life* era, *The Great American Magazine,* organized the investigation. We learned that a woman in Chicago claimed to have given Smith lessons in Russian—which wouldn't have been necessary if she had been Anastasia. Anthropologists compared blowups of Smith's features with photos of the teenage Anastasia without finding any convincing resemblances. Handwriting experts found variations between Smith's and Anastasia's signatures.

With great difficulty, we persuaded a Romanov cousin, Mrs. Paul Chave-havadze, to come from Massachusetts and talk with Smith for an hour.

As a child Chavehavadze had played with the real grand duchess, and she reported that Smith couldn't possibly be her second cousin. She told us privately that Smith might just possibly have been a Romanov servant, which would explain her familiarity with details of royal housekeeping. Smith had used the name Mrs. Marijan Smetisko on her immigration papers before anglicizing the last name to Smith. In Croatia, one Marijan Smetisko denied ever knowing anyone named Eugenia, let alone marrying her.

In a ten-page article, *Life* simply presented as a detective story, almost deadpan, all the evidence that had been uncovered. As we went to press, the Spellers hadn't yet thrown in the sponge. The book, entitled *Anastasia, the Autobiography of the Grand Duchess of Russia,* was printed. But shortly afterward, the Spellers conceded that Smith was a fake and moved to recall the copies.

Even though we doubted Smith, the romantic notion that an Anastasia somehow could have survived perhaps tempted us too long. I suppose it would have been just as effective to ignore what, by the time of publication, was obviously a waste of ten valuable pages in the magazine.

25

The Adamses and the Kennedys of Massachusetts

◯∾ While *Life* readers learned a lot about families called Adams and Kennedy, I treasure my personal contacts with the two families while our series about them were being prepared. *Life* contributions to the Massachusetts Historical Society gave us access to the Adams papers. The Kennedys shrewdly distributed favors for the maximum political effect, to be sure, but we were glad to work with this high-profile family.

The self-deprecating humor of the twentieth-century Adamses surfaced early in the negotiations for magazine rights to the family papers. Roy Larsen, president of Time Inc., was head of the *Life* group. We proposed a most difficult procedure, diving into bales of diaries and other documents to produce a series of magazine articles. The raw material, of course, included the work of two presidents, a lively first lady (Abigail), a Civil War ambassador to Great Britain, a distinguished writer (Henry), and a secretary of the navy of fairly recent memory. Lyman Butterfield, the historical society curator, was to spot material for *Life* and assemble a series of books for the society. He said gloomily, "This project will not be completed in my lifetime." (It was, incidentally.)

During a negotiating session I became aware of a middle-aged man off to one side who was scowling. He was Thomas Boylston Adams, a direct descendant of the presidents. I went over and explained that the questions we were asking weren't critical of the literary product of his family, the magazine simply had only a limited amount of space. He growled, "I don't see why you want that stuff at all. It's dull as dishwater."

When the arrangement was announced later, the living Adamses were on display. I went to Boston by train to a session of the historical society. Old John Adams, president of the society, presided. A fog closed Logan Airport, keeping Larsen airborne, so I had to fill in for him, silently wishing that the boys in the dingy pool hall in St. Thomas, North Dakota, could see me as a temporary Brahmin.

John handled the proceedings dictatorially. "I propose the name of Roy Edward Larsen to be an associate member of the Massachusetts Historical Society," he intoned. "And why, you may ask, should we admit Roy Edward Larsen? Because he's going to give us a lot of money, that's why. Do I hear any objections? No, I don't. He is accepted."

Tom Adams succeeded John as the senior Adams and as president of the society. He was particularly active in trying to improve polluted Walden Pond and its environs. In the process, as a creative curmudgeon, he fulminated savagely against the state establishment: "I refer to every blatherskite politician who would make a public swimming pool out of the font in St. Peters and a filling station out of the Taj Mahal if they were located in Massachusetts and it would net him a vote," he wrote. "Walden on a hot day in June looks more like the Ganges on a holy day than a place for Emerson and Thoreau to contemplate. But it's all right to copulate."

At various literary affairs observing the progress of the *Life* project, Tom Adams was a delight. He would advise the guests to have several cocktails before enduring the "ordeal" to which he was going to subject them. He had a disarming reason for arriving late at one of these: "I was reading *Alice in Wonderland* to my children before bedtime." I commented that, surprisingly, my own sons were bored and refused to listen to *Alice*. "My children," said Tom, "wouldn't dare not like it."

There were no sensational revelations in the Adams papers, but Lyman Butterfield's selections did a great deal to humanize the impression that younger citizens may have had that the Founding Fathers were unmitigatingly stern. As a young man teaching school and reading law in Worcester, for instance, John Adams confided to his diary that he was "too lazy, my mind is called off the law by a girl, a pipe, a poem." Just before he married Abigail he listed, at her request, her faults, which included "sitting with Leggs across . . . bad for the figure." She replied saucily that "a Gentleman has no business to concern himself with the Leggs of a Lady."

Tom Adams, who exulted in saying, "No respectable men's club should accept me," could be serious and eloquent, as when he presented some volumes of the diaries at the White House in 1961: "The independent historical society . . . has always been glad to welcome . . . cranks and eccentrics, as well as pillars of scholarship and society. It is old enough to know that sometimes the pillars crumble and sometimes the eccentrics turn out to be geniuses. . . . a working knowledge of the lessons of history is a necessity for survival. We have to know how we got here. If we step back into any of the old bogs we are done for."

On his deathbed, Thomas Jefferson perhaps predicted the importance that his fellow revolutionary and ideological opponent Adams—along with his descendants—would have. Jefferson is said to have asked about the condition of the first John Adams, who was also ill. Assured that he had not yet succumbed, Jefferson said, "The Republic lives."

Jefferson and Adams died the same day, July 4, 1826, but, with significant participation by Adams's descendants, the republic indeed lives.

If we take a hop, skip, and a jump through the centuries, it isn't difficult to fall in step with the Kennedys (and Fitzgeralds), who also helped keep the republic alive. To be sure, they may have resorted more to power politics than Founding Father John Adams would have displayed overtly. But he would have approved of President John F.'s handling of the Cuban missile crisis and of Attorney General Robert's determination to rid the republic of a blot like Jimmy Hoffa. The modern Kennedys, in turn, would have to agree with Jefferson's view of John Adams and no doubt applauded Tom Adams's campaign for a purer Walden Pond.

Over time, Massachusetts political power shifted inevitably, if not always smoothly, to the Irish Americans, then to the Italians, and so on. For instance, it was not at all incongruous to find Mike Ward, he of the wise Irish-American Catholic voice, serving on Boston's prestigious School Committee with a representative of old Massachusetts, a Mrs. Henry Wadsworth Longfellow no less, to their mutual satisfaction.

One day I was invited to the daily lunch of an informal Boston institution hosted by a Greek-American shipping magnate who was very big in the wholesale liquor business. Politicians from both parties would just drop in from time to time to mix fraternally, to shoot the breeze off the record. The topic of conversation was a supposedly authentic rumor of a secret medical report that Jack Kennedy's bad back (he was a senator then) was definitely going to end his political career. Surprisingly to me, this prospect was received with great equanimity by the Democrats.

Of the Kennedys, Joseph P. was a self-made tycoon, but let's not forget his father-in-law, "Honey Fitz" Fitzgerald, the former mayor of Boston and the personification of an old-time politician. Among Joe and Rose's children there were Joseph Jr., who had been the one destined for politics by his father, John Fitzgerald, and Robert, who preferred to be Bob rather than Bobby. All three died tragically. Today, of course, there is Edward (Ted), the senator.

As an ambassador for Roosevelt, Joe served at the Court of St. James's, where a youthful JFK got the idea for his book on prewar England, *Why England Slept*. Luce wrote the introduction. When JFK was nominated as the Democratic candidate for president, *Life* reporters and photographers hunted unsuccessfully all over the country to find Joe and get his reaction. It turned out, as Luce smugly told me later, that he himself had secretly spent the evening with Joe.

During the campaign, *Life* and *Time* were scrupulously fair, at least in the amount of space allotted to JFK and Nixon. In an editorial, however, the official endorsement, mostly on the grounds of domestic policy, went to Nixon.

I had solicited and obtained an article on the future of the Democratic Party from then Senator Kennedy after Stevenson's second defeat in 1956. It was relatively easy to get him to a *Life* editors' lunch. We were doing a story on the Kennedy and Fitzgerald families, and I asked him to come back after lunch to see some layouts. Word spread that he was there, as it had with the Duke of Windsor some years earlier, and he ran a gauntlet of breathless women employees. JFK outdrew the Duke.

The way the Kennedys got the most out of press coverage was, instead of granting exactly the same access to everyone, to make individual exclusives possible. There was a balance of sorts. If *Look* got exclusive photographs of the first family at Palm Beach, *Life* could photograph the children in the White House.

As president, JFK could make you feel you were his personal guest. He proposed to me, with convincing spontaneity, "Let me give you my tour of the White House," and led the way to the family quarters, leaving a senior speechwriter waiting outside the Oval Office. I was directed to note Eisenhower's golf-cleat marks outside his bedroom and the Kennedy display of American art—Remingtons, Russells, etc.

The rumors about Kennedy's personal life were extant before the 1960 Democratic convention. One writer, who had worked for me previously, announced pompously, using an Elizabethan term, "I will not have a whoremaster as President of the United States." He was on another Time Inc. payroll by this time and proposed an investigation. He persuaded me

With Senator John F. Kennedy and Harry Luce (1960, courtesy Time Inc.).

to meet a notorious private detective at my Los Angeles hotel. The writer's informant was to be a brothel proprietor, but he reported that he had lost touch with the madam, who had become the companion of a Tammany leader for the duration of the convention. He then named a colleague in the East who might help the writer.

The would-be investigative reporter was off on the next plane, but while he was airborne I had a check run on the eastern peeper. Before the writer landed I knew that his new source had a long record of nonpayment of alimony and traffic violations, so I told the reporter to knock off his search.

Luce heard about the writer's trip and asked—I don't know how seriously —"Why isn't *Life* telling me about this kind of thing?" I said I didn't think that *Life* should emulate *Confidential* magazine. I asked if, to be fair, he wanted a check run on Nixon's private life, too. No answer.

After the creation of the Peace Corps was announced, I went to Washington to make a pitch for a little advance notice on such sweeping proposals. We wouldn't ask for an exclusive on major announcements, but we would like to prepare some hold-for-release material showing the possible scope of any similar project.

JFK agreed to keep our request in mind, but it was easier to make potential deals with Robert Kennedy, attorney general, his brother's most trusted counselor. I had a standing invitation from him to chat when in town. Bob once said, "Ed, you've never violated a confidence."

The most dramatic result of our occasional meetings was his telling me confidentially about the legal task force that he had set up to pursue Jimmy Hoffa. The idea was to have our reporters knowledgeable enough ahead of time to reconstruct how the eventually successful conviction was achieved.

Life editors had seen Hoffa, the powerful Teamsters union boss and the target of the Bob Kennedy task force, up close at one point. A public relations man calculated that Hoffa's social graces at a lunch with us would improve his image. The idea was a dud. Hoffa came in very late, furious about a brush with a federal judge during the morning. "Everyone at this table has his price," Hoffa said, pointing at us one by one. "If I want to pay I can buy you all." He paid no attention to our quietly expressed demurrals, but we took some satisfaction when, the next day, a *Daily News* reporter turned the Hoffa spokesman over to the police for offering him a bribe.

Hoffa's end came, not in a federal prison as Bob Kennedy planned, but in a kidnapping and presumed rubout, gang style. One rumor is that his body was embedded in the concrete of Giants Stadium in East Rutherford, New Jersey, but no one has yet revealed his section, aisle, and seat numbers.

I was en route back from the Far East in 1963 when the president was assassinated. I had had a dubious promotion to a new position, editor of *Life,* and wanted to leave the new managing editor, George Hunt, some time without me looking over his shoulder. The *Life* coverage, which included the famous Zapruder film, was magnificent. However, I was not through with the Kennedys yet, even though I was no longer concerned with week-by-week news coverage.

As editor, I was in charge of very expensive projects, so I wheeled the *Life* checkbook into position to get the best possible firsthand account of the Kennedy years. One assistant, Ted Sorenson, signed elsewhere. I thought Arthur Schlesinger Jr. would bring the approach of a historian to the drama-filled years. I'm sure he would have wanted to take his time, but he rose to the competitive occasion and turned out enough of *A Thousand Days* for *Life* to publish several installments before Sorenson's series started. Arthur inscribed my copy with a tongue-in-cheek thanks for preparing an audience for the book.

26

Personal Notes about the
Quite Human Luces

❧ Naturally, I got to know various Luce family members reasonably well, better than I knew an Adams or a Kennedy. However, I would not count myself an intimate friend.

Harry claimed that anyone named Luce, anywhere, could trace ancestry to a small town in Scotland. In his words, the Luces were, "for 300 years, always solvent, sometimes distinguished, never rich." His father, Henry Winters Luce, was a Presbyterian missionary in China, where Harry spent his childhood before being sent to the States for prep school and, importantly, Yale University. I met the Reverend Mr. Luce once, briefly, in his son's office, and he seemed every inch the gentle, saintly man everyone said he was. Harry's mother was dead, and he had a sister, Elizabeth, and a half brother, Sheldon, the son of Henry W.'s second wife.

The blood relatives did not really figure importantly in Time Inc. affairs, but I hadn't realized this when, shortly after I came from Milwaukee in 1937, I was invited to lunch at the University Club by Sheldon, the titular business manager of *Life*. Pretty perceptive of a Luce, I thought, to have recognized within weeks the treasure they had acquired as an assistant picture editor, me.

Sheldon, who, then and later, couldn't have been nicer, leaned across our steak sandwiches and, in a confidential tone, asked: "Ed, I've been wondering, where does *Life* get all those pictures?" Sheldon soon departed for California, where, according to reports, he became the happy owner of a chicken ranch.

Harry's sister, with whom he had an affectionate relationship, was a far different type of Luce. Beth had all the graces he sometimes lacked, and seemed, as I gradually came to know her over the years, just as intelligent, in a low-key way. She was active in organizations such as the YWCA and in charities involving China. She was married to Maurice T. (Tex, after his native state) Moore, senior partner in Cravath, Swain and Moore, Time Inc.'s lawyers.

Tex, ever solicitous in protecting his brother-in-law's public relations, would have known how to handle a brash practical joker I met in Texas, where brashness abounds. I was at a Dallas social club when a far-from-sober small-time millionaire arrived with his secretary and kept asking me, "How's ol' Harry?" as he leaned against her. "Oh, boy," he said, "we sure scared him."

According to this little rich man, pranksters had staged a fake train holdup and caused Luce to dive under his seat. It was while his divorce from his first wife, Lila, was pending, and he was supposed to have thought the holdup was a new way to serve a subpoena. Harry confirmed later that, at least, there had been a fake train holdup.

Harry Luce's oldest son, Henry (by Lila, his first wife), became Henry III in later years, nickname Hank. He could have been somewhat of a problem. Although his abruptness of manner sometimes reminded one of his father, his talents didn't. I came, however, to respect his character and integrity. At Yale, he worked on the Hoover Commission, studying government. John Billings, before he retired, suspected that Hank was on his way to Time Inc. and, from his letters, realized that the young Luce's literary abilities were limited. Billings concluded unflatteringly, "There is no place to send him but *Life*." I said, "Okay, but he'll get tougher discipline than any other young writer there."

One Saturday night, when an issue of *Life* was closing, I got a summons to have dinner with Luce, to meet Hank and his wife. I thought, "Oops, here we go."

Lord Beaverbrook and a member of Parliament were there too, but left early for the theater. I braced myself. Harry said, "Henry is about to take a job on the *Cleveland Press*. You've worked on a newspaper. Tell him how to act, what clubs to join, etc."

Relieved, I made an honest effort, although I didn't know anything about clubs in Cleveland (or Milwaukee)—I was sure that Harry didn't mean the Press Club. There was then a custom among executives of publications to trade sons, presumably to give them experience useful for later jobs at home. I cited as a horrible example the scion of one of the *Baltimore Sun* families. He arrived in Milwaukee to become third assistant police reporter. He had a private airplane (with which to commute home on weekends) and a valet.

"Listen, Henry," Luce joked, "no valet."

I said, "You'll be considered a plant, so the thing for you to do is to behave from the beginning as if you were after Louis Seltzer's job." Louis, later also a friend of mine, was the editor of the *Press* and known as "Mr. Cleveland."

The move seemed to be a success. The young Luce became a good reporter. Whether my advice had anything to do with it, I don't know, although Hank's first wife, Betsy, told me it was the best thing that could have happened. Hank did resist trading on his father's eminence and later served creditably in various jobs around Time Inc.

A second son, Peter, successfully disassociated himself from the company.

The boss's wife must always be reckoned with. If she was Clare Boothe Luce, you would have reservations in commenting on her, but you might wish for the eloquence of Charlie Murphy. After Harry died, Clare was living in Washington when Murphy was unaccountably called on to be a character witness for her—she wanted to move into a Watergate apartment. Charlie testified that he "could hardly have been more comfortable had I been called on to vouch for the piety of the Sainted Mother Elizabeth Seton; for the courage of Molly Pitcher; for the civic zeal of Susan B. Anthony; for the rural grace of Emily Dickinson or for the acumen of a Hetty Green. All these gifts are summed up in a comely person and a radiant spirit."

Clare had a galaxy of careers. She had been a magazine editor of the old *Vanity Fair,* and on that level we treated each other as fellow professionals. She had decided opinions but scrupulously avoided direct contact with various Time Inc. editors. At first I gave her credit for admirable restraint, but later she told me that, early on in the marriage, when she thought Luce's longtime secretary, Corinne Thrasher, had been impertinent, her husband warned her that the magazines were not her business.

Clare occasionally conveyed her thoughts to Harry, who, if he found they made sense, would expose them tentatively with an offhand "Should we possibly do something about—?" The source was recognizable and, certainly, I turned down no ideas just because I thought they were hers. I felt no pressure to accept them, either.

When we were about to move into the then new Time & Life Building in 1938, we might have been close to getting her as a neighbor. She and

Dancing with Clare Boothe Luce at a birthday party she gave for the proprietor (mid-1950s, courtesy Time Inc.).

Harry toyed with the idea of living in a penthouse atop the building. They wisely gave up the plan when they realized that occasionally they would be returning home—in evening clothes—to face ink-stained wretches working late on one magazine or another.

If the night elevator operator had followed the unwritten code of his daytime counterpart, however, the magazine workers would not have had a chance to catch a glimpse of the Luces. Luce's approach was a signal for the operator to push everyone else away, shut the door in their faces, and whiz straight up to the corporate floor. Innocents who pulled hats down over their eyes, like Luce did, or had a vague resemblance to the boss would find themselves on an unexpected express ride before they could call out their floor number.

One time Harry heard about my plans for a vacation. "What do you want to go to Europe for?" he asked. "Everyone goes there. Why not North Africa or the Far East? I'll pay your expenses."

"It's my vacation, and I'm paying for it. I just think I'll enjoy Europe."

Possibly he didn't hear me. He resumed grumpily, "Well, don't expect me to pay for it."

"I told you I am paying, and, if you feel strongly about it, I won't even visit any of the *Time* and *Life* bureaus. I have personal friends in them, but they can meet me outside the offices."

This being settled, Harry became wholly gracious. Clare was ambassador to Italy, and he was being of considerable help to her. He called me in Sorrento with an invitation to a party at the embassy (my dinner clothes unfortunately were being sent from France to England for the voyage home, so I couldn't accept). He took the Thompson family out to dinner in Rome, and later Clare invited us to a family lunch at the ambassador's residence, the Villa Taverna.

The Borghese zoo was nearby and when we said we were going there with Harry, Clare, who was going to spend the afternoon with official papers, warned that I'd better have change because Harry never did. (He had a private office in Rome where there was a charge for the elevator. Time Inc. furnished the elevator operator with lira and several portraits of Harry from different angles so that the fees would be paid on his behalf.)

Sure enough, Harry didn't have any change for the zoo admission; he was also frustrated by not being able to find any of the sugar buns the Italians were feeding the polar bears. I pointed out that the kitchen of the Villa Taverna could provide buns for his next trip.

He then proposed what he called the Luce tour of Rome. We went to various places, mostly churches, on his regular route. He indulged himself thoroughly in his penchant for cross-examination. He had studied up on obscure facts about each stop on the tour and was absolutely devastating in astounding the guides, who usually had a set spiel but no more. For instance, in one church cellar he pointed out a trough that had been used to carry off bulls' blood in pagan sacrifices when the building was a temple.

It was only partly because Clare was a prominent convert to Catholicism (the eloquent radio priest, Monsignor Fulton J. Sheen, converted her after the tragic death of her only daughter, by a previous marriage) that it was arranged for us to meet Pope Pius XII. My wife, Marguerite, was a Catholic and so were my brother and his wife. We took rosaries to be blessed. A general audience was considered best because so-called "private audiences" were cut-and-dried affairs with His Holiness usually making a short, impersonal speech. At a general audience some can work their way up to the pontiff for a few words.

Our sponsors were a *Time* reporter, a papal knight (who was later stripped of membership and excommunicated for a scandalous extramarital affair), and the editor of the *Osservatore Romano,* the official Vatican newspaper. They were like Forrest Evashevski, who ran interference for Tommy Harmon. They shouldered other worshippers aside, pushing at the faces of one group of nuns who had traveled from Bavaria for the occasion.

Clare's secretary was in our group and was horrified when Pius momentarily mistook Marguerite for the ambassador (there was only a slight resemblance in facial bone structure). When corrected, the Pope said to the secretary, "Tell her she's working too hard." The rosaries we brought were duly blessed.

(We became aware that Ambassador Clare was the subject of petty malice in some parts of Roman society. One patently apocryphal story had her bending the Pope's ear with missionary zeal, and the Pope replying, "But, Mrs. Luce, I am already a Catholic.")

We had visited Assisi before Rome, and I remarked to Clare that the church there was one of only two we had seen where actual worship was going on. It contrasted, say, with St. Paul's-Outside-the-Walls, which seemed to be kind of a liquor store for the sale of monastery brandy. Clare brushed that aside and asked, "But surely you saw my namesake, St. Clare?"

We had, but I deplored the fact that the embalmed body of St. Francis was on display in a glass coffin on the main floor, while St. Clare (1194–1253, canonized in 1255) was in the basement, even though she was cofounder, with St. Francis, of the Order of the Poor Clares.

(Incidentally, Clare chided me from time to time for not working hard enough to find a female assistant managing editor. She was right. I should have found one.)

Throughout Italy I was dogged by calls from a prominent publisher of magazines and books. I knew what he wanted—free use of *Life* pictures—and was dodging him. Luce asked me why.

I said, "He's trying to take us for a free ride."

His temporary secretary, a contessa, was summoned, and Harry said, "Mr. Thompson here says your friend is a crook."

"Oh, no," she said.

"See?" said Harry. "What's the matter with him?"

"For one thing," I said, "of his four sons, one is a fascist, one is a Communist, one is a Christian Democrat, and one is a socialist. He plays each one according to the shifts in the political wind."

Harry was acclimated by this time, and he patiently explained the difference between what passed for Italian ethics and his and mine.

Shortly before Clare's term ended I got a long-distance call from Harry, still in Rome. "My wife is talking about writing her memoirs, but she wants to sell magazine rights to the *Saturday Evening Post.* She won't listen to me, but she may to you. She's in the States. Talk her out of it."

"It will have a big sale," he predicted. "All of the Republicans, Catholics, and feminists will have to read it, and so will the Democrats, Protestants, and male chauvinists—to see what she says about them."

I recalled an incident concerning the *Post* after she had made a trip to the Far East before Pearl Harbor. I was in John Billings's office, and he was talking to her on the phone. I guess he was a trifle tired of Clare's articles, although he had made good use of a closeup she wrote on MacArthur. It came in very handy after the Japanese attack. "Now, Clare," he was saying persuasively, "you don't want it said that you can sell only to your husband's magazines. Why don't you try the *Post* on this one?"

"This one" was the discovery by Clare of an American mercenary general, Homer Lee, who had informed his Chinese employers, in fairly exact detail, about how the Japanese would later start a war in the Pacific. Her article was a scoop of sorts.

When I talked to Clare about her book, I could see that she had an impressively well organized outline. It would be in sections, one each on her varied careers. There would be the entrance of an unknown American girl into society, her marriage to a Brokaw, her editorship of *Vanity Fair,* Clare the playwright (*The Women,* etc.), the politician and member of the House of Representatives, and the diplomat.

"I don't want to be regarded," she said, echoing Billings, "as an author who can only sell to my husband's magazine. Don't you think it would be more chic to appear in the *Post?*"

I didn't. I argued that she owed it to herself to get the widest possible audience—*Life's.* No. She was adamant. Ben Hibbs, editor of the *Post,* and Bob Sherrod, who would be her editor there, were both friends of hers.

Some time passed. The Luces returned from Rome, and I got a long-distance call from Harry, this time from Chicago. Was I free for lunch? No, but I could break a date. "Take my wife out," I was told. "I think she's changing her mind about selling to the *Post.*"

Indeed she was and gave as a reason that she would be required to write one installment at a time and would have only a week to produce the next. The *Post,* she said, wanted to start the series immediately. I found it hard to believe that any card-carrying editor would take such a chance on being left high and dry if the next chapter failed to come in. Almost as an afterthought she also said she had decided, on reflection, that she wouldn't get paid enough.

"Well, Clare, how much *do* you want?"

"Dear Harry will be my agent. See him about that."

Agent Harry asked me to forget Clare was Mrs. Luce and bid the amount I would be willing to pay her on her own. Remember, it was before inflation. I said $75,000, and he replied, "You have bid only half enough."

I said, "It's out of one of your pockets or another. A hundred and fifty thousand it is."

I later found out I had bid exactly what Clare had thought was too small a sum from the *Post.* A contract was duly drawn up, and Harper & Row got the book rights. *Life* was obligated to furnish research help and did, but Clare's signature on the contract was the last of her writing I was to see.

I kept making passes at the book from time to time. Once, at a Luce reception after the opening of a Chinese (Nationalist) art exhibition at the Metropolitan, I found myself sitting next to Clare. Nelson Rockefeller was on her other side, and, while he was saying "Hi, fella" to various passersby, I said, "Clare, I don't think you intend to write a line of that book."

"Oh, I want to," she said, "but Harry doesn't want me to."

Luce, who was drifting around the room, appeared and said, "What are you two talking about?"

I said, "I'm trying to get Clare's book back on the rails."

"Fine, finc," he said. "Good luck."

The Luce family's closeness to the Nationalist Chinese caused me some personal embarrassment in 1963. On a trip from the Far East I had stopped off in Taipei and made the obligatory call on Chiang Kai-shek. The interview was not very revealing for either one of us. As I was about to leave, Mme. Chiang, who had been expertly helping the official interpreter, proposed that I take some gifts with me for Clare and her sister-in-law, Beth Moore. The gifts arrived as I was leaving my hotel, two objects elaborately wrapped in silk. They weren't large. I tucked them in and thought no more about them until I was about to go through customs in Honolulu.

I sounded dubious even to myself when I said they were gifts from Mme. Chiang Kai-shek. Of course, I had no bill of sale and hadn't listed them on my declaration. The customs man disappeared. A last call for reboarding the plane was sounded. The customs man finally came out, said my name had sounded something like that of a known smuggler, apologized, stuck the packages in my bag, and summoned a jeep to take me to the plane.

I got a gracious note of thanks from Beth—the packages contained gold-embroidered heavy silk material. Nothing from Clare. Years later when I asked about the package, she said, "Oh, you brought it. I always wondered where it came from." The response by Beth and the silence from Clare were typical.

Once you accepted Clare for what you thought she was like, you could enjoy, as I did, the slightly off-color jokes she told Monsignor John Courtney Murray, her spiritual adviser. You found even more satisfaction when, in his suave Jesuit way, he topped her jokes with his own. Father Murray was also Harry's favorite opponent in theological bull sessions.

Clare had the grace to organize a farewell lunch for Harry's secretary, Corinne Thrasher. Corinne, with whom I had lunch after she retired from long, long service, and who was fiercely loyal to her boss, ruefully admitted that "Mr. Luce never thought of things like that."

Clare's book project was reconsidered periodically. At a lunch that stretched out for a full afternoon, Clare, still protesting that she intended to produce the book, said, "I want this to be honest, but I don't want to hurt people who are still alive." I began to deduce from bits of confidential comment on what it was like to be Mrs. Henry R. Luce that Harry was the main one she did not want to hurt.

As she approached eighty, Clare continued to say that she intended to write that book. She may, in fact, have written some of it. If so, it didn't surface after her death.

No one asked for my appraisal of Clare Booth Luce, but, shed of Charlie Murphy's hyperbole: yes, she was pious, brave, civically zealous—and she did have something in common with Emily Dickinson and Hetty Green.

27

When "Too Much Excellence" Became a Dirty Word

☙ The chip I sometimes wore on my shoulder like an epaulet might have indicated that I thought my performance so valuable that my job tenure could be as permanent as I wanted it to be. And, to be sure, Luce had mumbled a few times that he expected me to move upstairs "sometime." But I knew that precedent, Time Inc. style, indicated inexorably that a change of the guard would take place sooner rather than later.

So what next, in case "upstairs" became impossible? I had long thought that a medium-sized daily newspaper suited my experience and abilities. Enough might be going on to keep me interested—a weekly town would be too dull. If I could scrape up enough financing to buy the business, I would be indisputably my own boss.

My prospective purchase, ideally, might have an owner who didn't want a newspaper chain to come into his town, who was approaching retirement age and who had no heirs interested in the business. I had been in touch with a broker, W. H. Glover, who had an intimate knowledge of individual newspapers, including the health and actuarial expectations of each proprietor. And in 1956 my two sons and I spent a month of our vacations scouting papers that Glover recommended in Colorado, Wyoming, Idaho, Washington, and Oregon. We knew that officially none of these was for sale, but I hoped a family ownership might appeal to some owners. It didn't, as it turned out, though we did learn a good deal about the economics of running a daily.

Two years later, I had an outside chance to acquire a desirable newspaper. It was the morning *Sacramento Union,* which had first published Mark Twain's *Innocents Abroad* in installments. Its deceased proprietor's heir was married to a Los Angeles contractor and might be tempted. A resident manager had divulged to a new broker, Allen Kander, the confidential details of the *Union*'s remarkable profitability. Morning papers seemed to be gaining in most U.S. cities, partly because traffic made it difficult to deliver the afternoons at any meaningful time. The McClatchy chain's *Sacramento Bee* was powerful but not considered too dangerous to the *Union* because its broadcast interests had already put it under threat of antitrust action.

By that time my older son, Ed, had become a writer on *Fortune* and was frustrated because he wanted to be an editor and didn't feel he was being taken seriously for that kind of job. I didn't have enough assets to mount an acceptable bid on my own but proposed to throw what I had into a deal to be put together by a professional money finder from a nationally known firm. Ed used, I suspected, his slide rule from his M.I.T. undergraduate days and figured out a scenario for buying out our partners in a reasonably short time with the *Union*'s projected cash flow.

All calculations were predicated on the assumption that the Thompsons had to have 51 percent of the voting stock, and I specified to the money finder that no advertiser be included in the group being solicited to help swing the deal because that could bring trouble later if the paper were to be uncomplimentary about that company.

From a group that included a food processor, insurance executives, and other nonadvertising businessmen, we got promises of almost 95 percent of the capital needed. Being so close proved too much of a temptation for the money finder. He solicited an advertiser, who took one look at the balance sheet and went storming into the *Union* plant demanding a cut in his advertising rates because the paper was making so much money. The owner promptly took the property off the market.

My son Ed eventually became editor-in-chief of *Reader's Digest.* Colin became a CIA agent. I'm not sure we would have gotten along together in a business venture, but the effort to find a newspaper cemented a feeling of family closeness.

Life continued to be an aggressive and lively magazine. As background for the racial troubles in Little Rock, there was a graphic and thoughtful series, starting with the slave trade, on black segregation. With its publication we unwittingly caused a black schoolteacher and her husband, whom we quoted, to lose their jobs—we had included an account of their troubles in one installment. So we undertook to support them, as we should have, until they could relocate successfully.

We called the editorial team in Little Rock "war correspondents." One member was jailed on a charge of disorderly conduct for, as he put it, hitting a cop's fist with his face. Our air express packages of film came to us with the words "nigger bastards" scrawled on them.

Name-calling from the outside broke no bones, but by 1958 Life's profitability had slipped markedly, and business-side sniping at the editorial department became noticeable. Luce sensed, correctly, that I was getting a little testy, and he went out of his way to praise individual issues. (Sample: "Tops, absolutely tops. . . . if it makes you feel good for a moment you certainly deserve it." But he added that while Heiskell and Larsen liked recent issues very much, "we have fewer promotable items for newsstands than in the last few years.")

Harry continued to be supportive. He got angry when Life's use of lighthearted material was attacked by Lucius Beebe, a New York columnist. Beebe found the magazine's performance dangerous because it was "the most powerful influence on taste and social destiny. . . . It is hard to name a cheap, vulgar or meretricious aspect of the American chromium pigsty that has not received priceless publicity."

Naturally, I agreed with Luce's intracompany memo that followed. He allowed that Life should of course address itself to important issues, which we did—such things as the face of poverty—but he felt, as I did and do, that there was "no reason why Life should be a weekly headache and pain in the neck." Early in 1959 he expressed himself as satisfied with the editorial direction and said the rest was up to the promotion people.

During one discussion I had with Heiskell he said he viewed Life's attainment of status as an institution to be both good and not so good. When he commented that we were sometimes *too* earnest, I agreed that perhaps he had a point.

In March 1959 Heiskell unloaded with a blockbuster to Luce and me. Far from agreeing with Luce that promotion could take on all responsibility for keeping up sales, he concluded that the business side could just about maintain the magazine's present circulation position, but that any improvement in circulation and profitability would have to be generated by editorial. Ad pages had dropped in the last two years—by more than ten per issue.

For the first time in almost ten years there were some pointed Heiskell criticisms of editorial. Samples: "More and more of the news events of the world could never happen to the reader." "Are we telling the story of Man in terms that appeal to him?" "*Life* suffers from too much excellence"!

Look, which in its promotion called itself the magazine of the people (implying that *Life* wasn't), and the *Saturday Evening Post* had circulations approaching ours. I rated them low in competition because it seemed to me they were buying circulation at a cost that was prohibitive—premiums, lavish spending on direct-mail solicitation and other promotion, free grace periods for subscriptions.

At the time, I wrote a memo addressed to Heiskell's charges. Conferences, with some raised voices, followed. At one point Heiskell suggested that maybe he should leave. I suggested that maybe I should. I have some scrawled notes to the effect that each of us then said he didn't want the other to go.

Heiskell had made his points—something was askew—and felt that, temporarily, he couldn't go any further with Luce. As managing editor, with the self-confidence characteristic of that breed, I felt at first that I should drive the magazine closer to the concept of perfection, whether or not that had become a dirty word in some places. *Life* remained the big magazine which Luce continued to say had enabled the company to "build that skyscraper" (work was just starting on a new and much bigger Time & Life Building).

Tantalizingly, in retrospect, there *was* a serious—and possibly profitable—alternative to super bigness. Howard Black, the company's executive vice president for advertising, suggested an orderly drop in circulation from six million to four, saving millions of dollars on direct mail and production and retaining the kind of high-class advertising that was most profitable. Howard's jocular manner may have prevented his colleagues from taking him seriously. In any case, his suggestion was not pursued.

Instead, what emerged from the discussions about *Life* was a macho move to *raise* the circulation. Circulation had been going up only gradually during the late fifties. Now seven million would be the goal during the sixties. Taken with the approval of the board of directors, the "big decision" (Heiskell's term) included a cut in newsstand and subscription prices. Luce, who had assured me, "If we can't find any other way to fight [competition] except with dollars that's the way we'll fight," now sent a rousing wire to the 1959 ad sales convention: "We believe in a competitive economy, and we propose to compete the hell out of everybody on every front."

That all seemed to suit the combative aspect of my nature. I should note, though, that we were aware, at the same time, of a trend toward specialized publications. One assistant managing editor, Philip Wootton, came up with what he called a possible "quantum jump" in magazine making. The idea was to add supplements devoted to some of the areas in which *Life* excelled, charging a couple of dollars extra per year to special subscribers. Samples were made up, and the idea was tested by mail solicitation. My belief in an enthusiast who is convinced he has a workable idea is more fervent than my acceptance of a "scientific" test, but the returns on circulation tests did not support making a big investment in Phil's idea. The only subject that tested out favorably was an entertainment section, always a crowd pleaser, and this may have suggested that the company should then and there have embarked on a *People*-like publication.

Time Inc. hadn't had an editorial director since Billings retired in 1954, and Luce came to need one. He selected Hedley Donovan, who had succeeded Del Paine as managing editor of *Fortune*. Hedley had been in that job long enough to know what pains managing editors can be, so he suggested that Luce sound out Roy Alexander and me about his selection. Luce reported accurately to Hedley: "Your nomination was confirmed by the exclusive senate of two. . . . Roy was decidedly for having an editorial director and for you. I had a feeling that Ed didn't feel the appointment was entirely necessary although he was all for you."

I did respect Hedley's intellectual qualities, and he was scrupulously fair. My feet dragged a bit for purely selfish reasons. I would miss dealing directly with Luce on matters that he would now delegate to the editorial director.

The burning question in the upper reaches of Time Inc. increasingly became: what to do about *Life?* Could it—should it—be revamped? In mid-1960 Luce produced on his own what he called a "new prospectus" for the magazine, the first since the original in 1936. But in fact there was little new in it—"The New *Life,*" pronounced Luce, "is already inherent in the *Life* that is and has been." Not much guidance there.

Hedley had been musing about an editorial research and development operation. I now volunteered myself, Art Director Charlie Tudor, and Assistant M.E. George Hunt to form such a group to challenge the existing editorial content. There was no thought of a total remake ("The most discouraging thing about the *Life* situation," Hedley had recently observed, "is that the magazine is so good"). We concentrated almost exclusively on how to do better the kinds of things we already did well. In hindsight I shouldn't have limited the exercise to editorial. What was also needed was someone from the business side to challenge what was going on there. It might have been impossible, however, to find anyone to oppose the "big decision" to blow the competition out of the water with advertising and promotion expenditures.

In the R & D dry runs, with a lot of sweat and some ingenuity, a typographically tidier and cleaner-looking magazine took shape, displaying more effectively the kinds of wares we had. This was achieved in part by "stacking"—having some full-page advertisements face others, as many other magazines did. We knew that advertisers very much wanted to be placed next to editorial content, but we felt this would be a slight sacrifice. Sample issues were produced which were able to display five major stories instead of the three that normally ran, and with considerably greater impact.

Perhaps relieved not to have to think about the magazine for a while, Luce seemed to feel that we had invented something. His verdict: "We've just about got it. The New *Life*."

The results were approved by all hands, and I was quite willing to be convinced that we had contributed something more substantial than mere pleasing cosmetics. The new publisher, C. D. Jackson (Heiskell had become chairman of the board), wanting to get maximum promotional value out of the "new" magazine, wrote an enthusiastic introduction for the first issue. An invitation to trouble, as events proved, was that he mentioned the box-office poison (to advertisers) term *stacking*.

The first four issues of the revised product were praised by Luce and by many outside of the company. But then some advertisers voiced their unhappiness, and the business side lost its nerve. Stacking of ads went by the board, and with it a large part of the new magazine. Whether enough substance remained to be of great value quickly became moot because the task force's work was swept away in editorial staff changes. They started at the top—me.

Was Luce just kidding me along with an intention to deceive when he seemed to accept my version of a new *Life?* I have never thought so. He may have been kidding himself *and* me. What was happening was a buildup to a comeuppance, no matter what anyone thought or didn't think.

28

A "Promotion" the Ungrateful Recipient Felt Was a Kick Upstairs

༄ Was I being excessively romantic in adherence to my mystique of being a Time Inc. managing editor? I didn't like to compare what might happen to me with what I thought had happened to other managing editors when they were "promoted" to something called the editorship. Or to the concept of Del Paine, "debagged" into being publisher instead of managing editor of *Fortune*.

Luce, I supposed logically enough, had been musing about splitting the job of *Life* managing editor into those of managing editor and editor. Privately I should have conceded that there was possibly too much work in that big an operation for one man.

On June 8, 1961, I received a "nomination" from Luce proposing that I become editor, George Hunt managing editor, and Phil Wootton executive editor. Luce raised the question "Could the editor fire the managing editor?" He answered himself, "Yes, under certain circumstances." To me, the "certain circumstances" seemed most unlikely to develop.

I had been conscientious, I thought, in bringing along candidates to succeed me. If Luce wanted a certain kind of magazine, there was George. If he wanted a different sort, there was Phil. From his "nomination," I concluded that he had chosen George, but his memo indicated to me that it was a subject to be discussed. It turned out that I had little or no choice.

In trying to soothe me, Donovan said Luce probably thought he had discussed the change with me, and that I had assented. Hunt theorized that perhaps Luce had been afraid to propose it to my face. I decided it was too sore a point to bring up with Luce, and that my choice then was to go along or quit.

I really hoped I could work with Luce. He seemed serious about the editorship being a real job. It was understood that I would handle the big projects such as the astronauts and, later, MacArthur—anything that cost more than $50,000 was the rule of thumb. I would act as a sort of inspector general to ride herd on the troops. I would be the monitor of overall tone and policy, including editorials. If I had been able to adjust to not being a managing editor, perhaps I would have been able to goldbrick my way through to a state of genuine retirement.

But the arrangement didn't work for me or for *Life,* or—in the long run—for George Hunt, either. I should have quit. At that moment, however, I didn't have any alternative job waiting, and that fact caused me to look ahead to early retirement status at age sixty—six long years away. (Later, fifty-five became the routine early retirement age at Time Inc.) It turned out, though, that there was enough work for two in my job and George's.

I wanted to get along with George. At his request, for instance, I fired some old-timers whom he didn't think he could stand. "They will take it better from you," he said. All of them did take it well except one, who never spoke to me again.

To give him broader experience and administrative background, I had positioned George, when he came aboard after World War II, first as head of the *Life* Chicago office, then in Washington. In the New York office he had been an art editor (he was a painter himself), military affairs editor (he was a decorated Marine Corps officer) during the Korean War, and finally assistant managing editor. He was ready, and in fact impatient, to become managing editor.

On closing night of my last issue, two veteran associates, Hugh Moffett and Roy Rowan, hired two Dixieland jazz bands—one black and one white. At first the black musicians refused to perform with the "whiteys," but Moffett jollied them into it—no mean feat—and the two groups alternated in playing well into the morning. It was kind of like a New Orleans funeral, the musicians playing dirges on the way to the graveyard and swinging out on the way back. Next to country, Dixieland is my favorite music.

Neither George nor I succeeded in reestablishing the operation to the important business of making profits commensurate with costs. There were some shifts in editorial emphasis—some good and some doubtful. Hunt remained imbued with the marine spirit ("take the high ground"), which

resulted in more blockbuster articles, compelling when they had a genuine
sense of urgency, doubtful when they crowded out material which would
have made for a better-balanced magazine. In retrospect, I think *Life* began
to veer away from the kinder and gentler aspect of the world I felt we should
be interpreting. To be fair, although I wrote memos calling attention to what
I thought were unfortunate examples of gung-hoism, I failed to sound the
general alarm.

George paid no real attention to my remonstrances, although we did try to
have lunch on Mondays, the editorial day off, so he could keep me informed
about what he was up to. I would occasionally go over his head to complain
to Luce and Donovan, where I got kindly and understanding hearing. But
I would not have tried, in the words of that original Luce "nomination," to
fire the managing editor. I had helped set an example of managing editor
arrogance, which George tried to follow with zest. In my day, of course, I
didn't have anyone with the title of editor to deal with.

According to my own lights, I did try to make the managing editor/editor
combination work. All differences of opinion and content would have been
moot, of course, if the business side in the Hunt era had been improving the
profit picture.

Life was to have three more publishers as a weekly. They all wrestled
mightily with some problems over which they had insufficient control
or no control—increases in the cost of paper, rising postal rates, union-
negotiated pay minimums, and the "big decision" by the company to make
Life's circulation larger and larger. Whatever was being done to make the
magazine a more attractive home for ads—whether more effective selling
or increased editorial vigor—was not working well enough.

In general, I think I succeeded in keeping out of George's hair. Early on,
I volunteered to produce a booklet on defense from nuclear attack, not so
unrealistic a nightmare then. It would take the form of a manual instructing
people on how to neutralize the effects of nuclear fallout. President Kennedy
had promised one in every mailbox—fifty-some million. My offer was
accepted, and Robert McNamara assured the project preliminary funding
from the Department of Defense budget.

I knew better than to expect nonjournalists to envisage a booklet by
looking at photostats. A few of the reactions should have alarmed us. One
government think-tanker had an idea for a sketch with which to open the
booklet: A frontier family is besieged by Indians in a log cabin. Of the ten
family members, five would get scalped because they had no blast shelters,

and five would be saved because they did have a shelter. This idea man was of a low enough rank to ignore.

McNamara himself was something else. About a chapter on treating nuclear burns, he sent a terse message, "Kill it!" It seems that the Ford Motor Co., when he was chairman, had had an unfavorable public reaction on the subject of burns in a Ford public service ad campaign.

Sure enough, the Kennedy administration, which wasn't behind the door when public sensibility know-how was passed out, backed off from the fallout booklet. Something in the form of a rough paper miniature treatment was eventually printed, but not by us. It didn't go into every mailbox, but was left in the lobbies of all post offices.

At the time, I received no reaction on White House stationery, but later Kennedy aide Ken O'Donnell sent a message that the president appreciated the professionalism of our effort and thanked me. So, you lose a few.

If I had not imbued myself so thoroughly with the mystique of being a Time Inc. *managing* editor, I could rationalize satisfactory marks for the discharge of the duties of being editor of *Life*. What troubled me was the relatively small number of items in the finished magazine that I could tell myself I had originated or to which I had supplied major impetus. I *could* tell myself that it was of benefit to the magazine to have the most senior of its editors—me—knowledgeable in more and more significant areas. Certainly it didn't hurt.

For instance, what about the Far East, beyond general coverage of the events of a given week? There had been talk of a special issue on Japan. How were the liberated Philippine Islands and "our Chinese" on Taiwan doing? Why were American troops from the Korean DMZ serving as "advisers" in Vietnam and Laos? I went on a pulse-feeling trip in 1963. Marguerite and I had divorced, and in May, Lee Eitingon, of *Sports Illustrated,* and I married. She came along now, at our own expense, for the period of her vacation. I finished the two months alone.

As editor, I did have a role in making big decisions. I argued that the company should abandon its customary Republicanism, and I was for endorsing Johnson against Goldwater in the 1964 campaign, even though Clare Luce was co-chairperson of Goldwater's campaign. Johnson became our man. I heard a comment that Harry himself made to a *Newsweek* reporter—"There are issues on which my wife and I disagree. This is one of them." Surprisingly, *Newsweek* did not use the quote, which in my judgment was supernewsworthy.

I was also available for certain ceremonies. Sometimes they involved work on my part. A colleague from my Ultra days, Charlie Murnane, who had been to Bradley's HQ what I had been to SHAEF, had become president of the Minnesota Bar Association and wanted me to make a convention speech on the free press and fair trials. He hinted that Minnesota's two members of the Supreme Court, Warren Burger and Harry Blackmun, might attend. Time Inc. thought it was a good idea for me to speak. Although neither justice did attend, I did, and tiptoed carefully around the very delicate subject of my talk.

Once in a while, I would be called on for some high-level troubleshooting. For instance, people around Lyndon Johnson, now president with *Life*'s help, took alarm at a proposed *Life* investigation into the Johnson family finances. Luce volunteered the services of "that great editor," me, to keep the story fair. It was fair, okay, but not all that revealing.

What took up most of my working time during my last days at *Life* was another attempt at production R & D. This would pull together bits of the electronic age that were manifesting themselves into a rapid delivery system for all the editorial phases of *Life*. I nominated myself head of a small—too small—task force, which also included Paul Welch, a good and thoughtful reporter and bureau chief, and Howard Sochurek, an all-around photographer with superior technical skills. I was no technician, but I had discovered that every time an issue closed in Chicago the plant technicians there accomplished things they previously had considered impossible.

After about eighteen months of research in 1964 and 1965 we totted up our experiences and found that one, two, or all three of us had visited sixty-odd experimental facilities. These ranged from IBM on down to a one-man computer operation. We had been in the U.S., the U.K., and Germany. Finally we were able to project a scenario in which, by adapting state-of-the-art hardware that already existed or was about to, the thirty hours between a managing editor's okay of a page and the start of the presses could be cut to two.

The result was to be text, headlines, and photographs fed into a single transmission to the printing plant with prescreened copy ready to be put onto the press plates. I'll admit to putting some hype into an eighteen-page memo, but the dreams were all reasonable, and the top brass reaction seemed enthusiastic—Roy Larsen found it "the most exciting memo since Luce's original prospectus for *Life*."

In the event, though, no big changes were put into effect. But the vision of an electronic world resulted in my becoming chairman of a company-wide group to handle all proposals for pre-press projects. Editorial, business, and production executives were on the committee. *Time,* which pioneered in the electronic handling of word copy, was ahead of all the other magazines in practical progress. Related techniques were becoming visible down the road.

My feelings about the mostly good, not-so-old days as managing editor became vastly more poignant with Luce's decision, in 1964, to make Hedley Donovan editor-in-chief of Time Inc. in his place. There was no possible objection I could have to Hedley, a man I liked and understood. I even understood the overtones of a basic expression of Donovanese, an "ugh" written in the margin of a piece of copy. Still, when Harry called me to his office to reveal the impending change, I ventured to comment, "You can't expect anyone else to fill the office of editor-in-chief exactly as you have."

Almost as if talking to himself, he seemed to look past me and said, "Well, I do have all that stock, don't I?"

Harry took the title of editorial chairman, so I did not feel, for the time being, that I had ceased working for him altogether.

When Harry died in 1967, the Time Inc. I had worked for since 1937 came to a distinct end. I mourned him as a friend and as a respected boss. We didn't always quite agree on details, but overall I was aiming for the same kind of publication he was. By choice I had concentrated fiercely on *Life.* He could devote only part of his attention to that portion of his territory, but his absence created a full-scale void. I had a powerful reason for not continuing at *Life.*

By late in 1967 I felt intuitively that change was in the air. In advance of a scheduled lunch with Hedley, I delivered a four-page memo on what I believed was wrong (and in some cases, right) about what *Life* had become. I deplored the decline in the use of pictures as pictures, and, in particular, the absence of the photographic essay. Too many photographs were simply illustrations of text points, as in other magazines. In straining to be "with it," *Life* was in danger of becoming a national *East Village Other,* with too much attention to weirdos and the use of drugs. We were not dealing enough with what *Life* almost alone could celebrate—the satisfactions of normal living.

At the lunch Hedley waved at this and said, "Good memo!" But he asked why I hadn't done something about it. I suppose I exhibited some frustration in pointing out that the editor was inhibited from the top because the office of the editor-in-chief habitually dealt directly with the managing editor and from below by being virtually ignored. He indicated, without getting specific, that he didn't agree with me and went to the matter at hand. This

This gag picture of Mount Rushmore with my head added was used at a farewell party in 1968 (courtesy Time Inc.)

was unpleasant for me, and I thought for him too. He said it was about time for a change and that Thomas L. Griffith, who had been assistant to him, would become *Life*'s editor.

A job was available for me, at least for a while, as director of the company's editorial services. These included supervision of copy transmission, the photographic and text reference libraries, and the photo lab. The idea stemmed from my work as head of the R & D committee, and the position would have been an honorable one, to be sure. After sleeping on the matter, however, I decided to take retirement instead.

I did not think Hedley's decision unfair if only because, with Luce gone, he was entitled to his own team. Tom Griffith's book *How True: A Skeptic's Guide to Believing the News* records uncomplainingly Hedley's warning "that the odds might be against the magazine's survival, but . . . if *Life* couldn't last let it be its circumstances and not its editorial quality that was responsible." Shades of Heiskell's complaints in the late 1950s that it suffered from "too much excellence." In observing that "the managing editor's was the most powerful role," Tom notes that neither the M.E. nor the editor "was to report to the other; each only to Donovan." This was at least a clear description of a situation which had not been spelled out to me during the previous six years.

There was nothing ambivalent about the splendid farewell party that was thrown for me. It was as lavish as the Dixieland-band event of six years earlier had been unpretentious.

The company was in one of its periodic attempts at austerity, which were becoming much more frequent, but Hedley grandly waived the rules. Being a ham, I wallowed in sentimentality. It was rather like Tom Sawyer hiding in the church loft and hearing his own funeral sermon.

A connoisseur of tribal rites, Tom Griffith looked out at a sea of people massed under a sixteen-foot photo enlargement of me as I had posed, recumbent, like a team mascot, in front of the entire staff of *Life* photographers in 1960. He said, "Those are all your people out there." I guess they mostly were, because scores of them, who had fun at the wake along with the guest of honor, took the trouble to write me personal letters.

A few of the letters recalled undeniably rocky periods. Others predicted that I wouldn't be content to bask permanently in idleness. They, of course, were correct.

29

Smithsonian, a Magazine Waiting to Be Invented

૨૭ Upon leaving *Life* I didn't expect—and didn't get—a flood of job offers. At equal pay, I was priced out of the job market. An interesting feeler did come from William P. Bundy, an assistant secretary of state, who thought that my wartime intelligence experience might be combined with my journalistic knowledge in some patriotically useful way. (Yes, I did think pursuance of our aims in Vietnam was patriotic, although I was reasonably quick to disapprove of the way we were fighting.) My experience with the ill-fated booklet on atomic fallout might have been a warning, but I still thought Bob Lovett had something in his argument to me years before that purposeful communication with a few people who really make a difference is better than shotgun blasts at a mass audience.

Bill Bundy, who was Dean Acheson's son-in-law, might have had some reservations about me. He was in charge of the Department of State's Southeast Asian division. Time Inc. was hawkish enough for him, but what were my politics?

"I'm an independent," I told him. "My vote changes from election to election."

"Damn it, you're just like my brother, McGeorge [a member of JFK's brain trust]. He's always changing. I am a Democrat—first, last, and forever."

I had voted for Lyndon Johnson in 1964, so he allowed as how that would have to do and said, in effect, I'll get back to you in a few weeks.

Lee and I unwound with a trip to Greece. James Linen, the president of Time Inc., had family philanthropic ties to Greece and told me that the current Greek government, administered by a junta of colonels, wanted an outside adviser. I was doubtful, but he said, "Why don't you listen to them anyway?" I wisely refused an offer of a free trip. When we arrived in Athens, the first words from a butch-shorn colonel were: "The king [exiled] is giving a press conference in Rome tomorrow. Stop him."

I explained gently that I had not and would not sign on with his government.

After a week in Athens, happily free from any further official overtures, we paused in Paris, where a telex from Bundy caught up with me. I spent hours in the U.S. Embassy filling out reams of State Department job forms.

Back in the States, I was offered and accepted a post with Bill. My title would be Assistant to the Secretary of State rather than assistant to Bill, because that carried a somewhat higher salary. Bill hoped that I might be able to help explain our Far East policy to doubting VIPs.

By attending interminable meetings, sometimes with Bill, sometimes on my own, I somehow familiarized myself with what was going on in Washington. Attendants at these meetings included representatives of the Joint Chiefs, the CIA, the Defense Intelligence Agency. Once a week we all marched over to the White House—I had to trot because Bundy's legs were so long—to be received by Walt Rostow, an LBJ assistant. It may have been that the president wasn't telling Walt anything or that he didn't trust us because these, too, were pretty barren sessions. Walt had a red phone on his desk, a direct line to the president, but none of us ever heard it ring.

After my visit to Vietnam in 1963, when American troops were officially "advisers," I had thought, erroneously, that we should shed that euphemism and attack in adequate force. What really turned me off was that General William Westmoreland's top-secret reports to his superiors were almost word for word what he was telling the press. Those impressionable VIPs never materialized—luckily, because "Westy" would have been difficult to explain.

It was soon clear to me that I was in the wrong pew, and I resigned my appointment in the fall of 1968. It was to expire in January 1969 anyway.

Opportunity sometimes rears its welcome head at odd times. If I hadn't just happened to be in Washington, the secretary of the Smithsonian Institution, S. Dillon Ripley, might not have found me. Almost everyone in town except me knew that he was hell-bent on the Smithsonian's having a

*To Edward Thompson
With best wishes,*

Richard Nixon
May 6, 1969

Talking with President Nixon (1969, photo by Bill Bridges).

magazine. Unexpectedly, I received a luncheon invitation from William W. Warner, one of Ripley's assistant secretaries. He proceeded to sound me out on how to start a magazine.

Willie and I chatted inconclusively about the Institution. I hadn't visited it since 1930, during a vacation. I was aware that Ripley had imbued fusty old collections with a new spirit, and Warner confirmed this with specific examples. When it came time to explore the broad concepts and the nitty-gritty of starting a magazine, I didn't feel that Willie and I were speaking the same language. He had a memo with some ideas for articles, none of which turned into material that was eventually published. Willie's considerable abilities were to produce a book that was as charming as he was personally: *Beautiful Swimmers,* about the crabs and crabbers of Chesapeake Bay, won a Pulitzer Prize.

I figured I'd better get to know my prospective employer firsthand.

Briefly, the Smithsonian Institution consists of a collection of museums and is, by law, the national museum. It was founded by a private bequest of $500,000 in gold from a British scientist, James Smithson, illegitimate son of the Duke of Northumberland. It came to be supported largely by congressional appropriation and run by a board of regents, partly from the government, some from the private sector. The operating executive is the secretary, appointed by the board of regents.

Ripley hoped a magazine could make the national museum's scope more truly national instead of being limited to visitors from the Washington area and tourists like the Thompsons had been in 1930. Before my visit with the secretary, I reconstituted myself into a tourist and tramped the museum corridors.

The exhibits were a lot livelier, all right, but I concluded that a magazine confined to reporting on what the Institution had on view, including temporary shows, would run out of editorial material in a very short time. The turnover on the painstakingly fashioned exhibits was slow. I was wary and not at all interested in the kind of official publications that most other institutions were offering.

I met the secretary at the Ripley family base in Litchfield, Connecticut. As a working ornithologist, he conducted some of his research at a waterfowl complex, appropriately named Paddling Ponds. We sat under a tree, with a downy woodpecker tapping away above our heads. It was the beginning of a rewarding relationship, professional and personal.

My idle periods at the State Department had provided an opportunity to reflect on the magazine business. The death rattles at the *Saturday Evening Post,* to be followed by those at *Look,* were audible, but some special-interest magazines were doing well. Magazines generally were not going down the drain—mostly it was those with mass circulations to maintain that were in trouble. The national yearning for self-improvement was growing, and the prospective magazine readers continued to become better educated.

If there was no longer a mass market for a magazine that was everything to everyone, there might be a substantial opportunity for one that could do what nothing but a magazine could do. It would work if . . .

Like others, I found Ripley to have an aristocratic manner but also to be both engagingly self-deprecatory and most articulate. His elitist views on education were fine with me. He was prone to hamming it up at office parties by thumping a tambourine and, for photographers, riding the Institution's carousel—also fine.

In Litchfield, he started off by observing that the Institution should have had a magazine since the early 1900s—well before our times. Since I was obviously there as a possible editor, I said that I didn't want to run a house organ. He said he didn't want that either. After we had rambled over some possible subject matter, we agreed that the magazine's content could be about whatever the Institution was interested in—or might be interested in. I threw in, "And should be?" He agreed. That was about all that was articulated as a working idea, but an almost unlimited variety of subject matter was possible under such a concept.

It became apparent that, as far as Ripley was concerned, I could have a free hand in giving shape to the magazine. As a practical matter, no one in the Institution knew anything about either editing or publishing. I felt I was an editor incarnate; I had plenty of views on running a business. We would see if they were valid. As a matter of pride, I would insist on its being profitable. I would also insist on being publisher as well as editor.

The important catch was that, financially, the enterprise was on its own from day one. Naturally, the secretary said, he understood that substantial start-up funds would be needed before the enterprise was self-sufficient, but I wasn't to worry about that. The secretary would solicit the necessary advances. He told me about his past success in tapping private sources for other purposes.

One of my own ifs about the project was if I could get along with the secretary. I was now satisfied that I could.

The magazine I envisioned would be based on, but I hoped ahead of, the country's rising educational level. It would spur on the upward movement encouraged by the GI bill. It would stir curiosity in already receptive minds. It would deal with history as it is relevant to the present. It would present art, since true art is never dated, in the richest possible reproduction. It would peer into the future via coverage of social progress and of science and technology. Technical matters would be digested and made intelligible by skilled writers who would stimulate readers to reach upward while not turning them off with jargon. We would find the best writers and the best photographers—not unlike the best of the old *Life.*

If I had once been more inclined to headline news than to cultural matters, I had somehow elevated my own tastes. It was just as well. The kind of audience we had to attract to succeed was not only well educated, but also rather affluent. It would turn out that the new magazine would have to show a profit soon.

I would not suggest undertaking a quixotic quest for quality just for the sake of having a publication to run. I feel no empathy with the wispy figure sometimes observed at track meets. He is the one with the sweaty handkerchief around his head, who gets cheered just for finishing a long-distance race, even though he has been lapped several times by the field. Receiving polite applause for being a jolly good sport doesn't pay any bills—or salaries.

My jack-of-all-trades professional life had given me insight into how to recruit the circulation, advertising, and production personnel who would have nitty-gritty know-how in those areas. I needed on-the-job training as a publisher. It was just as well that I did not know that, at the time, *Psychology Today* and *New York* magazines were spending about $5 million each to get into publication.

My priority, while Ripley was supposed to be soliciting seed money, was to line up people with successful track records who could be enticed away from the so-called commercial sector. A training program from scratch would be lengthy. I needed a combat-hardened staff, ready to operate.

The day I sat down in a temporary office, I found a pile of applications for jobs on a magazine I hadn't known was about to be born. Quality was the primary commodity we would have for sale, and it would take a quality staff to produce this. I was not after youth particularly. I had felt conscience-bound to ask Ripley if he really wanted a sixty-year-old running the magazine, and he had answered that he preferred someone who would not use the job as a stepping stone to something else.

I had decided not to proselytize from Time Inc., although if someone I knew sought a job on his or her own, that was different. Volunteers wouldn't complete the minimum staff. I had to rely on a conviction that veteran firehorses will respond to the clang of the bell.

I enlisted some I already knew. Other names were suggested by friends. A former art editor of *Life,* for instance, who wasn't interested for herself, thought a former managing editor of *Horizon,* Ralph Backlund, could be lured away from a job in the State Department. He could and was.

Of the applications piled up when I reported for work, only one or-ganization, the *National Geographic,* was represented by more than one name. Bloodbaths there had dispelled the illusion that the *Geographic* was

Security Incorporated. There are discontented angels even in paradise. One such refugee, Edwards Park, was a star editor/writer in the essential area of history.

It developed from a chance restaurant encounter that an old colleague at *Life,* Grayce Northcross, would leave the United States Information Agency to become chief of research. Thus three out of the four key editorial problems got long-term solutions. A fourth, the science editorship, was more difficult to fill—not until 1973, after the weekly *Life* folded, did I find Don Moser. He eventually succeeded me as editor.

It would probably horrify an expert on management to hear how the business staff of what was to become a multimillion-dollar enterprise was assembled. A former *Life* employee who had been editor of *Natural History* and gone to *Scientific American* said no thanks to an offer of a job for himself but said the circulation manager of *Natural History* was restive. Anne Keating had a remarkable record and was being underpaid, so we got a circulation boss. Among possible advertising managers, we didn't look to be a safe bet to any good one except Thomas H. Black, Howard's son, who had confidence in the venture because he recalled how I had operated at *Life.* A mutual friend phoned me to expect a call from Joseph Bonsignore, who worked for Time Inc. corporate production in Chicago. His worth was appreciated by visiting *Life* task forces for his general savvy and ability to spot errors. I called him and offered him a job.

There were other important holes to fill. A new magazine needed a fresh design. I went to Allen Hurlburtt, whose new look for *Look* I had admired, although it had come too late. He in turn sent me to Bradbury Thompson (no relation), the dean of book and magazine designers. The magazine retains his tasteful, practical, elegantly simple visual plan.

Most important was an authoritative projection of the embryo magazine's chances of success. I turned to another friend, Arthur Murphy, who had held responsible business jobs at Time Inc., notably as general manager of *Life* and publisher of *Sports Illustrated,* and had since acquired a consulting firm. As I now reexamine his figures, I realize that he made a couple of very optimistic assumptions on which to base conclusions for us. He came out with a prediction of success for about the time it actually occurred.

A most vital reason I was glad to have Art Murphy's projection was that the start-up fund that Dillon Ripley thought could be raised wasn't making its appearance. "I get asked all the time," I wrote Ripley, "where the big money is coming from. . . . It will not surprise you that my cynical mind suspects that the Smithsonian officials detect some kind of threat to their own disposable funds."

He wrote on my memo: "We must have a huddle on this. . . . I should certainly try to raise (with some assist from you) in the neighborhood of $500,000." That had to do for the time being, although, even in those pre-inflation days, it wasn't much.

The "assist" to which Ripley referred included some time-consuming explorations of a possible joint venture with former senator William Benton and his *Encyclopedia Britannica.* I never thought I was good at fund-raising. Thus Benton, who in the meantime had been expressing doubts to Hubert Humphrey as to whether Dillon Ripley was a businessman, came through with the munificent contribution of $5,000.

To skip ahead, the only other contribution recorded was $50,000 by Thomas J. Watson Jr., then chairman of IBM and also a regent of the Smithsonian. He told me only that he was encouraged by my work at Time Inc., where he had served on the board of directors for a considerable period. Years later, Ripley said in a newspaper interview that Tom Watson had agreed to underwrite losses if the magazine project collapsed. I might have felt more confident if I had known about that safety net, but I spent no time on iffy speculation, only on making the magazine a critical *and* a financial success.

It wasn't exactly a contribution, but a first subscription was requested in a pretty cheery manner. At a party, Joseph Hirshhorn fished out a wad of bills, peeled a C-note off, and demanded to be put on our roll as subscriber number 1. I passed the $100 on to Ripley, but one of his aides picked his pocket and put it in an office safe for fear that the boss would absentmindedly assume it was his.

Correctly anticipating inflation, we weren't trying to sell long-term subscriptions, but we entered Joe for life anyway. He was, by the way, in the process of endowing a Smithsonian art museum, the Hirshhorn, no less.

Prepublication procedure went on without any Ripley suggestions, although his faith was not universally shared. It was certainly the job of the Institution treasurer to cast a fishy eye at what might seem to be excavation for a rathole down which to pour money. Ames Wheeler had come to the Smithsonian after he had retired as treasurer of one of the big steel companies. Although he steadfastly opposed the magazine through the planning stages, he couldn't have been nicer and more gentlemanly about it. After I introduced myself, he said mildly, "You should realize, of

Standing outside the Smithsonian Castle near the statue of Joseph Henry, the Institution's first secretary (1970, photo by Charles Phillips).

course, that the Smithsonian Institution is bankrupt." At that time I was still expecting Ripley to raise outside money.

Later, when it became evident that the magazine would have to prove its worth as a profit-maker, I tried to talk Wheeler's business language. "Now, Ames," I said, "you're running Allegheny Steel and want to make more money. You invest in more furnaces, right? Then you'll have more product to sell."

That gave him only momentary pause. He came back, "But suppose you make that extra steel and then can't sell it?"

He became a believer later, but I learned that at the last minute before the go signal for start-up of production, he called Ripley at home and pleaded in vain for half an hour for abandonment of this rash course. Ripley reported his cavalier rejection: "I said, 'Go to hell, Ames.'"

An essential next step was approval by the ultimate rulers, by statute, of the Institution—the board of regents. The administrative staff in the Castle, the Institution's original building and headquarters, did not take the regents lightly. As the time approached for a presentation to them of what the magazine would be like, there was a tizzy of nervous activity.

In late 1968 I had supplemented my examination of the Washington exhibition buildings with a trip abroad (Ceylon—now Sri Lanka—plus

Israel and India) to observe how Smithsonian field expeditions work. Ideas for some early articles came from that trip.

From Bradbury Thompson's designs, we made up sample pages and two-page spreads in full color to show what the magazine would look like. From these I prepared a slide presentation for Ripley, an indefatigable trouper, for delivery to the assembled regents. While he was performing, I was in an office outside the meeting, ready to answer technical questions if they came up.

The chief justice of the U.S. Supreme Court is ex-officio chancellor of the Smithsonian Institution. Earl Warren, who had announced his retirement pending President Nixon's appointment of a successor, stuck his head into my temporary office and asked me to excuse myself while he took a telephone call. I heard him say, "Splendid, Mr. President," through the office walls and realized later that he had been hearing about the selection of Warren Burger to head the Court.

Ripley finished, and no one actually objected to the launching of the magazine. We just assumed that silence meant consent and, living dangerously, went ahead. The news of a new chief justice and Smithsonian chancellor just may have interested the regents more at the time. Certainly it seemed so at the dinner, which I attended, following the meeting. A television set was wheeled in for the announcement and introduction of Burger, with his resplendent head of snowy-white hair. Out of the darkness came a comment from one unidentified regent: "Where did Nixon get him, central casting?"

30

A Launch into Perilous
Financial Waters

 Once committed to tempt fate, there is nothing for it except to plunge in. In early January 1970, we took out full-page ads in the *New York Times,* the *Wall Street Journal,* and *Ad Age* announcing a first issue for April of that year. The name would be *Smithsonian.*

The staff and the Institution as a whole had discussed names—we couldn't go on calling ourselves "it." A halfhearted idea was *Smithson's Monthly,* after the Institution's original benefactor. Someone suggested *Diffusion* because Smithson's bequest had been for the "increase & diffusion of knowledge among men," but to indicate that the contents might be diffuse was poor salesmanship. In the end, *Smithsonian*—the most obvious—won without much protest except for grumbles from the purists among the curators, who didn't want a group of non-academicians producing an official publication.

I was determined that *Smithsonian* would have—within its eminently stretchable concept—variety, visual impact, and . . . elegance. It would have class, as the Ethel Merman song went, "with a capital K."

Thus, we would use paper of high enough quality to give us faithful reproduction of the most subtle shades. We would have capacity for four-color reproduction throughout, even though in some cases black and white would prove more effective than color. I didn't share the conviction of my successors at *Life* that a large page size is a must if one is dealing with graphic material. After all, *Impact* had effectively displayed on *Time*-size pages how arresting the sights of war in the air can be.

Since 1927, I had been working toward the most desirable jobs on a publication. Now I had something approximating the ideal in sight. I needed to know more than a smattering of all details of publication. I felt confident about production. I already knew something about circulation and advertising, although it was mostly as an observer. I could learn anything else I needed to know as we went along.

Smithsonian, to survive, would need advertising revenue, of course, but we were prepared to wait for the traditionally deliberate recognition from Madison Avenue. I decided in advance, however, that because of the health issue we would not accept cigarette ads. Another decision on advertising involved the readability of the magazine. As a reader myself, I have been annoyed by the weary-looking back portions of many magazines. *Smithsonian,* then, which was starting out with a clean slate, would present each article in one piece. We would not start it in the front half of an issue and jump its last portions to the rear of an issue, where the text would meander through an interminable series of half- or quarter-page ads. In the beginning this wasn't much of a problem because there were so few ads. Later, when we had 200 or more pages in an issue, nearly half of them ads, it took skill to maintain the plan as conceived.

As 1969 came to an end, a first issue was being prepared. Anne Keating had already conducted a fall circulation test, which produced promising implications. To be convincing, however, a test must consist of more than getting expressions of interest; *paid* orders must be obtained.

The January 1970 ads announcing *Smithsonian*'s forthcoming appearance contained a prospectus written by the editors and signed by me and Tom Black, who was lining up advertising.

Another regents meeting was scheduled for January. As usual, it was preceded by a meeting of the executive committee, for the purpose of making recommendations (which are usually followed). This was duly held on January 27, 1970, but what happened and what was reported in the *Washington Post* were quite different. According to the *Post,* the executive committee voted to recommend that the magazine project be dropped. The article made it sound as if the project were dead.

Ripley telephoned me during breakfast to assure me that the matter hadn't even come up at the executive committee meeting. When the full board of regents met on January 29, the magazine was approved with no dissenting votes, although there were a couple of abstentions.

The damage, while real, was only temporary. It did affect the opening subscription campaign, however, and it may have scared away some early advertisers.

My general manager, Joe Bonsignore, had moved his family to Washington just in time to read the erroneous article. He had no telephone yet, so I could not relay Ripley's reassurance to him. Afterwards, he was so nervous that I offered him a division of labor: he could do all the worrying for the enterprise; I would furnish the voice of confidence. I gave Joe the best members of the staff I had pried from the Institution, headed by Carey Randall, who later became his associate publisher.

How to explain the *Post* story? There was a report that an aide to a U.S. senator, a member of the executive committee, had put some anti-magazine material into the folder for the meeting, perhaps concluding that the senator would introduce it, and this would settle matters. Whether or not the reporter was misled by the senator's office, the falsehood was in print. And although the correction was put out on the *Post–Los Angeles Times* Syndicate wire, it is a truism that a retraction never quite catches up to a misstatement. The *Post* did make a short correction on January 29 and a handsome, full retraction the next day.

We on the skeleton staff had a first issue deadline facing us. The editorial staff, plus Bonsignore, worked in crannies of the old Arts and Industries Building. Circulation and advertising had temporary quarters in a shabby New York hotel. I lobbied Ripley for better conditions, but he was singularly immune to my efforts at first. Our first editorial-production office was in space formerly used to store spare cartons. I lured Ripley over from the Castle. He looked briefly from his six-foot-plus height and observed, with apparent relish, "How quaint."

Smithsonian's prepublication circulation campaign provided us with a respectable 175,000 guarantee. No one kidded himself that our enticing words about the new magazine were chiefly responsible. The sponsorship of the Institution and the name *Smithsonian* were what moved prospective readers to expect a quality product. Only after publication began could it be established that the magazine would have a sufficiently appealing personality of its own.

Ames Wheeler, despite his doubts, loyally found money in the private-sector coffers of the *Smithsonian* to keep us going until subscription payments started coming in. The Institution never again had to spend any actual cash on us—our cash flow was always positive.

One good thing about the magazine business is that subscriptions are paid in advance. The money is carried as a debit in conventional accounting practice because future issues of the magazine are owed to the subscriber. Thus, although the magazine was not technically in the black until some-time in its third year, it always had money in pocket with which to pay its bills.

For the hard-pressed original settlers, a dozen of us in editorial and business, who produced it, the first issue provided an outline, in part, for what was to come.

The lead was an eloquent and witty treatment by renowned biologist René Dubos of the give-and-take between man and his environment; cartoonist Robert Osborn illustrated Dubos's somewhat abstract points. Other major article subjects, lavishly illustrated for the most part, included an experiment in Ceylon in breeding female domestic elephants to bulls from the wild; an eclectic selection of treasures from the Metropolitan Museum of Art, which was celebrating its 100th birthday; the crown-of-thorns starfish which were devouring Pacific coral reefs; a new black studies program at the University of Maryland; and controversial conclusions about human overpopulation that had been drawn from an experiment with Norway rats.

Reader reaction was quick and positive. The comment that pleased me most came from fellow-pro Tom Griffith at *Life: Smithsonian* "looks as if it had been in being for some time; it starts out established in form and content, no look of trial and error or slapdash about it."

But a first issue is only that. We owed our charter subscribers eleven more, and we had to give those who were selling memberships and ads something to talk about. (I have no intellectual qualms about calling magazines products; they have at least a few things in common with soap.)

I couldn't, in advance, have predicted precisely how successful *Smithsonian* would be, but it turned out that I had few worries. The staff, as we worked into place, had to execute the ideas we had had to begin with, resolutely throw away the ones that weren't working, and expand into other promising creative areas. We assumed there were prospective readers as curious as we were—or, we hoped, more so.

Readers began to respond to our early efforts, and their word-of-mouth enthusiasm complemented Anne Keating's exploitation of sound circulation-attracting procedures. For the ten years I was editor and publisher, circulation always accounted for about two-thirds of net profits. The better part of *Smithsonian* income still comes from circulation.

Early studies of our demographics showed that about 85 percent of our readers had attended college. Tom Black and Anne Keating, professional reader surveyors, allowed that, given the way the magazine had started out, such an elevated reader educational level was to be expected. We were happy about this but were in no position to be smug or self-satisfied. Fresh material and increased revenues did not flow in unsolicited. We still had to scrounge.

31

The World Is So Full of a Number of Things

෬ Substance plus variety put *Smithsonian* over. Without taking ourselves too seriously, we worked out a menu that led the reader to partake of everything, leaving him with the satisfaction of being adequately nourished.

Consider our covers: A great many magazines depend for significant sales on the impression projected from the newsstand and thus feel they must opt for screaming covers. *Smithsonian*'s revenues come so preponderantly from subscribers that its cover can, without impacting business, contribute to the overall beauty of an issue, or to its visual impact, its provocative quality.

If a *Smithsonian* cover tempted a subscriber to read the article it illustrated, it did its job. It could be a stunning young girl dressed in Victorian high style from a Frederick Leighton painting, or a stroboscopic portrait of a breathtakingly handsome bird of paradise. Artist Robert Osborn rose to depicting pleasure—he promised that his drawing of a beaming human face would "simply make you feel good." It did.

Our photographers, particularly the mostly semiprofessionals who illustrated articles involving remote places, shot mostly in color. But some of our most distinguished covers were in black and white. Nicholas Brady photographed himself, in frock coat and straw boater, looking at the Gettysburg battlefield. Alfred Eisenstaedt took one of a member of the Shakers, a shrinking religious sect, Sister Mildred, age seventy-seven, playing the organ. She had some qualms about being on a magazine cover, so she made a personal phone call to me and was assured that the editor's mother, if alive, would have liked to be on our cover.

Other superior black-and-white photography, when available, furnished a welcome visual change of pace inside the magazine. Irving Penn, who persuaded all kinds of primitive peoples to pose in his portable studio, and David Plowden, whose sensitive studies of the American landscape showed what was grand and what was alarming, were equal to other masters who shot in color, such as Dmitri Kessel, Eliot Elisofon, and Lee Boltin.

The normal magazine front cover is a vertical image of approximately eight-by-ten-inch proportions. The back cover is usually sold to an advertiser. *Smithsonian* did not guarantee positions for ads, so if the picture editor, Caroline Despard, could convince Editor Thompson that a cover candidate was worth a double-page horizontal wraparound, Publisher Thompson could usually be convinced that he should put whatever ad was scheduled for the back cover someplace else in the issue. Thus, an occasional double-page cover became a specialty.

How better to emphasize the length of a Texas longhorn's horns than to stretch them around two pages, with the fold or spine of the issue dissecting the nostrils? How better to show hordes of flamingos, settled on a lake in Kenya, than to have the birds extend, apparently into infinity, off the top, bottom, and sides of the two pages? While visiting an international wildlife office in Switzerland, I was mesmerized by a picture of a wild Bengal tiger dozing off a full meal and made that a double-page cover for an article on saving the tiger.

I am not dangerously modern, but I enjoyed and encouraged articles involving contemporary artists. They were amply represented in our pages, along with old masters and sculpture, which lent itself admirably to imaginative photography. By being a patient listener, I became appreciative enough of abstract art to approve articles on Mark Tobey, Ellsworth Kelly, Robert Rauschenberg, Jasper Johns, and Paul Klee. And a dadaist cover by Max Ernst, a landscape with owls, was a delight.

One of my favorite covers, by Dmitri Kessel—an example of graveyard humor at its best—was from Père LaChaise Cemetery in Paris. It showed a tomb figure of a man, recumbent, holding up the beautiful but disembodied head of a young woman, his beloved.

Thumbing back over my decade at *Smithsonian,* I find most of the articles well written. No science, for instance, has to be regarded as dismal. Articles were meticulously and respectfully researched. For the more complicated stories, specialists were required. The aim always was to achieve

Lee and I at our country home near Mahopac, New York (1974, photograph by Dmitri Kessel).

clarity without insulting the reader with oversimplification. Lightheartedness doesn't have to be lightheadedness.

For the most part our writers were freelance—Robert Wallace, Emmet Hughes, and Paul O'Neil come immediately to mind (I wish we could have paid them better). Robert Wernick was the most prolific. He seemed equally at home in a Mesolithic-era dig in Yugoslavia and with Gerald van der Camp, curator of a gloriously restored Versailles. As an issue was being assembled, there always seemed to be a supply of finished Wernick articles ready to go in, although we used no more than three in any given year.

Members of the editorial staff wrote signed articles only occasionally, but Edwards Park, a descendant of the redoubtable colonial theologian Jonathan Edwards, invented writing projects, a job which he preferred—vastly—to editing the work of others. Ted liked to specialize in history, for which *Smithsonian* always had a need. He made history himself with an irresistible modern newspeg when he proposed a monthly column, "200 Years Ago This Month," looking ahead to the Bicentennial. It started in 1973 with a report that "vessels bound for America with the ironwork for Boston's street lamps" had left the Thames. "The rest of the cargoes are chests of tea." The series of columns continued until April 1975, when Lexington and Concord signaled the actual start of war.

The Bicentennial was the basis for a number of articles. I had known Bill Mauldin in World War II when he created his immortal "Willie and Joe" cartoon for *Stars and Stripes*. I had hired him, as the GIs' cartoonist, to illustrate the memoirs of the GIs' general, Omar Bradley, for *Life*. Now, he transported himself back in time to Valley Forge. He had a spit-and-polish Von Steuben confronting a shivering 1777 GI, his feet wrapped in cloth. "Ven I yell 'Achtung!,'" the caption said, "I vant to hear doze rags click."

More factual, but no less humorous than Mauldin, was our article setting Henry W. Longfellow straight on the facts of Paul Revere's ride. Cruelly, we revealed that Revere had actually been captured by the British and had told them everything he knew about the patriots' plans. Surely, though, no one would consider it unpatriotic to reveal that neither Henry nor Paul knew that the requisitioned horse was named Brown Beauty.

Also on the light side, we defended the pesky dandelion. We furthered the tall-tale tradition with an examination of Sasquatch, or Bigfoot, the American answer to the Abominable Snowman and the Loch Ness monster. This kind of thing reached a climax with writer Gerald Carson and illustrator Brenda Tilly, who recorded a glossary of mythological American beasts, from the weeping squonk to the gowrow, the goofus bird, and the spiny-backed hodag.

Tilly was one of the army of illustrators that Caroline Despard always seemed to have on call, along with Richard Erdoes, Arnold Roth, Rowland Emmett, James Flora, and John Huehnergarth, to name just a few.

Cartoons, which could all by themselves constitute a funny article, could also sometimes be valuable in illustrating text written in dead seriousness. A serious contemplation of the desirability of taxonomists' preserving by classification some of the ten million kinds of organisms before many of them disappear from earth was combined with a visual fable with critters of land, sea, and air. They rushed headlong, in a frieze, across the bottoms of six pages, apparently chased by a butterfly. On pages 7 and 8, a taxonomist chased the butterfly, but he presumably would catch up with and classify the other wild things too. The illustrator, Fred Gwynn, an actor who drew, furnished visual grace notes for the basso profundo of the eighteenth-century genius Carl Linnaeus, the father of taxonomy.

Meanwhile, *Smithsonian* was moving into a recognizable place in the publishing hierarchy with a solid bottom line. In our third year of publication, 1972, we did a little better than break even. By 1974, our net had jumped to $1.3 million.

I don't know how much the board of regents knew about our improving financial health, but they must have felt at least that they wouldn't have to preside over a distress bailout. They let Secretary Ripley persuade them to award me the Joseph Henry Medal, named after the first secretary and the Institution's highest award. It isn't easy to assess what recognition of a single person does to the morale of a whole staff, but I did try to convince the staff members that the medal was for the magazine. (There was some in-house joking about the wording of Dillon Ripley's citation: "Dauntless in purpose and rarely persuasive." Did that mean that I wasn't persuasive very often?)

The good humor with which the *Smithsonian* staff produced the magazine was echoed with convincing volume in reader reaction to what I considered a major goof. A cover photo transparency of lightning striking the city of Pittsburgh was somehow reversed. The resulting letters to the editor were warm, friendly, and mostly funny.

One letter said the mistake should be an example to the "idiots at city hall" not to tamper. Others: "Are you proposing massive urban renewal?" A

Dillon Ripley, secretary of the Smithsonian, presenting me with the Institution's highest award, the Joseph Henry Medal (1974).

city planner concluded, "We do have some mobility." One writer assumed that we were just seeing if the readers were paying attention ("You made my day"), and another consoled us, "The quality of your magazine would make it worth reading with a mirror, don't feel bad." These responses made me feel so good that we published the corrections in what amounted to a promotion ad, with the picture reprinted as it should have appeared.

We could not, however, always sail along serenely, critically accepted and readily forgiven for a mistake, without irritating some people. There were occasional attempts to make us change our policies on advertising. I'll cite a couple of examples.

In general, the tobacco industry was resigned to our refusal to run cigarette ads, but one firm, a conglomerate that made food and other nontoxic products, lodged a protest when we rejected copy for one ad, which listed all the company's products in small type, including its cigarette brands.

We threw out the whole campaign of a major advertiser, Allied Chemical, because it was linked to a controversial pesticide called Kepone. That forced us to spend some time on Allied's chairman, John T. Connor. He seemed to be on a first-name basis both with Secretary Ripley and with Ambassador George C. McGhee, chairman of Smithsonian National Associates. Although his spokesman admitted that we had a legal right to reject an ad, Connor denounced me as an enemy of free speech. He demanded a conference with me and Ripley.

I pointed out to Ripley that, as a representative of an institution which deplored pollution, the magazine should not take any money from a corporation that was the defendant in scores of suits in Virginia, mostly for water pollution. Allied and a company called Life Sciences (which bought raw material from Allied and sold Kepone back to Allied for distribution) were about to be enjoined by the Environmental Protection Agency from handling the product.

Ripley's succinct advice was: "Tell Connor to go to hell."

The defection of an advertiser or two did not affect *Smithsonian*'s growth, but the competition from other publications for ad revenues might have been considered a threat. Neither Ripley nor I thought of the *National Geographic* as a threat—or at least we pretended not to. *Geographic* people told us in conversation that more than 70 percent of *Smithsonian* subscribers took the *Geographic* too. Their lists were closely guarded, so we couldn't check that, but fair enough. The *Geographic* reader, however, didn't have nearly as high an education or income level as *Smithsonian*'s. And while *Geographic* had seven million subscribers, compared with our less than a million, our greater number of advertising pages and, we thought, our cultural acceptance put us ahead in those categories at least.

Melville Grosvenor, editor of *Geographic* and a longtime friend of Ripley's and mine, demonstrated that *he* didn't think we were competitors when he proposed that he write an article for *Smithsonian* that I agreed was right down our alley. It was about: Melville's father, Gilbert, the first of three Grosvenors to be editor of *Geographic;* Melville's maternal grandfather, Alexander Graham Bell; James Smithson, on whose bequest the Smithsonian Institution was founded; Smithson's mortal remains; the Institution's regents, of whom Bell was one; and President Theodore Roosevelt.

Smithson, as previously noted, was the illegitimate issue of English nobility. Congress did nothing except accept the bequest and was not about to do anything, even when the Italian government started to destroy the cemetery in which Smithson was buried. Bell was a minority of one when the regents, perhaps influenced by a post-Victorian embarrassment about the illegitimacy, voted to make no effort to remove Smithson's bones to the United States. Bell's up-and-coming son-in-law, Gilbert Grosvenor, wrote

With my son Edward T., editor-in-chief of *Reader's Digest,* when we jointly received the Golden Plate award of the American Academy of Achievement (1977, *Orlando Sentinel* photograph).

a persuasive appeal, printed in the *New York Herald,* to have Smithson rest in the Institution that bore his name. The regents reversed themselves and appointed Bell a committee of one to get the bones transported "quietly and privately."

Gilbert persuaded the president, Theodore Roosevelt, to order a cavalry troop complete with horses and funeral caisson to meet a Coast Guard vessel that had removed the coffin from the German liner on which Bell had shipped it. The navy band played, and all available marines were on hand. The ceremony was neither quiet nor private. No arrangements for a permanent resting place had been made. What would even a reluctant Institution do when the cortege rolled up to the Castle entrance?

The coffin was duly received at the Castle and put into a spare room. Eventually, it was placed in a crypt near the entrance, where it rests today. Mel Grosvenor's article was published in January 1976.

For people who persist in thinking that the *Geographic* and *Smithsonian* are competitors, perhaps a comparison of the two business operations as of then will be of interest. At least it shows *Smithsonian*'s progress. I reported to Secretary Ripley that, disregarding a difference of opinion as to the value of the editorial content, *Smithsonian* was getting, as best we could estimate, a total net return equal to *Geographic*'s and a return vastly larger per employee. The *Geographic* magazine had an employee head count of 352, compared to *Smithsonian*'s 56. Our total broke down as follows: 23 editorial and 14 administration staff members in Washington, and 13 circulation and 6 advertising people in New York.

The *Geographic* listed 58 ad salesmen; we had 7, plus a half dozen advertising representatives across the country working on commission. Our 13 sold many more advertising pages than the *Geographic*'s 58. What this all added up to, roughly, was that the *Geographic*'s two magazines and its books grossed $176 million, with a net of $7.7 million. *Smithsonian,* on a gross of $28 million, netted $7 million with one magazine.

Whether it was the result of tidy business management or the way we perceived and fulfilled a need—or a combination of these—*Smithsonian*'s after-expense annual net surpluses ran from $6 million to $7 million in the late 1970s and enriched the Institution by those amounts.

In 1995 *Smithsonian* celebrated its twenty-fifth anniversary. Circulation today is more than two million.

32

The First Emperor's
Bid for Immortality

◁◁ Earlier the reader has seen how whole issues of *Life* were put together. Now allow me to describe the creation of a single article for *Smithsonian*. My sample is one I cherish, about a major archaeological discovery in China: Emperor Qin's terra-cotta army. Qin, the builder of the Great Wall, unified China some 200 years before the birth of Christ and called himself the "first sovereign emperor." We had the time and patience and pages to produce a truly memorable story. It should surprise no one that I involved myself more than was strictly necessary.

The article wasn't a scoop in the newspaper sense. First, there were scraps of news dispatches. Then I was able to make a personal reconnaissance on the spot in China. I got my hands on photographs that existed, and more were assigned. I enlisted an eloquent art historian to write the text. And with some tenacity and ingenuity we closed a cover and fourteen pages for the November 1979 issue. This was shortly before I left the magazine.

Farmers in the Xian area first discovered the buried pottery army early in the 1970s. The life-sized soldiers, nearly 7,800 of them, had been buried in three pits adjacent to the imperial tomb. They all had different faces, and they had been arranged in military formations facing in the direction from which Qin's last enemies had operated. They were to guard him on his journey toward the afterlife. In contemplating them, *Smithsonian* readers would be, vicariously, witnesses to the beginnings of Chinese sculpture. They would gain insights into the Chinese character, still valid in the time of Mao, who decided to approve of Qin as the wielder of a one-China policy.

No coherent explanation or publishable photographs came out of China immediately after the discovery, when the country was barely emerging from the disastrous Cultural Revolution. Journalism in China, particularly by foreigners, was practiced under severe restraints. Then, in 1979, the Smithsonian's chief botanist, Edward Ayensu, a native of Ghana, was invited to China to help scientists there classify herbs. With his support, Lee and I were approved to accompany him—without an itinerary fixed by the Chinese government.

Though neither Lee nor I could act like a botanist, we were the official responsibility of the Beijing Institute of Botany, which furnished us with the obligatory guide-translator. She was a Ms. Wang, who was a secretary of the Institute, and who would arrange for local guides at each stop. She and her husband had been exiled to farms during the Cultural Revolution, having to leave their children with relatives. But, although we became friends, she wouldn't discuss those events, and would accept from us only some *Smithsonian* posters for the children's room.

Our botanical sponsors asked where we wanted to visit. At the top of my list was Xian, but first we had to see the sights nearby.

In Beijing we visited the printing plant of *China Pictorial,* a propaganda magazine from which *Smithsonian* had bought pictures in the past. The magazine was produced on a flatbed press similar to that of the *Foster County Independent* but with color capacity of sorts—each of the three primary colors and black were printed in separate runs, with the sheets air-dried between impressions. The results, particularly of misty, poetic mountain views, were first rate.

At the ramshackle *Pictorial* offices, through an interpreter, I imparted some technical information about how Western publications operate. I also went through the photo files and found some early shots of the Xian excavations, but no overall views.

While in the city I sought out other photographers who had been to Xian. And we had one exceptional meal, a *China Pictorial* banquet at one of Beijing's three duck-only restaurants. Ours was Little Duck; there were also Big Duck and Sick Duck, the latter's name derived from its proximity to a hospital.

We flew to Xian. I had been briefed about the excavations, but I was not prepared for what lay under the hangar-type roof covering Pit No. 1. It was a museum in situ, in the process of preparing its exhibits. The area was as big as two football fields, but instead of forty-four players cavorting about (four times eleven), 6,000 life-sized soldiers had been crammed in. Toward the far end little tractors darted around, apparently in the process of further excavation. Nearer our small viewing spot were workmen going over figures with fine archaeological tools.

The original roofs over the army had been burned in 206 B.C. during the looting that followed the death of Qin. At the time, almost all the clay figures, weighing up to 300 pounds each, had been crushed by the falling roofs; now some had been removed for reassembly. There were a few complete figures in a room off the pit. In 1980, eight of them would tour half a dozen museums, starting with New York's Metropolitan.

The Met's photographer, Seth Joel, was the son of a talented *Life* photographer, Yale Joel. The Met had given us permission to publish Seth's pictures of individual soldiers, taken at Xian. But it became more and more obvious that the history of China under Qin and the narrative of discovery and restoration of the underground army added up to more than just a display of art.

Photographs were strictly forbidden in the pits, but I asked Seth to try to take a general view when he returned to Xian. I might have tried to sneak one myself, but the guards watched our every move, and I'm not that good a photographer anyway.

The Met connection gave us a chance to employ its assistant curator for Far Eastern art, Maxwell K. (Mike) Hearn, who was in charge of the touring exhibition, to write the article that would tie the whole story together. Mike had visited the site with Seth and—with help he acknowledged from Sima Qian, Qin's own historian and contemporary—he produced an authoritative essay. We could add complementing illustrations to Sima Qian's words and thus convey the spectacular scope of the discovery in a much more comprehensive way than the touring show would provide.

Let's look at what *Smithsonian* finally published:

The cover was a close-up of a chunky terra-cotta general, taken by Seth Joel, who lit still lifes in a way that made them seem almost alive. The general had a suitably baleful expression.

Inside, the article opened with pictures of the early excavations, when everything was still in the open air. One photograph, by Chinese freelancer Wang Yogui, showed soldiers out of the ground from the waist up. Another, from *Pictorial,* showed skilled archaeological workers with trowels and little brushes, clearing away dirt from several figures.

Next, going back in time, was a sketch of Qin from a French archaeology magazine—but of doubtful authenticity, so we ran it postage-stamp size. A large stylized diagram showed the soldiers and the colors of their uniforms. The 206 B.C. fire had blistered the paint from the figures, but Mike Hearn's research had revealed enough paint chips to justify the yellow that our artist, Nigel Holmes, chose for the predominant color of the foot soldiers' uniforms. Rows of archers wore green, armored spear bearers were in red. In the back were chariots and horses.

Pages 5 and 6 showed the Xian countryside today, with a map locating the pits and Qin's tomb. Before his death Qin had mobilized his wise men to find a potion that would enable him to live forever. They did not succeed, of course, and this so enraged the emperor that he executed 460 of them by burying them alive. Since he couldn't live forever, he decided to at least safeguard his journey into the hereafter. His solution: create his own protectors and put them into proper defensive positions.

The 6,000 men in Pit No. 1 were obviously intended for close combat. Pit No. 2 contained 1,400 figures, and the horse-drawn chariots there indicated mobility and the capacity for hit-and-run attacks. We were told that 368 more figures were in Pit No. 3, but none had yet been put on display.

Our next two pages included a meticulously drawn view of a trench showing soldiers, horses, and chariots as they were when crushed by the falling original roof. It had appeared in a 1979 issue of *Wenwe: Chinese Studies in Archaeology.* Opposite it were photos of individual figures standing while a head was being affixed to one of them.

Seth Joel had been watched closely, and was not able to get that one overall view needed to put the individual details into perspective. I knew *Time* had covered a visit to Xian of Vice President Walter Mondale, and I asked some pals there whether they had any overall pictures they weren't using. They did, and Managing Editor Henry Grunewald, an old friend, agreed that *Smithsonian* could have one.

Thus, our page 10 was a full-page picture of the Mondale visit, with the general scene I had wanted. Even though the photographer, Mark Meyer, had not been allowed to set up a battery of lights, his picture was effective. It showed the modern, Caucasian Mondale surrounded by the soldier statues, some of which had heads attached, some of which didn't. Sharp in the foreground, they faded in the background darkness.

The final four pages added details on which archaeologists based assumptions about the duties of individual soldiers—hands, footwear, hair

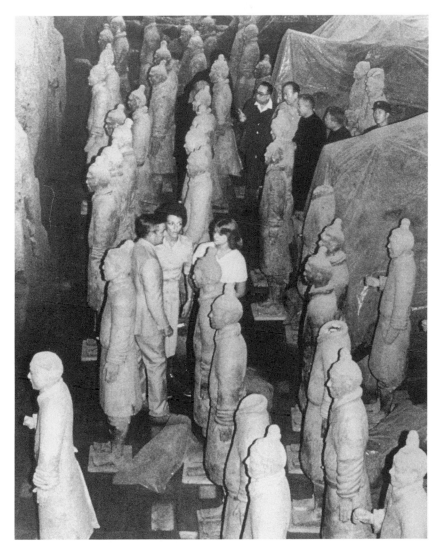

Vice President Walter Mondale, his wife, Joan, and daughter, Eleanor, tour one of the pits at Xian, China, filled with Emperor Qin's terra-cotta soldiers (1979, photo by Mark Meyer).

braids, and body attitudes. A Chinese photographer, Lo Zhonin, had been at hand when diggers uncovered a team of four chariot horses; he noted that paint particles revealed the animals had been painted light black or brown, with white hooves and teeth and red nostrils. We also showed pictures of successful reassemblage of individual figures.

The Chinese workers at Xian seemed to go about their duties in a deliberate fashion. The last I heard, nothing had yet been done about excavating Qin's tomb itself. The burial site may be rich in relics, but the scientists' attitude is: all in good time.

Our closing photograph (by Joel) was of a soldier without armor, poised for hand-to-hand combat, his head turned and his gaze directed as if into the future. Thus Qin, who couldn't live forever, did achieve a kind of immortality with this army that remained to guard him.

33

Exit (with Appropriate Smiles)
the Editor and Publisher

Traditionally, there are two things one does not believe about
oneself: that one has no sense of humor and that one snores. Perhaps I
should have taken a hint from the irascible North Dakota judge who found
my sense of humor distinctly perverse—when I printed his comments about
a mentally ill couple he had married—and verbally horsewhipped me for
it. Instead, I honor the adage in the George M. Cohan song title "Always
Leave 'Em Laughing When You Say Goodbye."

In this last chapter, then, I am leaving the reader with some examples of
the kind of journalism that can leaven the tone of material that frequently
runs to wars and depressions.

A trademark of a Thompson-edited publication became a last page that
leaves the reader with a pleasant aftertaste. It didn't have to be a belly laugh,
which in fact would have been out of character with what I had put together
in the other pages. My magazines were conceived as serious journalism,
which includes, as far as I am concerned, attention to what is right as well
as what is woefully awry. The former—comforting, even amusing—usually
doesn't lend itself to sensational treatment, either in pictures or in words.

At the same time, what is genuinely funny can be elusive. For instance,
a *Milwaukee Journal* photographer photographed a motorcycle daredevil
smashing a wooden fence. We published it, and I wrote a caption ending with
something like, "Any reader who has a fence he wants demolished can get
in touch with Ladislaus Pulaski. Adv." The *Journal*'s classified department
received a number of queries about the cost of such an "advertisement."

On *Impact,* during the grim air war of 1943–1945, one didn't of course overload with excessively lighthearted material. But a visual change of pace could still be achieved. I once used a parody of "The Ballad of Casey Jones," familiar to the flyboys, to caption a sequence of a train in Occupied France being caught by a formation of B-24s on a railway trestle:

> Smack on the viaduct, *nom du nom!*
> The train was a-facin' a quarter-ton bomb.
> The engineer shuddered, the fireman, too.
> Even the whistle screamed, *"SACRE BLEU!"*
> Conclusion: You can have good breaks and lots of traction,
>   but a train can't take evasive action.

Back on *Life,* more than a year before I became managing editor, I spotted an amateur photograph in the *Minneapolis Tribune.* It showed a sad-looking dog climbing a fence with obviously only deliberate speed, foot over foot. It was later considered to have been a model for the *Life* "Miscellany" page. At first any eye-stopping photo was a candidate for "Miscellany." Soon, though, humor dominated.

Looking back, I am amazed by the variety achieved on a relatively few subjects. Small children and animals produce an almost infinite number of smiles. A baby blissfully afloat in a pool encourages us all to enjoy vicariously the last days of summer; we share the outrage of a little flower girl as the ring bearer kissed the bride; and how can you resist a child attendant emerging from the back of a white gown?

Any right-thinking editor has to be revolted by the cutesiness of anthropomorphism, but it is fine to applaud when the pet rabbit of a Jacksonville grade school stands at attention during the Pledge of Allegiance, and to be touched when a canine waiter appears to be balancing dishes on his nose. (Writer Davie Scherman captioned that one "Old Dog Tray.")

The fun can be doubled when there is a juxtaposition of child and animal— for example, a little girl lapping up a saucer of milk while the kitten watches; a dog on the bed while his young master sleeps underneath; a mischievous puppy leaving a child with bottom bared by pulling off his pants.

Ideally, *Smithsonian* would have been born fully armed and confident. But a graceful "old soft-shoe" to end an issue was hardly appropriate until we had established a reasonably solid body for the magazine as a whole. In educating myself, I had been charmed by an authoritative but not-too-sobersided British magazine, *New Scientist.* Scattered among its serious articles were short essays, many signed "Patrick Ryan." Correspondence revealed that he was manager of a branch post office in London and considered himself the "only scientific humorist in captivity." He produced enough sample pages to convince me that he could deliver every month if desired. So in our eighth issue we announced that Ryan's column would start the following month. We could divulge that he grew up in a Cockney area, that his hobbies were "cooking, melancholy and in-depth research into the products of Arthur Guinness & Son Ltd."

Until the end of our second year, Ryan wrote all the back pages, ranging from how to answer voices that might come from space to how to remove a tattoo saying "I Love You, Mabel" when the heart has wandered elsewhere.

Patrick was a comforting friend in print to those without hair, those who couldn't sleep, and those who lacked physical stature—he listed famous baldies, insomniacs, and shorties. His recipe for outwitting polygraphs: render the machine inoperative by stuffing it with an overload of blatant lies.

The Ryan touch would persist through my time at *Smithsonian.* In our third year, however, we began to attract other back-page authors. Nan Lawler, noting scientific discoveries made by accident, made a case for having an ignoramus along on all scientific expeditions to capitalize on the fortuitous. Axel Hornas expatiated on the unlowly onion. Don H. Berkebile, noting the problems of modern solid waste, deplored the Bad Old Days of horse pollution, in convincing detail. Donald Gould, M.D., and serious confrere of Ryan's at *New Scientist,* was wide-eyed over the perks American physicians got on tax-deductible conventions at luxurious resorts.

For a while, until he died, H. Allen Smith, author of *Low Man on a Totem Pole,* was the most prolific substitute for Ryan. He had moved to Texas, about which it is relatively easy to be outrageous and funny. For us he reflected on water witchin', scorpions ("import 600 baboons from Africa to control them"), the loathsome bagpipes (on which he learned only "the sow caught the measles and died in the spring"). After the Department of Agriculture gave up on the pesky fire ant, he floated a proposal to parachute in giant anteaters from Argentina.

As I departed the earthly *Smithsonian* premises in 1980—yes, Virginia, it was finally time to retire—I could have been in a smug professional state. A letter on White House stationery, signed "Jimmy Carter," said I "had done as much as any figure in modern journalism to help Americans to learn about and enjoy the world around them." I had actually met Roosevelt,

Truman, Eisenhower, Kennedy, Johnson, Nixon, and Ford, but not Carter. I suspected that Hedley Donovan, former editor-in-chief of Time Inc. and then serving as a special assistant to the president, had put him up to it.

A letter on Supreme Court stationery predicted that "the American people will be in your debt a long time." I did know the signer, Warren Burger,

The January 1977 *Smithsonian* cover was a double-page wrap-around of the nine Supreme Court justices in an informal mood. The photograph by Yoichi R. Okamoto led into a story about the justices' human side. From left: John Paul Stevens III, Lewis F. Powell Jr., Harry A. Blackmun, William H. Rehnquist, Thurgood Marshall, William H. Brennan Jr., Chief Justice Warren E. Burger, Potter Stewart, and Byron R. White (©Okamoto Photographs).

also ex-officio chancellor of the Smithsonian Institution. It probably didn't hurt that we had brought off an article he suggested on the human side of the justices. It featured a double-page, wrap-around cover showing all nine members of the Court in civvies but still dignified, dangling their feet off a table. Perhaps he felt some personal rapport, too. After all, we were both born in Minnesota (although I left the state after nine days in the hospital) and on the very same day, September 17, 1907.

Logically, death was an ideal final-page subject. In one issue the redoubtable Ryan followed fellow Britons Somerset Maugham and Jessica Mitford with his own wry look at American burial rites. He saluted a 20-story necropolis in Nashville which stores ashes and thus saves 192 acres for agriculture (Père LaChaise Cemetery in Paris takes up 100 acres). I can see it now: urns full of pious Nashvillians rising in a flower-bedecked elevator, those who reach the tower being truly, as in the hymn, "Nearer My God to Thee."

Amen.

〰 *Edward K. Thompson* did *retire in 1980—to serve as a consultant to* Smithsonian, *to write this book, and to savor life in the country at his home in Mahopac, New York. Although he is now confined to a wheelchair and a nursing home (the result of a mild stroke in 1992), his mind is as active—and he is as clever and curmudgeonly—as ever. His wife, Lee, his two sons, his six grandchildren, assorted spouses, and his five great grandchildren are in frequent attendance.*

Index